EUROPEAN ARMAMENTS
COLLABORATION

Studies in Defence Economics

Edited by Keith Hartley and Nicholas Hooper, Center for Defence Economics, University of York, UK.

This monograph series adopts a wide definition of defence economics to cover all aspects of the political economy of defence, disarmament and peace.

This book is part of a series. The publisher will accept continuation orders which may be cancelled at any time and which provide for automatic billing and shipping of each title in the series upon publication. Please write for details.

EUROPEAN ARMAMENTS COLLABORATION
Policy, Problems and Prospects

RON MATTHEWS
Cranfield Institute of Technology
Swindon, UK

Routledge
Taylor & Francis Group

LONDON AND NEW YORK

First Published 1992 by Routledge

Copyright © 1992 by Routledge

by Routledge,
2 Park Square, Milton Park, Abingdon, Oxfordshire OX14 4RN
711 Third Avenue, New York, NY 10017

First issued in paperback 2014

Routledge is an imprint of the Taylor and Francis Group, an informa business

Library of Congress Cataloging-in-Publication Data

Matthews, Ron.
   European armaments collaboration : policy problems and prospects /
Ron Matthews.
      p.   cm. -- (Studies in defence economics ; v. 1)
   Includes bibliographical references and index.
   ISBN 3-7186-5244-7
   1. Defense industries--Europe--International cooperation.
2. Europe--Defenses--Economic aspects.   I. Title.   II. Series:
Studies in defence eonomics (Chur, Switzerland) ; v. 1.
HC240.9.D4M38   1992
338.4'76234'094--dc20   92-17039
                                                                  CIP

ISBN 13: 978-3-7186-5244-0 (hbk)
ISBN 13: 978-1-138-00219-7 (pbk)

CONTENTS

1 BACKGROUND

Introduction

A handful of years straddling the seam between the eighties and nineties have brought profound changes to the East–West security equation. The pace of these changes, political and strategic, has been frenetic. The new order is now irreversible: an unintended consequence of the August 1991 attempted *coup d'état* in Moscow. Although the West was initially slow to react to the Soviet transformation process, the coup ensured more active consideration of accommodating political and military responses. An important aspect of this process is that from an ex-post perspective, turbulence appears to be orchestrating the coming-together of an ordered political, economic and strategic jigsaw. International cooperation has, and will continue to be, a key variable in this evolving framework.

The Gulf crisis of the early 1990s represents an important part of the jigsaw. 'Desert Storm', aside from successfully bridling Iraqi President, Saddam Hussein, proved to be a milestone in several other significant ways. It revealed a sense of unity and purpose in NATO planning (including French), coordination and implementation of military policy. For the first time US-led strategic objectives were achieved under United Nations (UN) auspices, and with the approval of the Soviet authorities. In addition, the unimaginable also happened: an international military force, with global authorisation, upheld the rights of a community member. Moreover, the success of the operation soon led to speculation that this form of political and military cooperation represents the blueprint for the future.

Post Gulf war analysis highlighted two other key factors that assisted in securing a rapid and successful outcome to the Allied campaign. Firstly, there was the dominance enjoyed by the United States' (US) superior weapons systems. These emphasised the electronic dimension of contemporary military technology. High precision, laser-guided munitions; space telecommunications and surveillance; and sophisticated radar systems and electronic eavesdropping, all combined to give Allied forces an unassailable advantage in the conflict. The performance of the US military's electronic wizardry reinforced the American authorities' policy position

1

of eroding quantity by technological quality. No longer, it appears, is there a need for large and expensive standing armies; nor, indeed, for huge numbers of highly expensive fighter/bomber aircraft. A lesson of the Gulf conflict was 'economy of effort'. In this context, it has been claimed that the F-117A (Stealth) bomber, flying only about two per cent of Allied aircraft sorties, was responsible for hitting more than 40 per cent of the strategic targets.[1]

The second major lesson to emerge from the Gulf war related to the need for rapid deployment of mobile and flexible military forces. This is not to say that heavy weapons platforms, such as tanks, do not have a future role to play. They do, but for quick and decisive strategic advantage they too will need to emphasise mobility, adaptability, long-haul capability as well as lethality. The implications from official recognition of the need for high tech' weapons systems along with mobile and flexible multinational quick-reaction forces is the restructuring of NATO members' defence budgets, Armed Forces and defence–industrial bases. The political imperative of providing a peace dividend to western publics that have observed the threat from the Soviet Union not just dramatically reduce but dissolve, will ensure that this restructuring process occurs in a downward direction.

The restructuring process is a natural part of the new international security pattern. It has public finance, industrial and military linkages. Reduced military threats and adjusted force structures have led to falling levels of NATO military expenditure. The United Kingdom (UK) Ministry of Defence's (MoD) budget, at around £24 bn for 1991–92, is set to fall in real terms in the coming years of the decade.[2] In the US, reduced military spending has been a fact of life at the Pentagon for some time. The US defence budget fell 22 per cent in constant dollar terms between the fiscal years 1985 and 1991, and is projected to fall another 13 per cent between the fiscal years 1991 and 1996, when military expenditure to Gross National Product (GNP) is then expected to be down to 3.7 per cent.[3] Such declines in real defence expenditure are not untypical of spending trends in other NATO and erstwhile Warsaw Pact (WP) States. Indeed, although future events are uncertain it is a safe bet that declines in military expenditure will accelerate rather than decelerate.

The reduction in monies available for defence will force the restructuring of NATO's Armed Forces. Britain's 'Options for Change' policy document indicates that the Army will lose 40,000 soldiers. In fact, nearly half the remaining forces will be devoted to NATO's 100,000 strong Rapid Reaction Force. Less severe cuts will also affect the Royal Air Force and Navy. France intends to reduce its Army by up to 70,000 by 1998; that is a quarter of its current strength. Some 50,000 French

2

troops are due to leave Germany by 1995. Unified Germany plans to reduce its Armed Forces to 370,000 by the close of 1994 from the combined Germany total of the early 1990s. The US is taking similar action, closing a third of its 1,600 overseas bases by the end of 1995. Of the bases to be closed, around 80 US military facilities in Europe are to be staged out, bringing down the number of American troops stationed there from 287,000 to 150,000 by 1995.

Restructuring will also affect NATO countries' defence–industrial bases, but corporate strategy has been proactive in this regard, in that rationalisation, consolidation and diversification have been characteristics of the international arms industry since the late 1980s. The process will undoubtedly continue, though perhaps at a slower pace. There is really no choice, except to leave the defence sector altogether, an option which several major contractors have in fact decided to take. Nor is it easy to see how the export market can serve as a life-line in extending Western defence contractors' sales levels of the mid-1980s. Developed country arms imports are now in decline, while developing country imports, widely regarded as the best corporate option, have been in terminal decline for several years. According to SIPRI figures (World Armaments and Disarmament 1991), Third World imports fell from US $27.2 bn in 1987 to US $11.8 bn in 1990.

Compounding the problems of securing export orders to prop up flagging domestic sales, NATO's defence contractors also have to contend with the push for defence–industrialisation by developing States, aided by their ability to extract offsetting technology transfer from the advanced countries' arms vendors. This process will be difficult to halt, as the arms market in the 1990s is very much a buyers' market. Retro-fits to extend the life of existing operational kit will reduce the arms market still further, as will sales of redundant arms located in Europe. Already, at basement prices, tanks have been 'cascading'; that is, sold out-of-area. For example, US tanks have been shipped to Thailand and Egypt, while Czechoslovakian tanks have been sold to Iran and Syria. Finally, the projected emergence of an International Arms Register will act to stem prolific amounts of military equipment exports to unstable nations and regions.

Yet a further piece in the jigsaw has been the development of institutionalised East–West security mechanisms. The 35 nation Conference on Security and Cooperation in Europe (CSCE), including East and West Europe, Canada, the US and the Soviet Union, represents a forum for greater transparency and discussion on important issues affecting greater Europe. Political cooperation in the foreign policy domain has also been supplemented by cooperation in the military sphere by an additional mechanism, the agreement on Conventional Armed Forces in Europe (CFE). The CFE agreement has set in motion a process of controlled European arms reduction amongst East–West States. Conceptually, it is moving towards a position which Professor Taylor has coined 'legitimate defence'.[4] This describes a situation where national military capacity is recognised by friend and foe alike as being sufficient for solely defensive purposes. Politically, arms reductions make sense because the reduced WP threat calls for corresponding reductions in NATO military capacity, but there are implicit economic and military consequences of potentially greater significance for NATO. The fact is that negotiated maximum levels of conventional military equipment in Europe (Treaty limited items) constrains the ability of signatories to act unilaterally in raising national arms thresholds. Clearly, if national military quotas are broken, then Alliance agreed quotas will also be broken. A politically unacceptable position for other Alliance members. Three issues emerge from the CFE agreement:

1) A stimulus is provided for defence manufacturers to reorient research, development and production to those items that are not treaty limited. Here, SIPRI cites laser and railgun technologies (making gun calibre irrelevant for weapons performance), stating that . . . 'Therefore an armoured vehicle with a main armament based on either of these technologies may be unconstrained by CFE even if its mission is identical to that of a conventional battle tank.'[5]

2) Reducing numbers of helicopters, combat aircraft, tanks, artillery pieces, and armoured personnel carriers indirectly suggests that those that remain will require more sophisticated inputs reflecting the need for greater emphasis on intelligence-gathering, reconnaissance, command control and communications systems, as well as flexible state-of-the-art weapons systems. These more specialised requirements will, in turn, transform defence contractors not only in their product structure, i.e., increased emphasis on systems integration and electronic activities, but, in addition, industrial structure, through still further rationalisation and concentration. Huge numbers of defence workers will be affected by this process. For instance, it has been reported that over one million defence employees will lose their jobs in the US defence sector by the mid-1990s.[6] Over the same time-scale, it is expected that Europe's defence industry will contract by up to 30 per cent, leading to an upper boundary of job losses of half a million.[7] Clearly, those NATO countries and contractors most heavily dependent on defence will feel the pain more than others.

3) A further consequence of the CFE agreement will be its influence on NATO policy-making. The combined pressures of increased specialisa-

4

tion, reduced scale and commonality of equipment deployment by NATO States in Europe will act to encourage production and procurement integration amongst NATO countries. Decisions to unilaterally build-up national arms capacity are no longer sustainable. Arms procurement decisions will, in the future, have to be taken on a more integrative basis. This process naturally lends itself not only to arms production cooperation but also to standardisation; a logical goal for multinational forces. Thus, the jigsaw is complete.

This introductory section has attempted to sketch the turbulent but challenging environment in which NATO must now operate. It has also served to provide a backdrop for this book's subject-matter, NATO arms collaboration. A much discussed topic, and one that will have a greater role to play in the radically changing circumstances of the 1990s. The focus of discussion is directed towards the European dimension. The reason for this is straightforward: over the last decade, there has been a dramatic initiation and revitalisation of European cooperative institutions and policies, which, when combined with the defence–industrial restructuring that has recently been taking place, significantly alters the conditions for future NATO arms collaboration.

Chapter One discusses further some of the issues raised in this introduction as well as related aspects of the collaboration debate. The topics are interrelated within an economic, political and military framework, providing a background profile of the changed international system following the disturbances to the status quo. Chapter Two offers an historical review of post-war European policy initiatives aimed at promoting defence cooperation generally, and international arms collaboration in particular. To remind ourselves of the supposed benefits of arms collaboration, Chapter Three provides a theoretical overview of the principles involved. Progress towards constructing Europe's defence–industrial pillar is analysed in Chapter Four, emphasising especially the important contributions that the new technological bow wave industries of electronics and telecommunications are making. Chapter Five concerns itself with the changing industrial structure of Europe's defence industry, including an examination of the status and problems of the Defence Developing Industrial nations (DDI). In conjunction with the cooperative measures sponsored by NATO, the important and related topic of US attitudes, policy initiatives and responses is critically evaluated in Chapter Six. The penultimate chapter deals with the realities of arms collaboration. Here, the costs just as much as the more widely touted benefits are assessed. Finally, Chapter Eight provides a brief review of the subject matter, concluding with a prognosis of NATO arms collaborative developments.

Variations on a Theme of Uncertainty

Into the 1990s the only factor NATO can be certain about is the unpredictability of the situation. Since the mid-1980s the Alliance has been rocked by a series of events, such as the emergence of a benign Soviet Union; the INF Treaty; the democratisation of Eastern Europe, leading to the disintegration of the Warsaw Pact as a Military Alliance; reunification of Germany; the revitalisation and increased projection of European defence cooperation initiatives; substantial declines in defence expenditure on both sides of the East–West axis; changing demographic trends; and the existence of huge US federal budget and foreign deficits. Although this list is not exhaustive, it conveys the radical nature and pace of the changes taking place.

This is not the forum for discussing in detail the convulsive events which have occurred, but it would be a serious omission not to recognise their import since their cumulative impact has not left NATO unscathed. While much of what has happened affects all Alliance nations, the vortex of change is undeniably located in Europe.

In a very real sense, this maelstrom of change has left NATO searching for an aim. For forty years after the end of the Second World War NATO had been successful in its aim of preserving peace because it was operating in a hostile international climate, where a strong and unified Alliance was viewed as essential. In the new epoch currently taking shape, 'cold war' rhetoric and aggressive military postures appear counter-productive and remarkably out of place. The role of NATO must therefore reform correspondingly if the Alliance is to survive. There are several factors which NATO should consider in this reforming process:

(i) Credible Deterrence
As a public good, nations have always been prepared to fund defence for the insurance it affords in the event of external aggression. Clearly, as basic human characteristics have not altered, some minimal threshold of armed force will still be required in the 1990s and beyond. Indeed, the current economic and political instability in the former Soviet Union reinforces this view. If the strains of *Perestroika* and the political machinations of the loosely linked erstwhile Soviet States becomes too abrasive, stability may become threatened. What then? NATO's real threat at this time is that the unpredictability of the situation will be forgotten in the euphoria of liberalisation. Although rapid transition from international tension to peace is unlikely to be reversed, adequate and credible deterrence should remain NATO's goal.

(ii) Super-power Stalemate

The deliberate, institutionally-managed military stalemate of East–West military forces will contribute to change in the following associated areas:

- restructuring of each side's Armed Forces. NATO's efforts to establish multinational forces is an obvious impetus for arms standardisation policies to be made more effective;
- coupled with the demographic changes affecting most NATO States, there is likely to be an increasing emphasis on terminating or reducing conscription, to be replaced with volunteer forces;
- in combating the rise of terrorism and violence in society, NATO armies must be re-structured to play their part. The military in the Third World has been tackling this wider role for some time. For example, the Armed Forces of the Caribbean countries have been tasked with the para-military responsibilities of civil-oriented construction work for years; disaster management relief activities; the control of drug trafficking; ensuring internal stability; as well as the normal military goal of resisting external aggression.

(iii) 'Out-of-Area' Tasks

The greater stability in NATO's Central European front, wherever that may now lie, will allow NATO to refocus its attention to currently non-NATO strategic environments which are unstable, impinging on the security of Alliance States. Springing to mind in this context is the volatile Middle-East region bordering the southern flank of NATO. Due to the uncontrolled military activities of some Middle-Eastern countries it should be noted that Turkey, and to a lesser extent Greece, are unlikely to enjoy 'peace dividends' to the same extent as other NATO States.

Although these issues are pertinent to the circumstances NATO faces in the 1990s, the immediate priority is to ensure the establishment of a new and lasting economic and political order in Europe. At the core of this is the integration of Germany. Even though the problems are daunting, the inconceivable has already become reality. The cataclysmic nature of the changes Europe is now undergoing can be gauged by the *volte face* experienced by East Germany, almost overnight: from one of the most hardline of East Europe's military regimes to the world's first nation to possess a Ministry of *Disarmament* and Defence. In combination with this, note that prior to full reunification the German Democratic Republic announced that it intended, over several stages during the 1990s, to destroy around 2,000 MBTs, 4,300 armoured combat vehicles, 1,700 artillery systems (greater than 100 mm in calibre), and 160 combat aircraft.[8] Just as significantly, from 1991 onwards. 7,000–10,000 members of what used to be East Germany's Armed Forces are to be annually released into the civil sector. Also, as transitional measures, it was announced that a State Secretary for Disarmament and a Department Head for Military Conversion were to be appointed. The latter person would be at the helm of the planning mechanism for re-structuring the economy to accommodate the rising numbers of 'demobbed' military personnel.

The economic effects of the reunification of Germany will be profound, with increasing unemployment in the short-run inevitable. In addition, the rising unemployment is likely to be accompanied by inflationary pressure as the high cost of reunification makes itself felt. Fanning the inflationary flames will be the ill-considered costs of destroying military equipment, a major design aim of which was indestructibility. The costs of this process are likely to be substantial, much more so than the associated expenses of verification.

As reunified Germany is to remain an active member of the NATO Alliance, then a side-effect of unemployment, inflationary pressure and declining defence expenditures will be even further rationalisation in defence activity. This will, of course, affect Germany's defence–industrial base. The restructuring of its defence sector will be a scaling-down process, and will parallel similar developments in other NATO member economies. Interestingly, in the wave of rationalisation to date, it has been the 'captains of industry' rather than the military generals that have proved more deft in determining the nature of armaments supply. But it is to this issue that, for NATO, an imponderable remains: the shape and size of the Alliance's future defence–industrial capability. International armaments cooperation is certain to play its part.

Despite the fact that in practical terms the zest for collaboration fails to match the enthusiasm of political statements, collaborative arms projects will continue to be undertaken because the perceived economies they generate will become more important as defence activity declines. Economics has always been the prime-mover for collaboration. It was the principal reason why NATO countries embraced joint-venture projects in the 1970s and 1980s. Cost-saving provided the most popular rationale for the accelerated implementation of NATO cooperative programmes during this period. The speculated levels of collaborative savings have been enormous: Thomas A. Callaghan Jr., in his famous 1975 report on US/European economic cooperation, contended savings would approximate to $10 billion (in 1975 prices);[9] the US Senate Armed Services Committee in the late 1970s estimated Alliance savings of $10–15 billion per year;[10] while, more recently, a study performed by the US Department of Defence (DoD) estimated that over the last 25 years

8

NATO could have saved $50 billion in today's dollars by fully cooperating in the development, testing and procurement of a number of weapons systems.[11]

A further rationale for cooperation has been in terms of the military benefits of standardisation. The present diversity of NATO arms production signifies the importance of this objective, to the extent that one Allied Commander in Europe suggested that the Alliance was losing at least 30 per cent and in some cases 50 per cent of capability due to lack of standardisation.[12] However, in the present uncertain climate, international industrial collaboration has itself become the target of criticism. This has occurred for two reasons: firstly, for facilitating, indeed, even precipitating, the shrivelling of competitive forces, thus inducing industrial concentration, in the defence sector, and, secondly, for kindling the potential for political and military–industrial divergence between the US and European elements of NATO. As these issues set the scene for discussion in later chapters, it will be useful at this point to provide a fuller explanation of their importance.

NATO's Evolving Defence–Industrial Milieu

On the surface, NATO-wide defence–industrial policy during the 1980s has been clear-cut: closer cooperation at the planning, design, development and production stages. An important aspect of this process has been the emphasis given to the building-up of European defence–industrial capabilities; a policy supported by successive American administrations. The attractiveness of European defence industrialisation to NATO was that it would help reduce the divisiveness within its ranks over the Euro–US arms trading imbalance on the 'Two-way street', which was continually in America's favour. Moreover, greater equivalence between Europe and the US in terms of armaments development and production capabilities could only act to stimulate transatlantic weapons collaboration, thus decreasing costs at the same time as securing improvements in arms standardisation.

Behind the veneer of policy statements, developments at the defence–industrial level have been enigmatic and contradictory. Three separate, but interrelated areas stand out in this respect:

(i) Capriciousness of Competition Policy
Within NATO, the UK has been at the vanguard of competition policy. The cornerstone of its approach was the implementation of the 'Levene' proposals in 1985. These had regard to the efforts of the UK's Head of

Defence Procurement at the Ministry of Defence (MoD), Sir Peter Levene, to reform the system of procurement. They rest on three main principles: that suppliers should compete for development and production contracts (i.e. competitive tendering); that suppliers, and not customers, should bear the risk of failure, but should in return be rewarded for efficiency through higher profits (i.e. fixed-price contracts); and that budgetary control should be strengthened at all points (i.e. payment dependent on progress).[13] The thrust of these policy reforms was towards increasing competition and risk-exposure among defence contractors so that through resulting improvements in efficiency, the costs of equipment procurement could be reduced. This was the epitome of the Thatcher Government's market-oriented economic strategy. An essential strand of this classical philosophy was non-intervention. Government interference was regarded as a distortive influence on market signals, and should therefore be kept to a minimum.

This is fine in theory, but in practice during the mid- to late-1980s severe pressures were building-up in the UK defence industry for industrial concentration. The British Government, through its Monopolies and Mergers Commission (MMC), initially attempted to maintain competitive levels, in line with its market approach. In 1986, for example, GEC's bid to take over Plessey, a key defence electronics company, was rejected by the MMC on the grounds that it would restrict competition in Britain's defence electronics market. However, four years later, the premise on which that decision was reached was abandoned. The MMC in early 1990 approved a joint GEC–Siemens's bid for Plessey.

This policy turnaround by the government flags a segmenting of the UK defence market. It would seem that policy now discriminates between, on the one hand, the already powerful defence contractors, such as GEC, British Aerospace (B.Ae.) and Rolls Royce, and, on the other the components and subsystems producers at the lower end of the industrial scale; for these latter contractors, competition policy remains inviolable. For the big defence manufacturers, by contrast, the drive was for scale. To facilitate this objective, the government had been obliged to break the head of steam building up by allowing the UK's major defence firms the opportunity to engage in the restructuring taking place in Europe's defence–industrial base.

Suddenly, at the prime contractor level, 'bigness' became an imperative. As discussed in Chapter Five, a series of mergers and acquisitions took place in Europe during the late 1980s. The reasons for this rapid surge in European defence–industrial consolidation were twofold. Firstly, European consolidation was increasingly being seen as a considered response to the extant military–industrial power of the US, as well as the increasingly ominous strength of Japan's arms-related manufacturing capability. Secondly, there was a knee-jerk reaction operating, with corporate interests attempting to ensure that the most efficient cost structures were available prior to the 1992 trade liberalisation policies coming into effect. In a contradiction of terms, scale became a requisite for competition.

The revitalised Independent European Programme Group (IEPG) also played its part in the restructuring process through the approval of its Action Plan in the Autumn of 1988 (see Chapter Two). The aim of this policy document was the gradual evolution of a 'European' arms market. The two main features of the IEPG Action Plan relate to international cooperation in defence research and development (R&D) and the opening of European defence markets to competition (see Chapter Five). In both instances, the aim was to promote corporate efficiency. No longer would nationalism provide its own unique barrier to trade. With obstacles to cross-border competition progressively being removed, and a commitment by governments to buy foreign when justified (symbolically evidenced by Britain's purchase of American AWACs to replace the local, though disastrous, Nimrod venture), 'bigness' suddenly became respectable, indeed, essential, for market survival.

(ii) Military–Industrial Linkages
The apocalyptic changes affecting Soviet military policy over recent years has led to the complete collapse of the framework of assumptions on which NATO strategy was formulated. The dissolving Communist threat, as would be expected, has had ripple effects on defence expenditure plans by Alliance States. NATO's decade-long policy of three per cent increases in real defence spending was abandoned early on in the process. For the US, according to Pentagon-based General Powell, the consensus view is that the government is aiming for a defence budget reduction of around 25 per cent.[14] Moreover, although European nations continue to spend around $50 billion on defence annually, all national defence budgets are now coming under close scrutiny. In the UK, 'Options for Change' has signalled swingeing reductions in the military. France is scaling down planned military commitments. For Germany, across the board reductions in military spending are expected, with sustainable military manpower levels down to below 400,000. Defence reviews have been undertaken by the Norwegians and Danes, with the latter's projected defence spending poised on a steeply downward trajectory. The Belgians and Dutch also have plans for rationalisation of defence spending. The Netherlands, in particular, is considering severe cuts in defence spending: up to 15 per cent reductions in the 1990s on military

personnel and equipment; the de-commissioning of two submarines, 20 naval warfare helicopters, several frigates; the cancellation in the modernisation of Leopard-1 tanks; and the cancellation or delay in the acquisition of Stinger and Patriot missile systems. The only nations where defence budgets may hold up are the DDI countries of Greece, Portugal and Turkey, and also, perhaps, Spain.

The resultant reduction in defence equipment procurement will have a negative impact on capacity, investment and employment in the defence industry. In the former Soviet Union these scarce resources are required for civil purposes. Indeed, the pace of military to civilian production has been dramatic. Note the following comments excerpted from the Soviet weekly, *Ogonyok* (May 19, 1989):

'It has already been decided [by the Soviet government] to enlist the use of 345 defense plants and 200 defense-related scientific research institutes in peacetime production. Among these the Ministry of Aviation Industries has been assigned production of equipment for fruit and vegetable, starch, sugar syrup, and macaroni production as well as machinery for the canning industry; the Ministry of Defense Industries, the production of assemblies and production lines for processing meat and fowl, ice cream production, and the manufacture of metal canning containers; the Ministry of Medium Machine Building [nuclear weapons], development of milk production technology; the Ministry of Machine Building, production of equipment for the baking, sugar-refining, confectionary, brewing, butter and fat industries.'[15]

The wherewithal for this conversion will come from the anticipated annual 5 per cent falls in defence spending; reducing the production of tanks by 52 per cent; military aircraft by 12 per cent; military helicopters by 60 per cent; and munitions by 20 per cent, as compared to the Five Year military expenditure plan covering 1990.[16]

In the West, several of the key industrial actors are considering diversifying out of defence production. B.Ae. is laying more emphasis on civil production (even though currently the greater proportion of its profits come from defence contracts). VSEL Consortium, the UK's only submarine manufacturer, is seeking to return to commercial shipbuilding, after nearly a decade's absence; it has already acquired a 'beachhead' in the oil and gas industries' control equipment, power generation and telecommunications area, through purchase of the small but strategic Scottish firm, Sealand Industries. Racal has been successfully diversifying from military to civil markets.[17] Yet, while STC has been considering such a move, Thorn–EMI has already sought to divest, but has been unable to do so. On the Continent, Philips, the Dutch conglomerate, has been more successful (see Chapter Five). And in the US, Hughes Aircraft, a leading American defence electronics group is, in the face of declining US defence budgets, restructuring its seven operating units into three business areas by the mid-1990s: aerospace and defence; telecommunications and space; and new commercial business. Reducing corporate dependency on defence is now the name of the game.

For those companies staying in the defence sector, it is inevitable that most will be obliged to restructure production. Changing Force requirements will dictate the direction this takes. Irrespective of whether more emphasis will be given to 'defensive' as opposed to 'offensive' military systems, there is little dispute that electronics, telecommunications and surveillance equipment will be the dominant technological areas during the 1990s. In the post-CFE (Conventional Forces in Europe) Treaty, it can be anticipated that the core growth areas of defence sector production will be in the product fields charted below. The German Defence Industry is already restructuring production along these lines.

Reconnaissance	Command	Electronic
Verification	Control	Warfare &
	Communication	Countermeasures
	Information &	
	Intelligence	

For some economies, where there is a high level of industrial dependence on defence spending, military-to-civil industrial conversion will prove painful. This applies particularly to Britain, where, since the early 1970s, there has been a growing reliance by industry on defence funding. Military expenditure was especially vital during the early recessionary years of the 1980s. As proportions of manufacturing and engineering GDP, defence procurement rose from 6.3 to 12.2 per cent and 17.3 to 32.7 per cent, respectively, between 1976 and 1983.[18] A way of mitigating the trauma of transition is to opt for the 'Third Way'; that is for investment to be directed into the 'dual-use' technology industries. This enables defence firms to hedge their bets regarding the extent of the rise in the elasticity coefficients of defence goals. It also allows production to be geared to previously identified growth areas in defence equipment procurement. As the electronics and telecommunication areas of production are likely to become leading-edge, technology-drivers, significant cross-fertilisation of innovational effort can be expected to spread from the civil to military side of the business, rather than the reverse track.

(iii) Competition 'and' Concentration

Consolidation of Europe's defence industry has been forced by economic considerations. Fears of corporate alliances have led to the bevy of mergers and takeovers. French anxiety at being isolated in this process has softened its traditionally nationalistic stance over the sovereignty of local defence industry, though there continues to be hostility towards US investment. Economics appears to be achieving in Europe what two and a half decades of NATO collaborative policies have failed to deliver: convergence towards a unified defence–industrial complex. From a previous amorphous entity, the complex is now taking shape. It is dominated by Germany, Britain and France, through the powerful corporate conglomerates of Daimler–Benz, B.Ae. and GEC, Thomson–CSF, Aerospatiale and Dassault; with the convergence increasing through the speculated merger of these latter two companies.

Clearly, though this military–industrial convergence is good for standardisation, it is bad for competition and possibly technological dynamism, also. Some commentators have suggested this dilemma can be overcome through competing consortia, where transnational defence firms team up to compete against each other for particular major items of defence equipment. However, the outcome of such competitions will have to be institutionally orchestrated, enabling the losers to be sufficiently compensated to ensure their commercial survival for future competitions. Moreover, it is difficult to conceive how such consortia can increase competition beyond the 'big three' Euro nations' defence companies. This augurs badly for both the DDI nations and possibly also the US. These topics are discussed further in Chapter Five. However, with regard to the US–Euro defence cooperative position, it is worth offering a few comments at this juncture.

Europe's push for defence industrialisation has conspicously been to the neglect of its US ally. This, as will be discussed in the next section, has bred transatlantic acrimony. In particular cases, collaborative programmes have been pursued with great success; the US–UK co-production of the Harrier AV-8B is a good example. Major transatlantic procurement contracts have also been awarded: the French winning an order to supply their RITA telecommunications equipment to the US, while the US has taken French and British orders for AWACs aircraft. However, two points need to be made concerning transatlantic arms trade and transatlantic cooperation.

Firstly, stepping aside from the progress made on the 'two-way street' and comparative weapons testing policies in the US, the degree of penetration into the US defence market was worse in 1989 than it was ten years earlier in 1979. Table 1.1 shows that while there were eight non-US firms (including non-European defence companies) on the Pentagon's 'Top 100' firms of prime defence contract awards in 1989, there were 10 on the list in 1979. Furthermore, the value of the 1979 awards was $1.714 billion, or 2.71 per cent of Pentagon contracts compared to only $1.554 billion or 1.17 per cent of DoD contracts in 1989.[19] It should also be noted that these non-US awards were only a fraction of total DoD contracts in FY 1989. While McDonnell Douglas, General Dynamics and General Electric were awarded contracts valued at $8.6 billion, $6.9 billion, and $5.8 billion, respectively, the top non-US firm in Table 1.1,

Table 1.1: Non US-Firms on Pentagon's 'Top-100' Contract Awards List (FY 1989)

Rank	Company	$ ('000)
52	Royal Dutch Petroleum	306,245
63	Philips Gloeilampenfabrieken	220,486
70	Rolls Royce Plc	207,587
71	Montedison Spa	196,487
72	CAE Industries Ltd	184,358
78	MIP Instandsetzungsbetric	165,467
79	Smiths Industries Plc	163,340
100	Nisshin Service Co Ltd	109,861
	Total	$1,533,822

Source: *Armed Forces Journal International* (May 1990), p. 18.

Royal Dutch (which in any case is not an arms contractor), captured $306 million, representing only 0.23 per cent of total Pentagon contracts in FY 1989. Thus, although the latest figures for transatlantic arms trade suggest that the imbalance is now only 1:2 in favour of the US, as opposed to 1:10 at the start of the decade, the suggestion is that NATO is moving towards balance but at a lower level of trade.

This leads to the second point, which concerns transatlantic industrial collaboration. The danger is that increased emphasis on European Defence industrialisation and intra-European collaboration will initiate a permanent trend in this direction, rather than establishing a base for improving the degree of Euro–US cooperative ventures. The current pattern of such European ventures appears to be aimed at complete local-sourcing of electronics, avionics; indeed, all components under all circumstances. On their own, these are not optimistic signs for integrative NATO-wide ventures, but there are other less sanguine portents. Since the start of the 1990s, there has been a rising number of withdrawals from

Euro–US collaborative programmes. The depletion of participants leading to the cancellation of the NFR-90 project is a classic example in this context. However, although there may be other reasons accounting for the apparent fragility of Euro–US arms cooperation, only one conclusion can be drawn from the US Government's reduction in the funds it makes available for cooperative research and weapons testing under the 1985 Nunn Amendment. For further discussion on this point, see Chapter Six.

Political Turbulence : NATO Consensus Vs Intra-European Collaboration

There has been no single reason why NATO European members have endeared themselves to collaborative ventures, but rather a *pot pourri* of motives, some of which are entirely European in character. Self-sufficiency, for instance, could be cited as an important explanatory variable, but why should Europe seek to be self-reliant within NATO? Significantly, some observers have advanced the argument that it has been the contemporary widening of the diplomatic, political and economic schism between Europe and the US that European policy-emphasis towards intra-regional defence collaboration has been predicated. Others have rejected this argument, suggesting instead that 'preferential' intra-European collaboration has been the causal factor for much of the transatlantic friction and distrust.

Either way, a 'two-way street' now exists in abrasiveness. From the US side the former US Ambassador to NATO, David Abshire, is reported to have acknowledged . . . 'there is concern in the US that when Europeans talk about defence industry "cooperation" what they mean is putting up a united front to compete against US defence industries.'[20] More explicitly, Deputy Secretary Taft states . . . 'there are some European collaborative projects which the Europeans want to exclude the US from participating, like the European Fighter Aircraft (EFa) project'.[21] Boeing President, Mr Shrontz further comments, 'while defence had traditionally lain outside European competence, discussion in the European Commission of adding customs duties to non-lethal defence imports into the Community . . . (has) . . . fanned fears of protectionism in the US . . . the American impression is that there is a growing attitude in Europe to buy European wherever possible, if necessary at a premium'.[22] These US concerns regarding European nationalism in the defence sphere are already being translated in Congress into protectionist sentiment: the Secretary of Commerce has been given the right to appeal to the President to overturn any Memorandum of Understanding (MoU) affecting the competitiveness of the US; the Trade Secretary has been requested to report to the President and Congress over the procurement practices of US allies and trading partners under the presumption that American industrial and hi-technological markets are more competitive than those in Europe; and legislation has already been introduced aimed at abolishing bilateral MoUs in 5 years.[23]

By contrast, European anxieties over US motives on security and trade issues can be gauged from the following events and comments: firstly, in response to the US Government's blunt and direct statement to the Western European Nations (WEU) that the US saw no need to revitalise the WEU as any larger European role in defence should take place within NATO,[24] the Belgian diplomat, Mr Alfred Cahen, who became the revived WEU's Secretary-General, was open about the various motives for its revitalisation, citing the quality and stamina of leadership in Washington as being amongst them.[25] At about the same time, Sir Geoffrey Howe made the candid statement that . . . 'We need to be alert to trends in American thinking which might diminsh our security – perhaps not today or tomorrow, but possibly in the longer term'.[26] Also, more recently, the French Defence Minister, Jean-Pierre Chevenement issued the admonition that European governments are duty-bound to look first to European sources;[27] a similar sentiment also being expressed by Spain's Minister for Defence.[28] Europeanist views such as these have also appeared in supra-national reports on European defence–industrialisation. In this context, note the recommendation contained in the IEPG report, *Towards A Stronger Europe*, prepared by the Dutch diplomat Mr Vredeling: . . . 'Nations should be willing to contemplate cooperation *within Europe* as a *first* course of action for suitably sized projects'.[29] (Italics added.)

Although it is difficult to disentangle the web of criticism and counter-criticism to establish cause and effect, a major aspect of the current crisis of consensus in NATO is here again dictated by economics. For the Americans, many of the problems are rooted in the alleged inequities of defence burden-sharing: in this respect, the Europeans, in similarity with the Japanese, are accused of 'free-riding' on the backs of the American taxpayer. In support of this view, simplistic comparisons have been made using the rate of defence expenditure to Gross Domestic Product (GDP). According to this comparative yardstick the US proportion is double that of most of its NATO Allies.[30] When measured in absolute terms, US military expenditure committed to NATO is $160–170 billion, representing 60 per cent of the defence budget, which is significantly more than the defence contributions of the other 15 NATO members put together.[31]

Two factors makes this burden more difficult to carry. Firstly, the degree of gearing underpinning the US economy. Foreign indebtedness, in particular, is at crisis level: in 1988 net US foreign debt reached $532 billion showing an increase of $154 billion from 1987; foreign interest alone tops $200 billion each year. Yet, in 1983, at about the time US defence spending was increasing, America was a creditor nation. Rightly or wrongly, this led to the widespread belief that US budget deficits and defence spending are connected, as epitomised by the acerbic comment made by one US Defence Department official, 'that if the US were to spend 3 per cent of GDP like West Germany, instead of 6 per cent as it does, it would wipe out its federal budget deficit'.[32]

The second irritant causing US discomfort is the alleged ungratefulness of the Europeans for what America perceives as the disproportionate share of its largesse transferred across the Atlantic. For ungratefulness, read non-reciprocity. The Europeans have been regarded as offering only token support for US sanctions against Iran over the US hostages, and against the Soviet Union over its invasion of Afghanistan; worse still was the hostile reaction to US military action in Grenada, and similarly over the US bombing of Libya. There was also the Spanish Government's insistence that US F-16 fighters of the 401st Tactical Fighter Wing depart Spain; a NATO ally. Although European support during the Gulf war was acknowledged by the US, the perception of inequality still remains.

America's fetish over burden-sharing is matched by Europe's fixation with the military trade balance. Since the 1970s, NATO Europe has been obsessed with balancing military trade along the 'two-way street'. America supports this goal, but the scale of the problem is not the same. For instance, the 1987 US–Euro defence trade ratio was expected to have increased in favour of the US by at least 25 per cent over the 1.6:1 recorded for 1986. The 1987 ratio would thus be about 1:2 in favour of the US. In the larger scheme of things, however, these figures represent only about two per cent of total US defence procurement and a fraction of one per cent of the US national trade balance.[33] For Europe, on the other hand, the need to balance military trade with the US is more urgent. The ratio has taken on symbolic value, reflecting Europe's industrial and technological self-reliance in defence development and production. There is a growing under-current of thought in Europe articulating the need for self-sufficiency in this area, fuelled by such events as: the strong streak of unilateralism running through President Reagan's 'Star Wars' plan; the President's apparent willingness to bargain away nuclear deterrence at Reykjavik; the perceived manner in which the Intermediate Nuclear Forces Treaty was negotiated over the Europeans' heads; and, finally, the belief that the US contemplates military withdrawal from Europe.[34]

To foster the goal of defence self-reliance, relevant institutions have flowered. The creation and revitalisation of policy-discussion forums by European States have been aimed at developing a unified European approach to defence issues as well as foreign policy. Recent efforts in this direction fit into the current epoch, beginning with publication of the Klepsch Report in 1979, which seeks a strong European defence–industrial base as a necessary preliminary for Europe to effectively compete on the 'two-way street'. Since then two European institutions have developed in importance. There is firstly the IEPG. This was established in the mid-1970s to promote European collaboration in the research, development and production of defence equipment, and to maintain a healthy European industrial and technological defence base while working towards improving transatlantic arms cooperation. With an integrated Europe on the horizon in 1992, 13 IEPG countries met in Luxembourg in November 1988, and approved a 'Euro Arms' development plan for encouraging the evolvement of a Defence Common Market,[35] representing a more modest version of the Vredeling Group's proposals.[36]

The second European Institution is the WEU, deriving from the revised Brussels Treaty of 1954. Its membership comprises nine of the most important European States. The WEU, besides representing a military relationship, is the source of a significant collective defence–industrial strategy framework, the 1987 'Platform of Security Interests'. This policy-approach links security cooperation and increased integration, with the Single European Market (SEA) playing a key role, and either the WEU or the EC as the appropriate policy-making forum for defence matters. Although, from the defence perspective, the 1986 SEA is open to interpretation, the European Commission President has stated on several occasions that the SEA and its title III, in particular, makes the European Community the competent body for discussion of security and defence issues.[37]

In promoting the drive towards transatlantic arms collaboration, the US has introduced a number of initiatives since the late 1970s. The process began in 1977 with the Culver–Nunn Amendment to the Defence Authorisation Act. Even though its passage merely institutionalised measures that were already policy, such as the waiver provisions of the 1933 'Buy American' Act and the recognition of Rationalization, Standardization and Interoperability (RSI) as a US objective (albeit that it was already an agreed NATO aim), the Amendment provided a positive signal to Europe that the US was solidly behind NATO cooperative effort. In 1983, the Glen–Roth–Nunn Amendment was passed, re-establishing the commitment to RSI, but intending that it be achieved by the creation of an open, competitive market in defence equipment, and a trading structure that would accomplish more than the 'piecemeal' government MoUs of past administrations.[38] The last Nunn Amendment in 1986 was aimed at fostering cooperative R&D by the US and its NATO Allies through comparative evaluation. The 1986 measure supplements the Foreign Weapons Evaluation (FWE) programme which has been in existence since the early 1980s.[39] The results, particularly from the latter measures, have been especially evident in the aerospace sector. Air force programmes such as the Modular Stand Off Weapon (MSOW), Multifunctional Information Distribution System (MIDS), NATO Identification System (NIS), and Enhanced Fighter Manoeuverability, are all proceeding under the auspices of the most recent Nunn Amendment, requiring co-development wherever possible.[40]

Examining whether intra-European collaboration is a divisive rather than unifying experience for the Alliance throws up contradictory signals. There is no doubting that arms collaboration is proceeding apace whatever the political fall-out. Table 1.2, showing the list of UK collaborative programmes is evidence of this. However, its coercive force is changing: the threat from the former Soviet Union and the East European States has effectively disappeared, with the main enemy now viewed as the increasingly large claims against scarce resources demanded by defence budgets. Inevitably, this begs the question: what is the appropriate level of defence required?

Appropriate Level of Defence

The response to this question falls into the politico-strategic domain. Threat perception primarily determines military need, which in democratic countries must be prudently balanced against the social, infrastructural and economic responsibilities of government in respect of the civil sector. In this sense, Mikhail Gorbachev's 'charm' offensive succeeded in forcing NATO to re-assess its long-held judgement that continued military build-up is necessary to match the omnipotent WP threat. During his term in office, President Gorbachev's gritty political determination and personal charisma enabled him to bring to fruition a remarkable number of radical diplomatic initiatives, spanning the withdrawal of Soviet military forces from Afghanistan; the conclusion of the INF and START Treaties; and, incredibly, the dissolution of the 'Soviet Union', as it was known, along with communism. A likely consequence of the shrinking nuclear arsenal in Europe will be a greater reliance on conventional military capability. This process will consolidate the ongoing search for cost reductions in the production of conventional military equipment. NATO efforts to secure such cost reductions have been predicated on pressures to raise the level of return on given levels of defence expenditure. Although there have recently been real declines in monies devoted to defence, defence expenditure during the 1980s had exhibited an upward trend. For example, between 1980 and 1987 (in constant 1986 prices) American defence outlays rose from US $195 to 275 billion; French, from US $26 to 29 billion; and British from US $23 to 27 billion.[41] Nor were the Warsaw Pact States isolated from this trend. Over the same period, the German Democratic Republic's defence expenditure rose from US $3,142 to 5,388 billion, while Hungary's nearly doubled from US $513 to 936 billion.[42]

This rise in defence expenditure was associated with a number of characteristics, which remain valid in the 1990s even though defence spending is now contracting. Firstly, the cost in absolute terms of new weapons systems is extremely high. The most notorious example being the US B-2 'Stealth' bomber, presently costed at an incredible US $530 million per plane.[43] Compounding the problem of high costs, however, is their rate of increase. It is generally held that cost escalation of weapons systems proceeds at a pace faster than the rate of inflation. A major reason for this increase in cost relates to the rise in development effort inherent in producing increasingly sophisticated weapons systems. The case of US fighter aircraft provides a good example. Thirty years ago, the first F-84 was rolled out only three years and three months after the programme began; the F-104 a few years later took about five years; the F-14 took more than seven years; the F-15 and F-16 each stretched to ten years; the F-18 more than eleven years, while the first operational Advanced Tactical Fighter (ATF) is scheduled for fifteen years.[44]

The phenomenon of defence equipment costs rising faster than defence budgets has been described by Thomas A. Callaghan Jr. as 'structural disarmament'. Its impact on NATO thinking has led logically to a second issue being addressed: What are the most cost-effective means for attaining a specified level of defence commitment? A much lauded approach in this respect are the strictures of the UK Government's 'competitive markets' orthodoxy. Value-for-money initiatives touch all government departments, but none more than Britain's MoD.

Their purpose is unequivocal: to make government leaner and to save money. In achieving this goal, economy, efficiency and effectiveness have become buzzwords. In fact, policies are being introduced (i.e., New Management Strategy (NMS)) in which the gospel of budgetary discipline is intended to enlighten even field commanders.

At the NATO level, the UK has sought improvements in defence–industrial performance through the medium of collaboration. The

Table 1.2: UK Collaborative Projects (March 1990)

in production or service:

	AUSTRALIA	BELGIUM	CANADA	DENMARK	FRANCE	FRG	GREECE	ITALY	NETHERLANDS	NORWAY	SPAIN	TURKEY	US
Naval Equipment:													
Sea Gnat decoy system				●									●
Barra sonobuoys	●												
Land Equipment:													
FH70 Howitzer						●		●					
M483A1 Artillery Shell									●				●
Scorpion Reconnaisance Vehicle		●											
Multiple-Launch Rocket System – Phase 1					●	●		●					●
Missiles:													
Martel Air-to-Surface					●								
Sidewinder Air-to-Air						●		●		●			●
Milan Anti-Tank (inc. improvements)					●	●							
Air Systems:													
Jaguar					●								
Lynx					●								

22

Puma

Gazelle

Tornado

Harrier AV8B/GR5

Joint Tactical Information Distribution System

Other Equipment:

Midge Drone

in development or earlier study phases:

Naval Equipment:

Ships Low-Cost Inertial Navigation System

Talisman – Surface Ship Torpedo Defence System[1]

NATO Improved Link 11[2]

Land Equipment:

COBRA (Counter Battery Radar)

EUROPEAN ARMS COLLABORATION

	US	TURKEY	SPAIN	NORWAY	NETHERLANDS	ITALY	GREECE	FRG	FRANCE	DENMARK	CANADA	BELGIUM	AUSTRALIA
Multiple-Launch Rocket System Phase III	●							●	●				
Aimed Control Effect Anti-Tank mine								●	●				
Electro-magnetic Launcher	●												
Missiles:													
TRIGAT (Third Generation Anti-Tank Guided Weapon)								●	●				
Advanced Short-Range Air-to-Air Missile				●									
Family of Anti-Air Missile Systems			●			●			●				
Air Systems:													
Airborne Radar Demonstrator System[1]	●								●				
European Fighter Aircraft			●			●		●					
EH101 Helicopter						●							
A129 Light Attack Helicopter			●		●	●							
RTM322 Helicopter Engine									●				
Allied Standard Avionics Architecture Initiative	●							●	●				

Other Equipment:

NATO Identification System (NIS) Information Exchange[1]

NIS Question & Answer Component Development[1]

Ada Computer Language Project Support Environment[1]

Tactical Communications Systems for the Land Combat Zone post 2000[1]

Universal Modem for Satellite Communications

Allied Data Systems Interoperability Agency NATO Procedural Interoperability Standards[1]

Stand-off Radar Programme of Studies[1]

Notes:
1 US share of these projects includes Nunn Amendment funding.
2 Link 11 is the principal Maritime Tactical Data Link used by NATO nations.

Source: *Statement on Defence Estimates* 1990.

reduction of trade barriers either through removal (the 1986 SEA) or waivers (by MoU dispensations of the Buy American Act) has hastened the pace of collaboration. However, the fear remains that because of national predilections to conserve domestic defence–industrial capacity, even within this collaborative framework, the approach is an institutional second-best attempt at enjoying the benefits of competition *and* scale.

Doubts regarding the validity of collaborative doctrine only surface when discussion moves from the theoretical to the empirical. The principal underlying defect concerns the degree of governmental interference. Political constrictions cause inefficiency. It is because of this that awkward questions can, and indeed, sometimes are raised concerning: the costs international collaboration imposes on political consensus, particularly in relation to perceived regionalisation within NATO of common defence–industrial objectives; the cost-effectiveness of joint-ventures; the influence of collaboration on the character of NATO's evolving defence–industrial structure, trading relationships, and competitive forces; the role of the DDI nations; and, not least, the effect collaboration has on the standardisation of weaponry and logistical equipment.

Conclusion

The close of the 1980s has witnessed quite remarkable events in the international arena. Changes in the strategic environment look set to elevate the importance of arms collaboration in the Alliance. This chapter has introduced the factors which have helped to shape this process. It is important to note that discussion has not emphasised any one feature as being overridingly important. Instead, the focus has been on the interrelationship between events: budgetary pressures; crises in the Gulf, Eastern Europe and the Soviet Union; high technology and high cost weapons development; changed force levels and structure; industrial restructuring; and institutionalised agreements have all acted in concert to raise the profile of political cooperation and military collaboration.

A key conclusion to emerge from this opening chapter, then, is that NATO arms collaboration in the 1990s, facing an entirely new set of strategic, political and economic conditions and prospects, is on the threshold of acceptance in an environment where nationalistic defence–industrial policies have become obsolete. CFE-induced interdependence and declining defence budgets have narrowed the scope for nationalism in arms procurement and production. The chapters that follow trace and describe the major characteristics of NATO arms collaboration in reaching the position where it is today.

2 HISTORY

Introduction

NATO collaboration is not a recent phenomenon. It has been an aim of the Alliance for a long time. The purpose of this chapter is to historically review policy developments in this field, with particular emphasis on the contribution that Europe has made in this process. Three phases in a continuum of policy initiatives will be identified. These are discussed in detail, beginning with an appraisal of the post-war task of securing some form of European identity to assuage the threat of further intra-European conflict. The second stage, Europe's political and economic growing pains, is then examined. This phase is characterised by numerous ambitious cooperative proposals failing to find consensus in an era of US military dominance. Finally, there is the third phase, which is in effect a transitionary stage for perhaps the ultimate goal of defence Europeanisation. The EC has an outside chance of assuming this responsibility, though as indicated in the chapter, ambiguities surround the constitutional possibilities in this regard.

A feature of post-war cooperative endeavour is that the momentum of policy accelerated noticeably during the 1980s. This is clearly the case in terms of European developments, but it also applies to NATO's efforts in encouraging Alliance-wide collaborative links, as discussed in the latter part of this chapter.

The First Phase: European Rehabilitation

European defence–industrial initiatives have a long history. The Second World War acted as the catalyst for change, in the sense that pre-war defence policy was very much a national domain, whereas in the post-war period there has been a far greater emphasis on a collectivist European approach to the subject. The initial rationale for this change of policy direction was to ensure that Germany was fully integrated not just into a European economic and political framework, but an interdependent defence arrangement also. A re-industrialising Germany would pose less of a military threat to its European neighbours as a consequence.

The first step towards European interdependence was not long in coming. In the immediate post-war period, a grouping of several countries was formed, including Belgium, France, Luxembourg, the Netherlands and the United Kingdom. The signing of this Alliance on the 17 March 1948 created the first rung on the ladder of Europe's quest for common security. The entity formed was officially called the Brussels Treaty Organisation (BTO), though it was better known as simply the 'Western Union'. From this modest beginning, a panoply of policy measures ensued. Several of these measures focused on the importance of cultivating foreign policy and defence arrangements that were entirely European in character; others were premised on the development of a security posture that included Europe's North American allies, the US and Canada. This vision of an Atlantic security arrangement led, of course, to the creation, in April 1949, of the Atlantic Alliance – the North Atlantic Treaty Organisation (NATO) – heralding an unbroken era of American involvement in European security matters. The creation of NATO, moulded as it was, and still is to a great extent, around American military strength, overshadowed Europe's incipient policy efforts aimed at securing defence autonomy. Indeed, it is fair to say that the BTO's *raison d'être* was eclipsed by the formation of NATO even though the European organisation embodied a stronger military commitment than NATO. Note that while the BTO's Article V, which still remains in force today, commits member States *automatically* to the defence of one another in the event of attack, the Alliance Treaty merely commits member States to take *whatever steps* are constitutionally necessary to come to each other's defence. This distinction, however, is more apparent than real because in the event of an attack against an Alliance State, NATO's Integrated Military Structure is activated.[1] As one source eloquently couches the situation:

> 'NATO, to borrow Joseph Frankel's distinction, circumscribes rather than overrides its signatories' sovereignty. It has no provision for the type of majority voting which would allow some members to declare war on others' behalf. But it ensures, in effect, that no such vote need ever take place. If Soviet tanks cross the West German border, NATO's Supreme Commander will commit the forces of half-a-dozen countries to the conflict without asking half-a-dozen Parliaments first.'[2]

The US Position

Clearly, then, from the time of America's entrance into the Second World War, its influence in Europe's security arrangements was pervasive. Moreover, US dominance also extended into the defence procurement area. After the Second World War, due to its massive and unrivalled armaments manufacturing capacity, the US found itself in a dominant position in relation to NATO. In the late 1950s, the Lockheed F-104G *Starfighter* was chosen by Belgium, Canada, Denmark, Germany, Greece, Italy, Norway, Portugal and Turkey. Also, the American M47/48 Patton tank was acquired by Belgium, France, Germany, Greece, Italy, Norway, Portugal and Turkey. Thus, whereas common military procurement in the Warsaw Pact had been achieved by edict, by virtue of the Soviet Union's monopolist position as a manufacturer of tanks, aircraft and missiles for the East European captive market, NATO at that time was securing the same through economic and industrial circumstance. Neither system in the long term had much to commend it.

In recognition of the growing disquiet felt by European NATO Governments over American domination of Europe's arms market during the early 1960s, the US' authorities put forward proposals ostensibly encouraging the expansion of European defence–industrial activity through a common trading framework. This recourse to a limited free trading network in military equipment (*á la* David Ricardo's comparative advantage theorem, see Chapter Three) almost certainly had its roots in the United States through the Canada Hyde Park Agreement signed around two decades earlier in 1941. Known as the North American Common Defence Market (NACDM), the arrangement took on a more definite and permanent shape with the signing of a further pact between the two countries in 1960. The essence of the NACDM was that Canada abrogated its right to produce major weapons systems which were henceforth procured from its southern neighbour, whilst the US waived customs duty on most defence material manufactured by Canadian contractors; the latter, in other words, being given preferential access into the American defence market.

This arrangement, albeit with intermittent strains, worked reasonably successfully. In 1965 an American proposal hinted that this more 'egalitarian' trading arrangement should be employed as a standard of reference for a reform of defence procurement practices between Europe and the US. This was the US Secretary of Defence, Mr Robert S. McNamara's, much vaunted 'Defence Common Market' (DCM) scheme. Here, the law of comparative advantage would be allowed to operate. Each NATO State producing the weapons systems and military equipment in which its defence sector was the most efficient, and selling the product to its Alliance partners at uniform prices. Presented as a triumph for the course of standardisation, which it would have been, the scheme would also have ensured that the US achieved a veritable monopoly of the sophisticated weapons market within NATO for as long as the Alliance lasted.[3] However, as one official US source sardonically observed at the time, the defence common market would have constituted little more than . . . 'an arena for arms competition between resentful pygmies and an affable giant'.[4]

Thus the McNamara initiative never got past the drawing board stage, though this did not stem the US' readiness to discuss with its NATO European allies the notion of a concrete Atlantic partnership based on a wider 'grand design' for US–European relations. This, indeed, had been the policy backdrop to Mr McNamara's suggestion. The notion of a 'grand design' resulted from President Kennedy's 1962 speech in which he supported the 'twin-pillar' approach to the NATO Alliance. The President's position was that a stronger Europe, both politically and economically, would strengthen the Atlantic partnership. However, as with the DCM, serious discussions never began. Europe was beset with anxiety: a more united Europe could lead to a weakening of the US' resolve to defend Europe; that Europe would become the junior partner in such a relationship; that for the French, the European pillar would be dominated by Britain and Germany, while for the British, it would lead to the erosion of the UK–US special relationship. As a consequence, NATO remained the primary defence mechanism for Europe and North America, with proposals aimed at collectivising European Defence policy emerging from within Europe.

European Policy Proposals

The BTO within a year of its creation had been effectively emasculated by the signing of The Alliance Treaty. Nevertheless there continued to be pressure from within Europe to form a European body responsible for defence matters, complementing rather than substituting the role played by NATO. Over the early 1950s this viewpoint evolved and crystalised into a European armaments free trading goal: the European Defence Community (EDC). This policy proposal had quite revolutionary characteristics. Shaped at a time when the Korean war was heightening the menace of the Soviet Union, the EDC was planned to create a unified European defence policy, based around a European army and a centralised procurement system. However, the steam generated for a wholly European defence organisation quickly evaporated. This was caused by a number of factors. As Professor Taylor, argues: Britain declined to be involved, thus accentuating French insecurities that the EDC would be dominated by the Germans; the Korean war ended and Stalin died, hence reducing the threat posed by the Soviet Union; and, finally, two French political groupings hostile to the EDC, the Gaullists and the Communists. strengthened their representation in the National Assembly between 1950 and 1954 so that, when the treaty was finally presented for ratification to the Assembly in 1954 by an unenthusiastic Prime Minister, it failed to win majority support.[5] At that point, the proposal to institute the EDC had effectively failed. With this ambitious plan defeated, a watered-down cooperative European approach on defence matters was successfully adopted. This had regard to the Paris Agreements of October 1954, alternatively known as the Paris Protocol. The Agreement represented an enlargement of the BTO, to include Germany and Italy. Also, what had previously come to be known as the Western Union, was now officially termed, the Western European Union (WEU).

It is clear, then, that although the WEU rose from the ashes of the EDC, its lineage more certainly derives from the Brussels Treaty Organisation. Moreover, as with the BTO, it was envisaged that the WEU would work in parallel with NATO. Indeed, the Paris Protocol formally established the relationship by providing for a new Article to be inserted into the Brussels Treaty. The relationship of the WEU to NATO was specified thus:

'In the execution of the Treaty, the High Contracting Parties and any organisations established by them under the Treaty shall work in close cooperation with the North Atlantic Treaty Organisation.
Recognising the undesirability of duplicating the military staffs of NATO, the Council and its Agency will rely on the appropriate military authorities of NATO for information and advice on military matters.'[6]

Although the WEU was a modest policy initiative compared with the proposed EDC, it nevertheless carried European defence cooperation further forward. Several important features of the WEU can be singled out: the creation of a Parliamentary Assembly; a committee to promote cooperation among member States in the field of armaments manufacture, which would in turn foster armaments standardisation; an Agency to oversee that armaments production by particularly Germany could be inspected, ensuring that imposed constraints were honoured; and Britain's undertaking to maintain specified Armed Forces on the European mainland. The WEU also served a most valuable function during this early post-war phase of European economic and political rehabilitation: by accepting Germany as a fully fledged member of the Union, it eased German entry into NATO – a contentious issue at that time. Thus, in the following year, 1955, Germany was welcomed as a new member of the NATO club.

Germany's entry into NATO provided added strength not only to the Alliance but also to the growing pressures of European defence cooperation, including armaments collaboration. This is evidenced by Germany's membership of FINABEL in 1956. FINABEL was set up in 1953 following an initiative by the French Chief-of-Staff. It comprised the Chiefs-of-Staff of France, Italy, Belgium, the Netherlands and Luxembourg. Britain joined in 1972. The purpose of FINABEL was, and still is, the fostering of cooperation among member States in respect of land armaments. More specifically, cooperation was to be encouraged in the following areas: definition of qualitative requirements of military equipment and joint definition of the military characteristics of such equipment; joint testing of such equipment and procedures; tactical and logistical studies; and exchange of information.[7] In pursuit of these aims FINABEL has worked closely with the WEU and NATO. FINABEL liaises with these organisations to ensure that collaborative requirements and intentions are coordinated. It influences the work of both the WEU's Standing Armaments Committee (SAC), which is responsible for laying down the criteria for new weapons development, and also SAC's NATO counterpart, the Military Agency for Standardisation (MAS). This latter body issues Standardisation Agreements (STANAGS) covering the procedures, doctrines and equipment characteristics to facilitate 'inter-operability'. It should be noted that the MAS is but one arm of NATO's effort to encourage cooperative equipment programmes; the other is the Conference of National Armaments Directors (CNAD). This represents the principal civilian body working under the North Atlantic Council. Its area of concern lies with the exchange of views between national staffs over defence equipment for the Army, Navy and Air Force. Here, the objective is to find common areas of interest between two or more countries concerning the replacement of weapons systems that are to be phased out or the development or purchase of new weapons systems.[8]

Thus, from what has been stated, it would appear that during this initial phase of European defence cooperation, local ambitions were to some extent stultified by the omnipotence of NATO. Although a start had been made with the creation of the WEU and FINABEL, they were neither decision-making nor dynamic organisations. Their purpose was solely liaison and advice. Although these early attempts to secure greater European defence cooperation brought little in the way of practical results, they did illustrate a recognition of the importance of the cooperation concept. However, the real success of this recognition pertained to the civil side of European affairs. It was here that there was a growing sense of political and economic identity. The Paris Treaty had established the European Coal and Steel Community; the Rome Treaty of the Economic Community (EC) had come into force in 1957; and such ventures as the European Space Research Organisation and the European Launcher Development Organisation were on the horizon. The UK remained outside these Treaties until 1973. Until that year its major institutional link to the EC States was through the Assembly of the WEU. However, once Britain joined the Community the WEU took on a rather moribund character.

The Treaty of Rome, which created the EC, had little to say on defence. The only important references were contained in Articles 223 to 225. Article 223 is the one of significance. It asserts that:

Any member State may take the measures which it considers necessary for the protection of all the essential interests of its security and which are connected with the production of or trade in arms, ammunition and war material; such measures shall not, however, prejudice conditions of competition in the Common Market in respect of products not intended for specifically military purposes.

This Article, coupled with the other two, with Article 224 vaguely referring to the consultation of member States if the EC was threatened with civil and international disorder, and Article 225 the enablement of the Court of Justice to become involved, in the event that Articles 223 and 225 became applicable, gave the sense of excluding defence equipment from the EC's sphere of competence. The potential for the EC to become involved in defence–industrial matters is still very much an interpretative issue awaiting resolution.

At the close of the 1950s the French in particular were under no illusion that the EC's defence posture was inadequate. In 1959 de Gaulle proposed the creation of a political union incorporating defence and foreign affairs. The response from the other members of the EC was sufficient for a committee to be established to investigate the worth of such a union. The Chairman of the Committee was French; a M. Fouchet. Fouchet's recommendations regarding a European Political Union never came to fruition due to member States fearing such a body would erode the power of both NATO and the EEC Commission. There were also objections by some States, notably the Netherlands, that Britain was being excluded from negotiations. The failure of this French initiative to construct a unified European approach to defence left Europe almost totally reliant on NATO for defence policy and related industrial considerations. No European consensus or dialogue existed on this question, and there the issue lay, until fresh developments began to emerge around the late 1960s and onwards into the seventies.

The Second Phase: Political and Economic Growing Pains

There was no radical *demarche* towards European defence cooperation during this early postwar phase of economic and political reconstruction. Several initiatives had been introduced but with limited tangible results. This should not be taken to infer that cooperation at the corporate level was not taking place. Indeed, there had been a profusion of activity. Since the late 1950s industrial collaboration in armaments production had been concentrated in the air and ground sectors. Table 2.1 lists the principal ventures in this area, dominated by the three big European

Table 2.1: Selected European Collaborative Projects

Project	Participants
Aircraft	
Jaguar Fighter Bomber	Anglo/French
Puma/Gazelle/Lynx helicopters	Anglo/French
Alpha Trainer/ground attack figher	Franco/German
Breguet Atlantique Maritime Patrol aircraft	Franco/German/Italian/NL
Tornado fighter/bomber	Anglo/German/Italian
Missiles	
Roland surface-to-air missile	Franco/German
Kormoran long range air-to-ship missile	Franco/German
Milan and Hot wire-guided anti-tank missile	Franco/German
Martel air-to-ground guided missile	Anglo/French
Atlas light anti-tank missile	Anglo/Belgian
Third Generation Anti-Tank Guided Weapons (TRIGAT)	Britain/France/Germany (EMDG)

weapons producing nations, Britain, France and the late West Germany. The greatest cooperative progress had been in aerospace. The Jaguar, a supersonic strike and trainer aircraft, was jointly developed by Britain and France. Production of the aircraft was shared equally between the two nations with the fabrication of the airframe undertaken by the British Aircraft Corporation and Dassault–Breguet, and the manufacture of the engine by Rolls Royce and Turbomeca. Britain and France also collaborated in the co-production package of the Puma/Gazelle/Lynx helicopters, with Westland and Aerospatiale being the principal contractors. Similarly, Franco–German cooperation led to the development of the ground-attack/trainer Alpha jet, which was developed and built by Dassault–Breguet and Dornier. In addition, there was the Breguet

Atlantique maritime-patrol aircraft, servicing the needs of France, Germany, Italy, and the Netherlands. A consortium was involved in this particular project, incorporating the following companies: Dornier (FRG); ABAP (Belgium); Fokker–VFW (Netherlands); Breguet and Aerospatiale (France); with Aeritalia (Italy) subsequently joining the group. Another major cooperative project was the Multi-Role Combat Aircraft (MRCA) Tornado. The project was first mooted in the 1960s. An international consortium comprising Britain, West Germany and Italy, was established to manage the production of the aircraft. It centred around two organisations: (i) PANAVIA, taking managerial responsibility for the manufacture of the airframe with ownership and staff in proportions of 42.5 per cent – British Aerospace, 42.5 per cent – MBB, and 15 per cent – Aeritalia, and (ii) TURBO–UNION, having the engine as its responsibility, with ownership and staff in shares of 40 per cent – Rolls Royce, 40 per cent – Motoren und Turbinen Union (MTU), and 20 per cent – Fiat Aviazione. The project planning of the avionics, including the coordinating work of the contractors, was undertaken by the creation of a company called Avionca Systems Engineering. Dramatic collaborative progress also occurred in other end-product areas. In missiles, for instance, there was the impressive Franco–German joint venture to produce the ROLAND low-level surface-to-air guided weapon. France and West Germany also combined to produce the long-range air-to-ship missile, the KORMORAN, and various high-speed anti-tank wire-guided missiles, such as MILAN and HOT. Britain also figured in a number of cooperative programmes, including the Anglo–French air-to-ground guided missile, MARTEL, and an arrangement with Belgium for the development of the ATLAS lightweight anti-tank missile. There was also the missile venture jointly formalised by Britain, France and West Germany in 1980, called the Euromissile Dynamics Group (EMDG). By bringing together the anti-tank guided weapons resources of British Aerospace's Dynamics Group, Aerospatiale's Engins Tactiques Division, and MBB's Unternehmensbereich Apparate, EMDG began life with a formidable reservoir of technological ability from which to draw.[9] In ground equipment, the FH-70 provides a good example of European collaboration and in the maritime area, looking to the future, is the speculated cooperation between Britain and France in the development of a future frigate; this project rising from the ashes of NFR-90.

In contrast to these and many other cooperative ventures, many of which evolved through the 1960s, European defence–industrial *policy* appeared to stagnate. It was inconceivable, however, that growing collaboration at the industrial level would not generate political pressures to develop a supporting European defence–industrial strategy. Inevitably, not least because of a rapidly expanding corporate defence sector, with its associated political lobby, fresh policy initiatives began to surface around the late 1960s. First there were initiatives from the EC, none of which came to anything. Then in 1967, the 'Colonna Plan', the Commission's memorandum on industrial policy, was floated. Later, in December 1973, the Heads of Government referred to the need for industrial cooperation (though not explicitly in the defence area), declaring that Community Member States should . . . 'develop more actively between them a common policy on industrial, scientific and technological cooperation in all fields.'[10] In the mid-1970s, there were a series of further proposals: a suggestion from the European Commission (1976) that the establishment of a jointly organised European Military aircraft procurement agency should be considered; a proposal by Mr Tindermans in his report on European Union (1975), that a European Armaments Agency be established; and the Klepsch ('Two-way street') report (1978) that a European Common Industrial Policy should be considered for the development and production of conventional armaments.

Certain organisations were also formed either directly under the auspices of NATO or through its encouragement. In 1968, Eurogroup was established as an informal grouping of European governments within the framework of NATO. Its aim was, and continues to be, to ensure that the European contribution to the common defence is as strong, cohesive and effective as possible.[11] Its founder members were Belgium, Denmark, Germany, Greece, Italy, Luxembourg, the Netherlands, Norway, Turkey and the United Kingdom. Portugal later joined in 1976, and Spain in 1982. The work of the Eurogroup is informal. It provides a twice-yearly forum in which member country Defence Ministers can discuss defence matters, fostering cooperation through sub-groups, covering: Eurocom (interoperability of tactical communications systems); Eurolog (cooperation in logistics); Eurolongterm (concepts collaboration in the field of defence equipment); Euromed (cooperation in the military medical area); and Euronad (defence equipment cooperation).

The major flaw in the make-up of Eurogroup, however, relates to the refusal by France to participate. It was clear that without French participation, European defence–industrial policy becomes rather a vacuous objective. It was because of this, and with the approval of NATO, that in 1976 the Independent European Programme Group (IEPG) was established. The IEPG and other defence organisations are shown in Figure 2.1. The important feature of the IEPG is that France agreed to become a full member, joining with existing Eurogroup countries. Indeed, it was at the insistence of the French that the title of the body was pre-fixed with the word 'Independent', characterising their

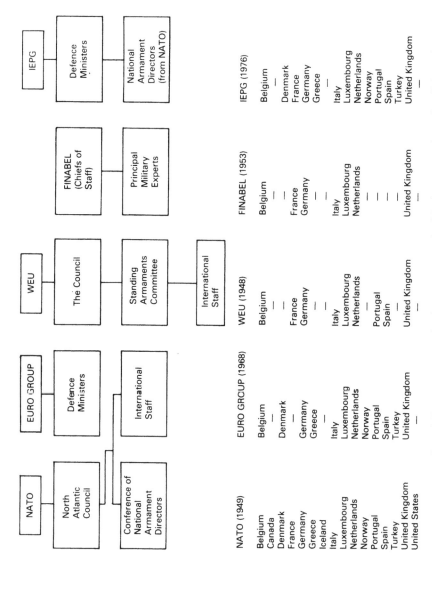

Figure 2.1: NATO and European organisations concerned with the promotion of collaboration

opposition to what was perceived as American domination of the Alliance. For the French, Eurogroup was too closely intertwined with NATO machinery. In their view, cooperation was synonymous with Americanisation.

Thus, the IEPG was established, being independent of both NATO and the Eurogroup. With the inclusion of France, it was believed the organisation could make practical progress in defence–industrial collaboration. The IEPG's objectives reflected this optimism. They are as follows:

– to permit the most efficient use of funds for research, development and procurement;
– to increase standardisation and interoperability of equipment;
– to maintain a healthy European defence industrial and technological base; and,
– to encourage a better balanced 'two-way street' in armaments cooperation between Europe and North America.

But although the *casus necessitatis* of the IEPG's creation was the participation of France, enabling European nations to speak and act together on defence issues, there was still criticism in the final years of the 1970s that progress in European defence cooperation continued to be tardy. As mentioned earlier, the way ahead was widely felt to be via a European Armaments Procurement Agency; a viewpoint which to a greater or lesser extent mirrored ideas expressed by: Mr Leo Tindeman in his report on European Union; Mr Spinelli, a former member of the Commission; Lord Gladwyn, in his report on the effects of a 'European Foreign Policy on Defence Questions'; and Dr T. A. Callaghan Jr. in his monogram on 'US–European Economic Cooperation in Military and Civil Technology'. Dr Klepsch in his celebrated 'Two way street' report, argues that such an Agency could operate through some form of relationship with the EC, though stressing that the IEPG would require strengthening through provision of a permanent secretariat and ministerial representation. However, a major political problem in any EC–IEPG liaison would be how to accommodate Ireland, a neutral country, in the deliberations between the EC (to which Ireland belongs) and the IEPG on this matter.

The Third Phase: Preparing for Europeanisation

The onset of the 1980s signalled a sense of determination and, indeed, realism into endeavours aimed at Europeanising defence policy and production. Although there had been no new institutions created or any dramatic shifts in policy, a conviction appeared pervasive that a singularly European approach to defence was inevitable. Interestingly, it was in the political arena where the signs of European consensus in this respect were growing.

European Political Cooperation (EPC) can really be traced back to the late sixties and early seventies, when Summit meetings and Foreign Minister gatherings agreed on the harmonization of national foreign policies so that a European position might be taken on key international events. Intense diplomatic consultation between the EC Foreign Ministers then became the norm so that common statements could be mutually agreed. Despite the fact that political cooperation appeared to work, EPC statements were hollow in substance because 'defence matters' were specifically excluded from its sphere of influence. It is difficult to comprehend a unified EC foreign policy stance without the supporting structure of a common security policy. Although there have been attempts to regularise this situation, most notably during the early years of the 1980s through the Genscher–Colombo initiative, none have been successful. Indeed, when, in 1983, the 'Solemn Declaration on European Union' was adopted, the EPC mechanism was held to relate only to the political and economic aspects of security. Its mandate was limited to these areas, because three Community States, Denmark, Greece and Ireland, for a number of reasons, insisted it went no further. The result of this was that the EC continued to lack competence on defence issues. It clearly possessed an economic dimension, which could now be coupled with the newly developed political consensus. But a security aspect, seemingly vital, for a complete approach to 'Union' continued to be missing. Two schools of thought emerged during the decade to pontificate on how this missing defence link could be established, providing the European pillar to the Alliance. Each of these standpoints will now be addressed.

First School of Thought: Resurrection of the WEU

There are those, and particularly the French, who view the revitalisation of the WEU as the way forward for projecting a European defence posture. Frustrated by the objections of a minority of smaller States to allow the EC to speak on defence topics, the remaining seven of what were the ten EC countries decided to go it alone and reactivate the WEU. This occurred in 1984, after a lapse of almost ten years during which the body, save for its Assembly, had lain dormant. In October 1984, the Rome ministerial meeting adopted a Declaration which, in a way, was the 'Certificate of Rebirth' for the WEU, specifying the Union's task and the context in which it was to be accomplished.[12] Its object has unequivocably been interpreted as the creation of a European defence identity. This was to be achieved, moreover, not by replacing NATO, but by raising Europe's contribution, encompassing the political, economic and defence–industrial elements, to the Alliance. Through this approach, the interdependence of the European and North American components of NATO would be strengthened. Stemming from the Declaration of Rome, the WEU has therefore been viewed as having a dual role to play:

– as a beginning to a European security division; and
– as a base for a European pillar within the Atlantic Alliance.[13]

Phoenix-like, the WEU had thus re-emerged to become an important mouthpiece for Europe to speak on defence. Events have underscored this, notably when the EC member States agreed through the WEU in the Autumn of 1987 to send warships to the Persian Gulf to assist in keeping it open for navigation. In addition, the WEU played an important role in the decision by EC countries to send troops and provide support for the Allied war effort in the second Gulf crisis in 1990. Also relevent is the WEU's approach agreed in its 'Platform on European Security Interests' (1987) that emphasised Europe's determination that NATO incorporate both a nuclear and conventional deterrent. The 'Defence Platform' also articulated the member countries' intention to develop for the first time a 'more cohesive defence identity' within the Atlantic Alliance and the need for a major European contribution to Western defence. Even though such a position may have been precipitated by the progress made at that time in the US–Soviet arms control negotiations, raising fears of a possible 'de-coupling' of the US from Europe, it is clear that the WEU had begun to harness the forces working towards a European defence policy. It provided for 'out-of-area' activities which NATO has until recently been reluctant to undertake; it is the only Western European body entirely devoted towards defence; and it includes France as a full member, which is important because the French do not belong to NATO's integrated military structure.[14]

Second School of Thought: The IEPG

In similarity to the WEU, the IEPG was also rejuvenated during the early 1980s. But, while the resurection of the WEU was very much driven by EC pressures, the revamping of the IEPG was predicated by calls from the US that Europe should make a greater contribution towards its own defence. Until 1984 the work of the IEPG lay primarily in fostering a common understanding of member nations' procurement processes and the assessment of management paradigms for collaborative projects. But in the November of that year, the IEPG met for the first time at Defence Minister level. A decision was then taken that the organisation would lay greater stress on 'European' cooperation, and on how best to rationalise and increase the effectiveness of Europe's defence–industrial base.

For the purpose of encouraging arms collaboration among European members of NATO, the IEPG had developed close relations with a parallel body, the European Defence Industrial Group (EDIG). EDIG was created in 1976 with the purpose of becoming the formal advisory group to the IEPG. This was difficult in practice as it was not until 1984 that the IEPG officially recognised EDIG. Since that time relations have been swiftly cemented; the strong link being reflected in the four *ad hoc* working groups EDIG formed to correspond to the IEPG's working groups on its European Defence Industrial Study (EDIS). It is also important to note the close links EDIG enjoys with NATO. For instance, the EDIG Council is formed from the Heads of Delegations to the NATO Industrial Advisory Group of the IEPG. EDIG's key objectives in the early 1980s were ambitious, covering:

– harmonisation of programmes and procurement practices;
– early involvement of industry in operational requirements planning;
– achievement of economies of scale;
– strengthening of the IEPG industrial base; and
– definition of IEPG market rules.[15]

Since 1988 the structure of the IEPG has been characterised by three Panels. EDIG as a response has established three focal points to act as bridges to the IEPG Panels. Figure 2.2, below, illustrates this network. It can be observed that the IEPG's three Panels are concerned with Operational Requirements and Programmes; Research and Technology; and Procedural and Economic Matters. The various *ad hoc* working groups supplement the work of these Panels. In addition there is a Sub-Group reporting to Panel III whose remit is to formulate measures to assist the smaller European economies in encouraging developing defence industries. The reporting chain runs from the Panels to the National Armaments Directors (NADs) who in turn report to the Defence Ministers currently meeting twice-yearly.

The progress the IEPG has made since 1984 in terms of forging a unified European perspective on defence has been solid. The commissioning in 1985 of the EDIS report, following the decision to revitalise the IEPG, provided the turning point. Also widely known as the 'Wisemen's Report', it was presented to the IEPG Defence Ministers in 1987. The

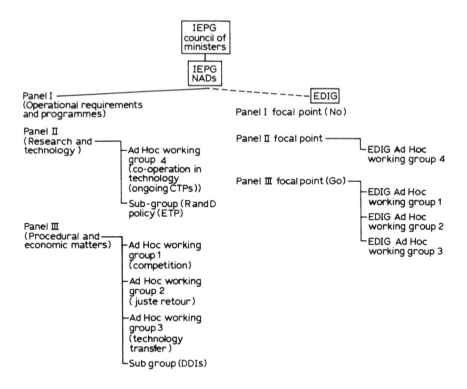

Figure 2.2: Relationship between the IEPG and the EDIG

Action Plan deriving from this report and prepared by the NADs was adopted in 1988. The gist of the EDIS Report, officially called 'Towards a Stronger Europe' was that . . .

'the root cause of the transatlantic arms trade imbalance was the fragmentation of the European market on national lines, which translates into high R&D-to-production cost ratios and elevated unit costs. Only greater inter-European competition and extensive industry linkages, combined with a far more liberal sharing of technology, could lessen this handicap.'[16]

The road to the report's adoption in 1988 was not smooth. At the June 1987 IEPG Meeting in Seville, Spain, the ministers rejected the recommendations of Mr Vredeling (the Dutch Defence Minister who was Chairman of the study team) for a common R&D fund and a permanent IEPG secretariat. The eventual adoption of these objectives a year later reflected the change in the mood of ministers, anxious over the increasing trade and political frictions between Europe and the US. In the November 1988 IEPG meeting held in Luxembourg, the Defence Ministers also agreed to start exchanging information on forthcoming arms purchases.

The need for greater information to assist European harmonisation of defence procurement and promulgate economic efficiency through increased scale and competitive bidding opportunities has long been recognised. The Greenwood Report of 1980, for instance, put forward several proposals in this respect: the establishment of a European Public Procurement Task Force, ensuring the most effective use of government purchasing power; a European Defence Analysis Bureau, acting as a clearing-house for information; the identification of procurement possi-bilities; and the analysis of options.[17] This centralised Bureau has not yet happened, though the IEPG's Action Plan is making the reality of it a definite possibility. The proposals already adopted favour the creation of a research and procurement office to be operated along the lines of the European Space Agency; the latter's operations being funded on a percentage basis by the countries benefiting from its work. Unlike current practice in NATO, where a nation purchasing a foreign weapon often wants an accompanying share in its production, the IEPG's proposed Central Agency would parcel out the work based on open competition without regard to national borders. Britain and France already have an agreement up and running whereby each country makes available a 'contracts bulletin' listing equipment requirements that are open to tender. In addition Britain and France have set up small-scale 'reciprocal purchasing' arrangements in an effort to avoid duplication. Building upon this pioneer cooperative scheme, with the aim of making the European armaments industry more competitive, has been the IEPG's encourage-ment of transnational arms trading. In support of this, the European Defence Ministers meeting at Gleneagles, Scotland, in February 1990, agreed that each of the thirteen countries represented produce contracts bulletins which would be regularly published and distributed to other European NATO members, with an invitation to tender. This step, though relatively insignificant taken on its own, fits in with the trend of developments consolidating the European pillar within NATO. But what of NATO in this process towards cooperation? A few comments are in order here before briefly examining the controversial debate over the EC's role in the defence area.

NATO Policy
For more than thirty years NATO has advocated the importance of armaments cooperation through commonly agreed standardisation

procedures and multi-national arms collaborative ventures. One of the earliest NATO inspired schemes was the NATO co-production programme agreed by the Alliance in 1957. At that time the emphasis lay on the military benefits of standardisation or at least interoperability. More recently, the high cost of not developing and producing the defence equipment of the Alliance in an efficient and rational manner has come to the fore, especially as limited resources buy less and less modern equipment. The cost factor has always been recognised as important, but throughout the fifties and sixties the US vision carried sway. This viewed standardisation as the Allied adoption of US equipment, especially since a good proportion of the more than \$20 bn the US supplied in military assistance to European nations in the thirty years following the Second World War was recycled back to US defence contractors. With the reconstruction of Europe and a growing European arms trade imbalance with the US, the 1970s led to a re-evaluation of NATO procurement practices. Although it was the increasingly divergent sourcing of NATO weapons systems that sowed the seeds for NATO's cooperative measures, it was probably the Callaghan Report of 1975 that provided the germinating force. The report's evidence of duplication and wasted resources galvanised official opinion. As a result a plethora of standardisation measures was introduced by NATO during the 1980s.

The Alliance's approach to standardisation during this period incorporated an expanding number of initiatives. All of them faced the same problem, however: the need to harmonise technical requirements and life-cycle patterns, while, at the same time, overcoming the industrial and political obstacles to collaborative arms programmes. NATO's struggle with these difficulties meant that dramatic policy successes have been elusive. Nevertheless, there are clear benefits in the communication channels NATO established, and reforms to improve the institutional framework are regularly implemented. The history of NATO cooperative measures instituted in the 1980s is evidence of the Alliance's commitment to the cause.

The institutional approach begins with attempts to establish NATO military requirements. Figure 2.3 below diagrammatically traces the two-pronged approach NATO adopts in this respect. Following through Path A first, force proposals and material requirements are agreed by the Major NATO Commanders (MNCs). After deliberations regarding assigned missions and associated operational concepts, the MNCs submit their requirements via Mission Need Documents (MNDs) to the NATO Military Committee (MC). In turn, the MC initiates recommendations to the Defence Planning Committee (DPC) and North Atlantic Council

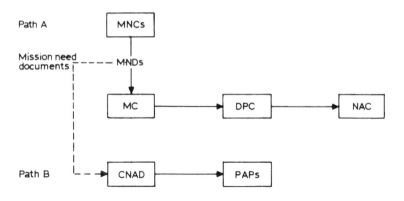

Figure 2.3: NATO's Twin Paths to Standardisation

(NAC) that programmes be commenced for the agreed requirements outlined in the MNDs. The other part of NATO's cooperative approach, Path B, represents a separate avenue for dialogue. Here, short-circuited out of the Path A system, the MNDs are channelled into the Conference of National Armaments Directors (CNAD), which then enters them into the NATO Phased Armaments Programming System (PAPS) for consideration for cooperative ventures. Although much effort is expended in discussions and information processing, this twin-track approach has been associated with limited coordination and hence disappointing results. While the acceptance by the MC of a Mission Need Document recognises that a piece of equipment needs to be developed to counter a specific threat, there is no guarantee that a collaborative approach will be pursued in achieving this end, any more, indeed, than when the MND has passed through the PAPS process. Yet, when PAPS was introduced in 1980 this was intended to be its *modus operandi*. The main objective of PAPS was to facilitate NATO weapons collaboration as well as to record progress regarding the Alliance's success in meeting material require-ments identified along Path A. PAPS uses 'milestones' to monitor the weapons systems acquisition process right from the requirements and feasibility stages through to the full life cycle of engineering to final manufacturing. Even though PAPS provides a mechanism common to the research, development and procurement stages of all NATO States' weapons systems, it has yet to distinguish itself in promoting armaments cooperation among NATO States.

Before the MND is processed by PAPS, it will have been discussed at the CNAD stage. It will be recalled that the National Armaments

Directors comprising CNAD also participate in the NATO-inspired Eurogroup meetings. This integration is important, as within the NATO framework CNAD is the superior body with responsibility for coordinating armaments activities. There are several groups, including those of land, sea and air warfare equipment, under the wing of the CNAD. Under these main groups are, in turn, around 200 smaller working parties, examining particular aspects of cooperation. For example, under the Naval Main Group was established an armaments project group tasked to consider the standardisation of NATO's frigates. Out of this grew the ambitious NATO Frigate Replacement (NFR-90) project. Such working groups are therefore an important cog in NATO's developing collaboration machinery. Through this medium, nations strive to harmonise the time scales, technical requirements, and development programmes for the economic and military benefits of standardisation and interoperability.

To assist the work of the CNAD working groups, NATO's international staff annually publish a document called *The Consolidated National Defence Equipment Schedule* (CNDES). This represents the procurement plans of NATO States in each mission area. The CNDES is informative. It does not stimulate cooperation between countries identified as being at similar stages in the development and acquisition of similar items of military equipment. This is mainly because many of the weapons projects were already too far down the road to facilitate easy harmonization. NATO's Long Term Planning initiative represents a move that is intended to rectify this deficiency. Long term defence planning added a new dimension to NATO's cooperative efforts. It has introduced a system that examines mission areas in a time frame beyond the current acquisition cycle.

Since the mid-1980s the pace of NATO's involvement in cooperation and standardisation work has noticeably accelerated. In 1985 the *Conventional Defence Improvement* (CDI) policy was instituted. This represented efforts by the MNCs, through their *Conceptual Military Framework*, and also CNAD, through its *Armaments Cooperation Improvement Strategy*, to respectively practice long term armaments planning and redress conventional arms deficiencies through more efficient coordination of national procurement efforts. The following year, 1986, saw the integration of the diverse sources of cooperative information flows in a document, entitled: *The Overall Review of CNAD Activities and Projects* (ORCAP). Specifically focussing on cooperation in conventional weapons systems, ORCAP provides a synthesis of the following areas: mission area technologies; weapons deficiencies; the work of CNAD project groups; and the status of collaborative ventures already in operation under the auspices of CNAD. Finally, in 1987, the then Secretary General of NATO, Lord Carrington, proposed that NATO establish a *Conventional Armaments Planning System* (CAPS) to weld long run planning and collaborative objectives into a single coordinated endeavour. The purpose of CAPS was to link both the Long Term Planning Guidelines emanating from *NATO's Long Term Planning System* and also the CDI's *Conceptual Military Framework* to national research, development and procurement plans so that international arms cooperation could be recognised very much earlier in the process. Indeed, the fountain-head for collaborative effort within NATO could then be the agreed priorities of the Mission Need Documents. To this end, a trial of CAPS was begun in 1988. The review procedure was undertaken by a NATO Conventional Armaments Review Committee. In 1988 this Review Committee accepted responsibility for collating and analysing the information obtained from an Armaments Planning Questionnaire circulated and completed by NATO member countries. From this process, NATO's first conventional armaments plan was submitted to CNAD in the Spring of 1989. The Plan represented an analysis, by functional area, of the plans and activities of member countries. It also contained associated recommendations for furthering cooperative effort, as based on this analysis.

NATO's endeavours to secure greater commonality in equipment and doctrine have been reflected in several other initiatives aimed at promoting standardisation. Firstly, there is the NATO *Standardisation Group*, which was established in 1985. The Group was tasked by the North Atlantic Council to satisfy the dual aims of standardisation policy; that is, improving NATO's military effectiveness as well as its economic efficiency. One of its goals in this respect was to create a NATO Standardisation Base to facilitate the identification of shortfalls and duplication in the Alliance's standardisation efforts. A second measure for the improvement of NATO standardisation concerned the *Infrastructure Programme*. This contributes to the funding of numerous projects assisting in the standardisation of common-funded facilities, such as oil storage networks, integrated command, control and communications systems and mobile war headquarters. In 1988, funding of $4.8 bn for the first two years of the present six year funding period (1991–1996) was agreed. Finally, there is, of course, the *Military Agency for Standardisation* (MAS), comprising Army, Navy and Airforce areas of operation, with 49 separate working parties seeking to maximise doctrine and tactics among NATO member States. This is an important first step in enabling the development of equipment standardisation.

It is clear therefore that NATO has been building up a momentum especially over the last decade to promote arms cooperation. NATO's European members have played their part in this process. As we have observed, Europe's contribution to the cooperation goal has additionally been promoted via initiatives to strengthen its defence base through rationalisation and coordination of European defence procurement. The WEU and the IEPG have been the vehicles for this objective. Increasingly, however, Europeans have asked whether the EC might be a more appropriate body to perform this role, taking foreign policy (note here the EC's peace-keeping role in the 1991 Yugoslavian crisis) and defence within its ambit of responsibility. The next section considers the main points in this regard.

The European Community: Defence Implications of 1992

Even though the Treaty of Rome, which gave birth to the EC, specifically excluded defence from its areas of competence, this has not deterred some commentators from arguing that the EC should be given responsibility for defence and security in addition to foreign policy. The 1986 Single European Act (SEA), aiming to create a Single European Market (free from barriers of trade) by 31 December 1992, acted as the catalyst for this view. There remains, of course, the difficulty of a neutralist Ireland to be overcome, but this was seen as a minor irritation compared to the increasing EC–US frictions concerning 'burden-sharing' and 'trade-war' disputes.

'In March 1987, European Commission President, M. Jaques Delors, went so far as to say that the Single European Act (SEA), and its Title III in particular, made the European Community (EC) the competent body for the discussion of security and defence issues. Title III codifies the previously informal cooperation between EC member States in foreign policy.'[18]

This call by M. Delors was not in isolation. In January 1989, while addressing the European Parliament, Spanish Foreign Minister Ordonez stated . . . 'If we are to give a new impetus to the dialogue with the Soviet Union and the other Warsaw Pact countries we shall have to be fully aware of the overriding importance of developing a security dimension within the process of constructing European Union.'[19] Equally significant is the fact that the WEU's 'Platform on European Security Interests' clearly linked security cooperation with increased integration of Western Europe, with the SEA playing a major role.[20] This was advocated because of the chequered success of the EC's informal EPC arrangements to that time.

The remarkable aspect of these calls is that like the Treaty of Rome, the SEA includes an Article appearing to bar the liberalisation commitments applicable to the defence sector. The Article in question is Article 30. Suitably vague, it reads that the . . .

> 'high contracting parties are determined to maintain the technological and industrial conditions necessary for their security. They shall work towards that end both at the national level and, where appropriate, within the framework of the competent institutions and bodies.'[21]

Although the SEA's Article 30 excludes the prospect of a common European defence and security policy, separate from the Alliance, there are two points which need to be emphasised:
1) The involvement of the Commission in EPC is now formally enshrined in Title III of the SEA. This makes sense as EPC and EC are obviously intertwined through the EC Council of Ministers.
2) It is also the case that the SEA provisions will *indirectly* apply to the European defence contractors operating both in the military and civilian industrial fields. The electronics sector, for example, comprises dual-user industries supplying materials and components for both defence and civil purposes. Semi-conductors drive Tornado and Efa fighters just as they do office equipment. The SEA, therefore, will apply to the European armaments industries through their integrative relationship with the civil sector.

Conclusion

Reading through the lengthy catalogue of collaboration policies detailed in this chapter, it is difficult not to be struck by the NATO members' revealed commitment to the aim of cooperation in arms production and procurement. But given the enormity of debate and political will in this area it is surprising that technology-sharing and procurement integration has not been advanced further. An important finding of this chapter is that the road to consensus in defence cooperation is clearly a long and tortuous journey. National considerations dictate that the pace of movement towards integration often slows the speed of change. But this is a healthy characteristic of the process, leading to a strengthing of dialogue through negotiated eclecticism. And the pressure to converge is constant.

The drift of argument in this chapter suggests that a salient feature of the collaborative movement over recent times has been the supportive relationship between Europe and NATO in the evolution of separate, though linked institutional mechanisms for furthering collaborative goals. But as we will observe in Chapter Six, the asymmetrical size of the US' military–industrial complex acts in practice as a formidable barrier to transatlantic NATO collaboration.

3 OVERVIEW OF PRINCIPLES

Introduction

The purpose of this chapter is to review the main advantages claimed to arise from arms collaboration. The discussion is theoretical in nature, particularly with regard to the arguments advanced for cost savings. Here, the focus is to explain in simple terms why arms collaboration and therefrom standardisation provokes such a rallying call when approached from an economic standpoint. The chapter details the primary sources of cost savings, illustrating the benefits to be obtained from trade, scale, learning effects, and non-duplication of R&D. The comparison between theory and practice is then briefly explored to determine the importance of collaborative cost savings in reality. The chapter closes with a summary discussion of the benefits collaboration is purported to confer on military efficiency.

Imperatives For Collaboration

During the early 1980s collaboration was viewed very much as the way forward by defence planners. Cooperation in the production of defence equipment was encouraged for a spectrum of reasons. In particular, it was held to economise on R&D and production costs, and this was a significant benefit when considered in the context of escalating costs of modern defence equipment. At the beginning of the 1990s, this feature remains unchanged, but now, in addition, most NATO States are experiencing (real) declines in defence expenditure, leading to falls in the scale of production. This will not leave defence sector costs and prices unaffected, especially since traditionally, as was mentioned in Chapter One, military equipment costs inflate at a faster rate than economy-wide costs.

Table 3.1, below, provides an indication of the dramatically rising procurement costs of modern military equipment. In absolute values the sums are staggering, leaving little uncertainty as to why continuance of several of the major NATO projects is now in question. For example, in US $, 1988 prices, the European Fighter Aircraft programme (765 units) is billed at 31.9–37.1 billion; the Harrier GR5 programme (62 units) at 1.9 billion; while a replacement frigate is costed at 280 billion.[1]

Table 3.1: Generation-on-Generation Real Cost Increases of UK Military Equipment

Defence Equipment	Escalation Factor
New Frigate	4 times price of predecessor
Harrier GRI fighter	3.75 times price of the *Hunter*
Sea Wolf Missile	3.25 times price of *Sea Cat*
Challenger Tank	2.25 times price of *Chieftan*

Source: Hartley, K., and Hooper, N., 'Economics: the Ultimate Arms Controller?' *NATO's Sixteen Nations* (Dec 1988–Jan 1989) p. 35. Original source: House of Commons Defence Committee, *Statement on the Defence Estimates 1988*; and *The Procurement of Major Defence Equipment*, 1988.

The case for industrial collaboration in armaments manufacture has been built up over the last two decades. The principles are by now well-known, but even so, for completeness of argument, it would be well to review the subject matter. In essence there are three main areas of benefit enjoyed by countries participating in defence technology-sharing. These are:

(i) cost reduction in R&D and production expenditure;
(ii) through standardisation of equipment, a more credible military combat and logistical set-up; and,
(iii) the political and military benefits arising through greater cohesion and unity of Western Europe's defence posture.

The remainder of this chapter reviews in detail the substance of cost reduction and military benefits derived from collaboration.

Cost Reduction

Of the oft-cited virtues that arms collaboration bestow on the NATO fraternity, the economic predominate. However, to maximise these putative economic benefits, it is necessary for States to give up production capacity. To date, only grudging progress has been made in this respect. Thus, where NATO States produce military equipment independent of each other, then economic efficiency in weapons production is sub-optimal. In the economic context, there are two principal avenues for improvements in efficiency: economies through trade and economies from the scale of operations, together with the associated learning effects.

52

Each of these will now be surveyed, beginning with trade-induced efficiency.

Efficiency Through Trade

The non-cooperative production approach leads to wastage of resources through lack of scale and the duplication of investment effort. It is for this reason that some commentators[2] have urged for increased specialisation among NATO countries, particularly of an intra-European nature. A few observers[3] have even mused over the possibilities of progressing toward a genuine international division of labour; that is a common market for defence equipment where single producers of military items ultimately evolve, based on cost and quality considerations. The notion that economic efficiency and hence cost and price reductions can be maximised via a greater emphasis on international specialisation is supported by a long history of economic thought. It will be valuable to briefly review some of the more important elements of the theorizing to which the protagonists of free trade in military equipment continually refer in support of their arguments.

The collaborative economic building blocks date back to the period spanning the 16th and 18th centuries. During that time, the easing of obstacles to international trade, especially the progressive availability of efficient and reliable transportation systems, led not only to an expansion of foreign trading but also to the intellectual development of a separate economic rationale for the same. Previously, foreign trade had been articulated through a mercantilist perspective: equating national economic wealth with power and prestige. Put simply, the mercantilists believed that a positive balance of trade, achieved through protection if necessary, had favourable repercussions on the stock of bullion; the primary indicator of national wealth. No thought was given to the inescapable consequence of such a system, that one country's surplus has necessarily to be matched by other countries' deficits.

The publication in 1752 of David Hume's book, *Political Discourses*, was the first major attack on mercantilist philosophy. Hume argued that the conscious pursuit of a favourable balance of trade was not only foolish but also self-defeating; his explanation for this was based on the working of the gold mechanism. He made the point that if a country's exports were to increase more than its imports, the associated inflow of gold would automatically lead to an increase in the money supply; this would occur according to the principles of the quantity theory of money, and domestic prices would inevitably inflate. It follows that the deficit country would experience totally opposite effects: a fall in the price level, because

53

the outflow of gold had reduced the money supply. Thus, increasing prices in the surplus country, combined with falling prices in the deficit country, naturally leads to a reduction in the former's imports and expansion in the latter's exports. Under Hume's reasoning, the result of such a system is the automatic correction of the trading imbalance. It therefore appears that mercantilist doctrine sows the seeds of its own destruction.

The mercantilist boat leaked even more alarmingly with the appearance of Adam Smith's *Wealth of Nations* some twenty years later. Smith's contribution to the debate was substantial. Through the incorporation of his division of labour concept into the international context, he became the first scholar to focus attention on the question of whether it is economic to import goods that technically could be manufactured domestically. Smith agreed that the international division of labour is essentially comparable to the *industrial* division of labour, both between people and between firms in the domestic economy. He also went further, arguing that by extension, nations just as much as households or firms would constrict the gains to be had from specialisation if attempts were made to become self-sufficient in production. The substance of the venerable professor's proposition cannot be bettered by quoting him directly on this point:

"It is the maxim of every prudent master of a family, never to attempt to make at home what it will cost him more to make than to buy. The tailor does not attempt to make his own shoes, but buys them from the shoemaker. The shoemaker does not attempt to make his own clothes but employs a tailor. The farmer attempts to make neither the one nor the other, but employs those different artificers. All of them, for it is for their interest to employ their whole industry in a way in which they have some advantage over their neighbours, and to purchase with a part of its produce, or what is the same thing, with the price of part of it, whatever else they have occasion for. What is prudence in the conduct of every private family, can scarce be folly in that of a great kingdom. If a foreign country can supply us with a commodity cheaper than we ourselves can make it, better buy off them with some part of the produce of our own industry, employed in a way we have some advantage."[4]

The basis of Adam Smith's thinking was that barriers (mercantilist policies, including tariffs, prohibitions on import, and export subsidies) to free trade were economically harmful in the long-run, and should be dismantled.[5] He was able to prove this by showing that if one country can produce a good with less labour than the other country, and the other country can produce some other good with less labour, they would both lose if they were to continue producing both goods. Each country should specialise in the production of the good that it can produce with lower labour costs, and then trade the surplus production. From this logic, Adam Smith demonstrated, in terms of labour units, the possible gains when countries are in a position of absolute advantage. Table 3.2, below, illustrates this point by reference to Britain and Portugal. It primarily shows what each country can produce before trade takes place.

Table 3.2: Specialisation Through Absolute Advantage

Production Possibilities	Wine		Guns
(Before Trade)			
Britain	20	or	80
Portugal	30	or	60
Self-Sufficiency			
(Before Trade, but with each country devoting 6 months			
for production of each category of goods)			
Britain	10	and	40
Portugal	15	and	30
Total	25		70
Specialisation			
(After Trade)			
Britain	0		80
Portugal	30		0
Total	30		80

Without affecting the nature of Adam Smith's conclusions, the approach is simplified by assuming that the same amount of labour is used by each country in the production of the respective amounts of wine or guns. Before trade, therefore, Britain has an absolute advantage in the production of guns, while Portugal has an absolute advantage in the production of wine. Thus, if it is assumed that Britain and Portugal are content with the production of 70 guns, the amount that can be produced under self-sufficiency, the question arises regarding the amount of labour resources required for production. The answer to this is straightforward. Take, for instance, the relatively efficient gun producer, Britain. To produce 70 guns it would need to spend 7/8ths of its labour-time, leaving 1/8th to produce wine (1/8 × 20), amounting to 2.5 units of wine. But given that the skills and opportunity costs differ between these two countries, in that the opportunity cost of Britain producing guns (the amount of wine that has to be given up to produce one extra gun) is only 1/4 compared to 1/2 for Portugal, then better for Britain to totally specialise in the production of guns and Portugal in wine. Of course, if this happens, trade is necessary so that each country has access to the good it is not producing. But note that when trade takes place, then output of both goods increases in comparison with self-sufficiency.

A short period of time was to elapse before another classical writer, David Ricardo, was to argue the possibility of gains where one country was more efficient than the other in producing 'both' commodities; this is the well-known theory of comparative advantage. In his *Principles of Political Economy* (1817), Ricardo illustrated his theory of comparative cost by reference to an imaginary pattern of trade between England and Portugal. His example related to wine and cloth, where England enjoyed absolute advantage in the production of *both* commodities. Again employing Britain and Portugal, Table 3.3, below, illustrates the mechanics of comparative advantage theory. Based on the same assumptions of labour input as were used in Table 3.2, our contemporary example examines the relative efficiencies of producing 'dual-use' trucks and tanks. As shown, Britain has an absolute advantage over Portugal in the production of both trucks and tanks because the British are better at producing both. Note, however, that Portugal has the least 'comparative disadvantage' in the manufacture of trucks. This is the lynchpin to Ricardo's model. Ricardo's concern was with both opportunity cost and comparative advantage, emphasising not so much the total amounts workers can produce but the sacrifice needed to produce an additional unit of a good. Thus if Portugal specialises in truck production, maximum output will be eight trucks. Britain can then allocate its resources accordingly. From Table 3.3, either;

(i) $16/30 \times 30 = 16$ tanks $+ [14/30 \times 60] = 28$ trucks
or
(ii) $34/60 \times 30 = 17$ tanks $+ [26/60 \times 60] = 26$ trucks

Irrespective of whether Britain chooses option (i) or (ii), when compared with self-sufficiency, trade through the international division of labour increases the output of either the amount of trucks or the amount of tanks, with no increases in labour inputs.

Economies of Scale

The previous discussion on the gains from trade dealt with efficiency improvements via the international division of labour. A further

Table 3.3: Comparative Advantage

Production Possibilities	Tanks		Trucks
(Before Trade)			
Britain	30	or	60
Portugal	2	or	8
Self-Sufficiency			
(Before trade, but with each country devoting 6 months			
for production of each category of goods)			
Britain	15	and	30
Portugal	1	and	4
Total	16		34
Specialisation			
(After Trade)			
Britain	16	and	28
Portugal	0	and	8
Total	16		36

important consideration has regard to scale economies. The impact of scale will be felt in both production and R&D areas. Moreover, because lengthening of activity cycles, by definition, involves repetition, economies through learning also become a relevant characteristic of defence–industrial operations. Each of these factors will be surveyed in turn.

(i) Production
The methodology here is straightforward. If economies of scale exist in some lines of production, but individual markets in the participating countries are too small to allow any country to fully exploit the advantages of long production runs, then it is beneficial for all States to let one country, or a few countries, specialise in the production of the item that has falling costs of production. Since falling costs, derived from internal economies of scale, not only benefits the defence contractor, through greater competitiveness, but also the public, through the release of public funds for either public expenditure-switching or reduction of the tax burden, it is prudent to encourage policies which expand output until the lowest point on the average cost has been reached. Figure 3.1 depicts this point as X, where costs per unit are minimised.

In the event that the optimal output level, X, cannot be reached by producing solely for the domestic market, it is in the interests of all Alliance members to accept that defence contractors in some States, or

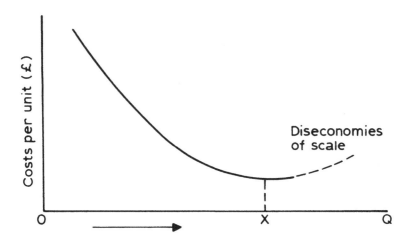

Figure 3.1: Economies of Scale-Production

even in one State only, specialise in the production of a good in which economies of scale can be reaped. Other countries, in turn, can then specialise in those goods in which they are able to obtain scale economies. If free trade were allowed to rise above nationalism, a constrained model of this comparative advantage approach could evolve within the NATO defence market. It would be a constrained version because the existing major defence–industrial States, such as the US, France, Britain and Germany, dominate production in all areas due to the size of their procurement demand and the extent of existing capacity and capability. It would be unlikely that other countries would naturally be able to evolve into efficient producers of major items of defence production.

Figure 3.2 shows the dual effects of several countries combining to produce defence equipment, and thus benefitting from both economies of scale and international division of labour effeciency effects. Running down LAC 1 (long-run average cost curve – one) is effected by raising output, and thus allows a defence contractor to operate at the optimal cost-output position Y on LAC 1. This is the 'economies of scale' effect. If this increased scale was achieved through international specialisation, it will result in productivity improvements leading to the lowered cost per unit, Z; that is, the new optimal cost-output point on LAC 2.

It was Adam Smith again who was the first observer to bring these two forms of efficiency together. He not only specified the critical significance of the division of labour but also provided the primary operational barrier to its effectiveness: the extent of the market. The size of the market is determined by a number of considerations: the size of the military

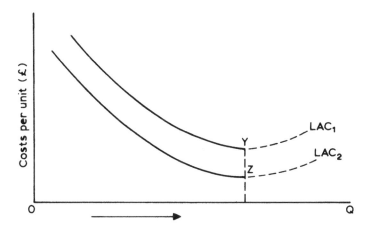

Figure 3.2: Efficiency Through Collaboration

establishment within the country in which the defence sector is located; the level of income; the nature of procurement policy (whether inward- or outward-oriented); and, finally, the accessibility of export markets. Clearly, all these considerations relate to effective demand, continuing to be relevant today.

Where effective demand is fragmented, as occurs in the NATO Alliance, then scale and division of labour effects are not maximised. This is usually referred to in the literature by comparing NATO's armaments production practices with those that prevailed in the now defunct WP (discussed further in Chapter Seven). It is commonly held that the Soviet Union obtained scale and specialisation cost reductions through the edict that all military equipment procured by Warsaw Pact States was sourced from the USSR. Thus, despite the relative backwardness and inefficiency of its civil industrial sector, the Soviet Union was nevertheless able to develop a big and diversified defence–industrial base. Indeed, some commentators have even argued that the Soviet Union did not possess a military–industrial complex; it was one.[6] Captive demand from the Warsaw Pact States during the post World War Two period enabled the Soviet Union to pursue a particular strategy in the production of conventional defence equipment. It was an approach focussing on cost-savings. Within this, several conditioning factors featured prominently: specialisation, standardisation (and interchangeability of components), and scale. The goal of Soviet defence–industrial policy was to obtain efficiency through long production runs of standardised equipment; an important consideration in a capital-scarce Soviet economy. The economic

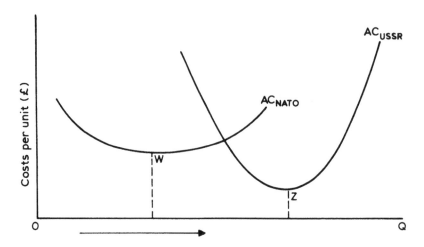

Figure 3.3: Comparison of Production Optimums Between the Soviet Union and Alliance Nations

effects of the Soviet Union's long production runs can be highlighted by a comparison of production optimums between defence manufacturers in the USSR and Alliance nations; this is depicted in Figure 3.3.

The differences in the shape of the cost curves derive from two factors: the level of demand, and the degree of flexibility of the defence contractors' productive operations. In the NATO economies, nationalism historically has not only limited effective demand but introduced inefficiency through building excess capacity into the plant. This has been due to uncertainty concerning the level and composition of future output, leading to a relatively high optimum production costs per unit, W. By contrast, in a planned economy geared to manufacturing single types of equipment, uncertainty is considerably reduced. The construction of defence–industrial manufacturing facilities yielding minimum average cost, Z, over a high level and narrow range of output then becomes rational.

(ii) Learning Effects

As these benefits derive from repetitive manufacturing activity it is appropriate at this juncture to examine their role. It is held that specialisation of repetitive tasks is economically beneficial because it increases the manual dexterity of the workforce; economises on time spent in production; and encourages innovation through the need to remove efficiency bottlenecks in constituent manufacturing activities. Learning curves, such as the one shown in Figure 3.4 represent declines in unit costs associated with increases in cumulative output.

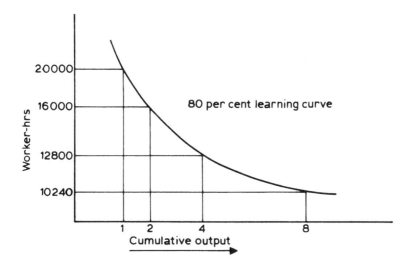

Figure 3.4: The Learning Curve Phenomenon

They are predicted on the belief that the greater the repetitiveness of task, the more efficiently it will be undertaken by labour. Thus, in Figure 3.4, man-hours required for unit production decline by 20 per cent for each doubling of cumulative output.

The most celebrated study in this area was that which examined the learning effects arising from the operation of a Swedish steel works over a 15 year period beginning around 1836. Often referred to as the 'Horndal effect', output per worker-hour rose by 2 per cent per year during this period in which neither machinery nor the size of the labour force was changed. After that 15 year period, however, further productivity improvement became progressively harder to secure. More recent studies continue to support the existence of learning effects: Hartley discovered an 80 per cent learning curve for the UK aircraft industry whilst a 75 per cent curve for the US aircraft frame industry has been reported,[7] and it has been suggested that tank manufacture approximates a 90 per cent curve.[8]

(iii) Research and Development

The argument applied to cost reductions in production through collaboration is also applicable in the sphere of R&D. As most NATO military projects can be expected to be at the sophisticated end of the technological spectrum it is to be expected that emerging technologies

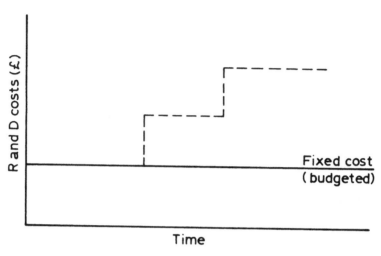

Figure 3.5: Constant R&D Costs

will take up an increasing proportion of the expenditure on defence equipment. In 1985 Hartley estimated that the ratio of national equipment expenditure in military R&D budgets was 1.4 to 1 for France, 2.25 to 1 for the UK and 2.2 to 1 for NATO Europe.[9] Moreover, the rate of increase of military R&D has been rapid. To illustrate, note that between 1965 and 1986 there was a 191 per cent increase in R&D to produce the next generation fighter plane: the estimated development of the Tornado in 1965 amounted to a 30 per cent increase over the previous R&D costs of a fighter aircraft (such as the British Lightning or the American Phantom), while the Harrier represented an 86 per cent increase on Tornado development costs and the Efa 105 per cent.[10]

Although R&D is a fixed cost, it is important to recognise that it is fixed in relation to output. In absolute terms R&D costs are not fixed, but are prone to substantial growth. Thus in the case of R&D costs on the Tornado, the R&D element rose continually during the period of the fighter's development. Figure 3.5 illustrates this relation between cost and development time. At given time intervals projected R&D costs are reassessed and revised upwards. The sad case of Britain's NIMROD AEW programme provides a good example of this process. By 1986 it was at least three years late, with its cost (it never reached the production stage) approaching twice the original estimate (in constant prices).[11] Although increases in R&D costs are both predictable and unwelcome, they may still be compensated for if the production run is substantial. Thus, referring again to the collaborative Tornado project, unit R&D costs were reduced substantially due to the aggregation of participating country orders. With the UK demanding 385 fighters; FRG 324; and Italy 100, the combined production total for the aircraft of 749 more realistically approached US scales of output. Figure 3.6 shows how unit R&D cost falls as output increases.

Clearly, then, collaboration *can* lead to savings in R&D. And the non-duplication of resources devoted to the development of armaments is a primary reason why. Obviously if three countries are cooperating in the development of a fighter the cost of R&D represents only one third of the costs of an individual country developing the aircraft independently. In addition to this factor is the scale of output. The longer the production run the lower the unit R&D and production cost, and this may outweigh any differences between nations in terms of comparative efficiency (advantage). Given the spectrum of cost saving possibilities theoretically achievable through collaboration however, it has to be acknowledged that few studies have empirically substantiated that such savings are actually achievable.

Cost Savings in Practice

Little evidence exists concerning economic efficiency deriving from collaboration. In fact, the most recent evidence conflicts with the notion of collaborative cost-savings. The 1991 National Audit Office (NAO) study of Defence Collaborative Projects examined ten collaborative defence projects to establish whether higher production costs are more than offset by development cost savings. The finding of the NAO's investigation (based on somewhat dubious assumptions) was that development cost growth on collaborative projects was, on average, higher than for non-collaborative projects.[12]

By contrast, for evidence on cost savings, Professor Hartley's studies provide the major sources. In his 1991 book (*The Economics of Defence Policy*) the author makes reference to industry studies showing scale efficiencies in Western Europe and North America in terms of unit cost reductions of 10 per cent when output is doubled from 50 per cent of 'minimum efficient scale'.[13] Professor Hartley in his celebrated 1983 book (NATO Arms Collaboration) supplemented the scale efficiency argument with evidence of 10 per cent unit cost declines through learning effects in aircraft production for each doubling in cumulative output, and 10 per cent reductions in average costs through international trade specialisation.[14] Moreover, a German study concerning the fly-away costs of a three-nation collaborative aircraft venture calculated that the project

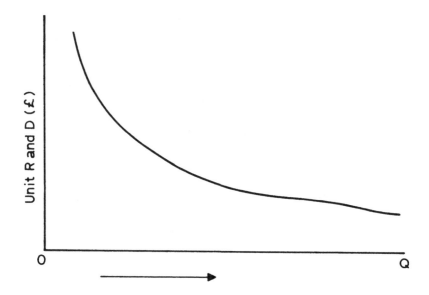

Figure 3.6: Falling R&D Unit Costs

would be 92 per cent of a national effort, while a UK government estimate of the European Fighter Aircraft project was that it would be 20 per cent cheaper than going it alone (saving the UK some £1.2 bn to £1.4 bn, 1987 prices).[15] According to Professor Hartley, the overall conclusion from this evidence is that if equipment standardisation leads to scale economies, learning effects and gains from free trade, it could result in unit cost savings in the region of 20–30 per cent (that is, 10 per cent from each source of cost saving).[16]

The Military Imperative

Aside from the strong financial pressures to standardise equipment through collaboration, there are also powerful military arguments in favour of cooperation. Notably, it promotes military and logistical efficiency. Examples of the lack of standardisation abound. For instance, it was reported in the mid-1980s that NATO States were fielding over two dozen antitank weapons, a variety of tanks, approximately 100 different tactical missiles, 50 kinds of ammunition, communication systems which are incompatible, and over two dozen families of combat aircraft, each with a different radius and ordnance capability and refuelling facility, so that when landing different fuel nozzles were required in order to refuel.[17] Note also the saga of the British Government's selection of Vickers Challenger II main battle tank; the final decision suggesting something awry in NATO defence procurement. Over a four year period, and the expenditure of huge amounts of money by European and US defence contractors, the final government order was for only 140 tanks. Thus, the Alliance continues to deploy four different tanks with three different guns and sets of ammunition under a total allowed under the CFE agreement of only 10,573 tanks on the Central European front for the four countries.[18]

Standardisation of military equipment is a term often employed to represent the fruits of collaboration. In practical terms, however, it more closely resembles the aim of commonality. The military benefit of closer commonality of equipment is based on the enhancement of NATO's operational effectiveness through its various Armed Forces employing equipment that is similar. Effective deployment of cross-national forces would only be possible if they could be fused into a single combatant force no longer reliant on separate national operational or logistics support.

It is not unknown for national variants and modifications to evolve in collaborative ventures, thus destroying the benefits of standardisation. Britain's Tornadoes, for example, were after delivery to the RAF fitted with bomb racks of different design to the racks used by the German and Italian air forces. Although Britain's Tornadoes have thus been 'de-standardised' they may nevertheless still be interoperable, so that different weapons systems, fuel and ammunition can be serviced and replenished by Allied nations. Interoperability (always favoured in preference to commonality by the French) is the short-run policy objective of NATO enshrined in its approach towards rationalisation. This rationalisation goal (RSI – Rationalisation, Standardisation and Interoperability) covers standardisation, interoperability, cross-servicing and general cooperation on military and non-military matters.

A further benefit claimed for arms collaboration is that it binds together the participating nations not only from the military perspective, but also industrially and politically. This is particularly important in the case of Europe where NATO member States are heterogenous in terms of history, society and culture. Indeed, the growing phenomenon of national and transnational mergers between defence sector undertakings has likely been encouraged by the increased collaboration between European States over the last ten years; that is, collaboration has probably assisted the specialisation and rationalisation of defence industry by a reduction in the number of small inefficient manufacturers operating in a fragmented market.

Finally, at the political level, consensus and unity are promoted through countries 'sharing' their defence sector. It is argued that besides strengthening the common purpose, collaboration, reflecting a political commitment, also holds the added benefit of making it more difficult for cooperative ventures to be cancelled or postponed. But this may not always be the virtue imagined (see Chapter Seven).

Conclusion

The important message to emerge from the discussion contained in this chapter is that there are considerable benefits associated with collaboration. The economic arguments are clearly the most compelling; though, of course, the Armed Forces would likely rank the military advantages higher. It is baffling, however, given the impressive theoretical paradigms underpinning the types of cost savings flowing from collaboration, why there is so little evidence available to support these propositions. A few studies have been mentioned which argue the existence of cost savings, but the paucity of research findings in support of collaboration is a cause for concern. The difficulty researchers face centres on the counterfactual. Comparing collaborative project costs with what they might have been if the venture had been undertaken as a national enterprise is clearly a speculative exercise. It is enough to highlight at this juncture that under optimal conditions collaboration is a provider of attractive benefits. Even in the second-best real world environment, in which collaboration is associated with cost premia, the presumption continues to be that the net effect will favour collaboration rather than 'go-it-alone' policies. Further discussion of this important point will be reserved until Chapter Seven when various inefficiencies of collaboration are examined.

4 EUROPE'S DEVELOPING DEFENCE INDUSTRIES

Introduction

For the purpose of assessing the possibilities of transatlantic cooperation as well as the pattern of intra-European cooperative effort it is necessary to appreciate the industrial status of Europe's defence capacity. Thus, this chapter and also Chapter Five, concentrate on examining the development attributes of Europe's defence–industrial base.

The present concern is to identify and analyse the key factors associated with defence–industrial activity in the 1990s. In beginning the discussion, the problems inherent in defining defence production are tackled. The policy difficulties raised here are then logically extended into a discussion of 'dual-use' industries. Many commentators see this area as the path forward for defence contractors through progressively greater reliance on civil capacity with cross-over relevance to the military–industrial domain. The aerospace, communications and electronics industries possess many of the dual-use characteristics advocated, and, accordingly, these engines of technological growth are analysed in some detail. The appraisal reveals the prospective industrial leaders in the changing market segments of Europe's defence industry. Discussion concludes with an examination of the policy initiatives Europe is introducing to stimulate R&D cooperative effort, particularly in dual-use activities.

Defining the DIB

Europe's Defence Industrial Base (DIB) is much discussed, though little understood. It clearly relates to the relationship between military output and the underlying manufacturing sector producing that output. Yet this much can be deduced from the term itself. For policy purposes, therefore, it is evident that further clarification is required. In this respect, two key and interrelated questions need to be asked: firstly, what exactly is meant by a DIB, whether on a European or a national scale? Secondly, is it possible to rigorously define the outputs and inputs constituent to a DIB? Both of these questions will now be considered, beginning with the problem of defining a DIB.

In the mid-1980s, the British Secretary of State for Defence, George Younger, told the House of Commons Defence Committee that . . . ' "the defence industrial base" is the term we adopt for convenience to describe the wide range of firms which supply the Ministry of Defence with the equipment and services it requires.'[1] This is an unhelpful categorisation. It encompasses various commercial operations which logically do not form part of the UK's DIB, while omitting many of those which logically are a part. For example, although Britain's farming sector supplies dairy food to the Armed Forces, it is stretching a point to include elements of the agricultural sector in the UK's DIB. However, national distinctions must always be recognised as influencing interpretation. Thus, in the former Soviet Union and India, where state-owned military farms are organised solely to provide dairy and agricultural produce to the troops, the judgement that farming activities lie outside the domain of defence production might be different. Equally, there are firms supplying the basic materials and equipment to the defence contractors, which appear to be excluded from the Defence Minister's definition of the DIB. Their activities would not be found at the industrial interface between the MoD and the prime-contractors supplying military equipment. Nevertheless, this substrata of contractors supply essential raw materials and equipment. For example, oil as well as other energy sources, and mechanical, electrical and electronic equipment. These intermediate and capital goods are not military items, but ought they to be part of a DIB? As yet, there is no consensus on this, and even the Secretary of State for Defence was hesitant regarding the contribution of UK business to the DIB . . . 'I would not like to put a firm percentage on it, but a significant proportion.'[2]

Table 4.1 shows the broad nature of defence–industrial activity in a mature technological economy, such as Britain's. It indicates forcefully how some leading-edge sectors, such as electronics and aerospace, are powerful players in defence production; others, such as food and textiles, also make contributions which cannot be described as insignificant. But these industries do not constitute, in conventional parlance, a defence sector or DIB. Conceptually, this is more narrow, applying to firms providing military equipment as also the supporting layer of businesses supplying the technology to produce defence output. According to this view, then, there are about 800 firms in the UK making equipment designed specifically for military use, with about 10,500 firms qualified on the MoD Defence Contractors list; their numbers increasing at the rate of 700 per annum.

Table 4.1: Defence Expenditure in the United Kingdom, By Commodity

£ million

	SIC (80) Group[1]	1983–84	1984–85	1985–86	1986–87	1987–88	1988–89
Total[2]		7,096	8,014	8,128	7,919	7,933	8,241
Solid fuels[3]	111,120	10	11	10	12	11	8
Petroleum products[3]	140	673	737	601	385	313	295
Gas, electricity and water supply[3]	161–170	182	195	213	231	220	230
Ordnance, small arms and ammunition	329	584	675	699	683	705	723
Other mechanical and marine engineering	320–328	410	407	415	427	685	671
Data processing equipment	330	97	104	121	130	197	225
Other electrical engineering	341–348, nes	119	136	135	145	131	141
Electronics	344, 345	1,550	1,638	1,697	1,599	1,546	1,754
Motor vehicles and parts	351–353	187	274	288	253	310	247
Shipbuilding and repairing	361	425	557	660	700	661	680
Aerospace equipment	364	2,070	2,461	2,391	2,418	2,150	2,176
Instrument engineering	371–374	125	115	118	114	126	131
Food[3]	411–429	113	126	132	127	126	128
Textiles, leather goods and clothing[3]	431–456	93	111	124	133	104	112
Other production industries	111–495, nes	243	237	271	290	353	318
Other industries and services	nes	215	230	253	272	295	409

1. Groups in the Standard Industrial Classification (1980 revision).
2. Gross expenditure at current prices excluding VAT, pay and allowances, general administrative expenses (amounting to some £864 million in 1988–89), Property Services Agency expenditure on behalf of the Ministry of Defence and other expenditure on land, buildings and works services.
3. Includes payments for goods and services purchased overseas.

Source: *Statement on the Defence Estimates 1990*, Vol. II, p., CM 1022–I.

Defence production in the UK is big business, amounting to around £8,296 billion, represented 39 per cent of the total defence budget in 1990. Many of Britain's biggest firms are involved in producing for defence. In fact, a report in 1990 showed that more than half of the top 50 companies listed on the stock exchange have links with producers and sellers of armaments.[3] A relatively small number of big defence contractors provide the apex to the pyramid shape of the UK's DIB, with a similar European pyramid also now emerging. At the top of the UK's pyramid are perched the huge engineering conglomerates, such as BAe, Rolls Royce, GKN, and so on. Moving towards the base come the myriad subcontractors to defence production. The scope of corporate involvement in military production, both at primary- and to some extent subcontractor level, may be gauged from Table 4.2, showing the list of those firms included in the annual *Statement on the Defence Estimates* as having more than £5 million worth of contracts.

Problems of Dual-Use Technology

If there is difficulty in defining the nature and scope of a DIB, the problems in specifying whether the output of a producer is military-oriented or not are no less intractable. This question was faced in the previous section in relation to agricultural items, but now attention is focused on primarily manufactured goods. It is an important consideration because although certain countries may be regarded as having limited DIBs, as represented by the degree of indigenous defence production, they may nevertheless possess potentially huge defence industrial capacity, if government policy were to change such that defence output was encouraged.

Japan provides the best example of a country with a latent defence manufacturing capacity. The country has a peace-oriented constitution; and a defence policy restraining defence expenditure to around one per cent of GNP level.[4] This obviously acts to suppress local defence production, especially when Japan additionally prohibits itself from exporting military equipment. However, Japan's GNP is the second largest in the world, so that one per cent of this is sufficient to provide for a sturdy incipient DIB, reckoned by the close of the 1980s to be the world's sixth largest.[5] Given a relaxation of government policy towards defence production, Japan's civil producers of electronic and heavy engineering equipment could quickly transfer resources and production to military output. To some extent, Indonesia is following a similar industrial development model. Through its industrialisation strategy. the Indonesian authorities are seeking to provide realisable defence–industrial

70

Table 4.2: UK-based MoD Contractors, Paid £5 million or more by MoD

Over £250 million

British Aerospace plc	Rolls Royce plc
The General Electric Co plc	VSEL Consortium plc
The Plessey Co plc	

£100–250 million

Boeing Aerospace Company	Hunting Associated Industries plc
Devonport Management Ltd	Thorn EMI plc
Ferranti plc	Vickers plc
FKI Babcock plc	Westland Group plc
GKN plc	

£50–100 million

Artix Ltd	Racal Electronics plc
The British Petroleum Co plc	Short Bros plc
British Telecommunications plc	STC plc
Dowty Group plc	Swan Hunter Shipbuilders Ltd

£25–50 million

British Airways plc	FR Group plc	Pilkington plc
British Railways Board	Harland & Wolff plc	Serco Ltd
BTR plc	Lucas Industries plc	The "Shell" Transport
Esso UK plc	Marshall of Cambridge	& Trading Co plc
	(Engineering) Ltd	Singer Link Miles Ltd
	Philips UK Ltd	Smiths Industries plc

£10 25 million

A C Cossor Ltd	Cranfield Institute of	NAAFI
Aerospatiale SNI	Technology	Notchlook Ltd
Avon Rubber plc	Cray Electronics	Northern Engineering
BET plc	Holdings plc	Industries plc
BMARC	Digital Equipment Co	SD Scicon plc
British &	Ltd	The Services Sound &
Commonwealth	DRG plc	Vision Corporation
Holdings plc	Hawker Siddeley Group	Shell Nederland
Cable & Wireless plc	plc	Raffinadrij BV
Cambridge Electronic	Hewlett Packard Ltd	UK Universities
Industries plc	Hillsdown Holdings plc	UK Atomic Energy
CAP Group plc	Hollandse	Authority
Civil Aviation Authority	Signaalapparaten BV	United Scientific
Coats Viyella plc	Honeywell Ltd	Holdings plc

Table 4.2: *continued*

Computing Devices Co Ltd	Inchcape plc	Varity Holdings Ltd
	Initial Contract Services Ltd	Vosper Thorneycroft Holdings Ltd
	Meggitt Holdings plc	William Cook plc
	Mobil Holdings Ltd	

£5–10 million

A & P Appledore Tyne Ltd	Kodak Ltd	RHP Group plc
AGIP Petroli SPA	Leyland DAF Ltd	Rohde & Schwarz UK Ltd
Chemring Group plc	Logica plc	
Conoco (UK) Ltd	Martin-Baker Aircraft Co Ltd	The RTZ Corporation plc
Courtaulds plc	McDonnell Douglas Corporation	SAFT (UK) Ltd
DFDS (UK) Ltd		Schlumberger Measurement & Control (UK) Ltd
Ferguson Industrial Holdings plc	ML Holdings plc	
Ford Motor Co Ltd	Optical & Medical International plc	Siebe plc
Frazer Nash Group Ltd	Paccar UK Ltd	Thomson-Brandt Armaments
General Motors Ltd	The Peninsular & Oriental Steam Navigation Company	Thomson-Sintra ASM
George Blair plc		Tracor Aerospace Inc
Grand Metropolitan plc	Petrofina (UK) Ltd	Trafalgar House plc
Hogg Robinson plc	Portsmouth Aviation Ltd	Trusthouse Forte plc
Hunting Communication Technology Ltd	Readicut International plc	Turbomeca SA
	Remploy Ltd	Wardle Storeys plc
		The Weir Group plc
		Williams Holdings plc

Notes:
1. Includes suppliers of food, fuels and services.
2. Within each financial bracket, contractors are listed in alphabetical order.
3. The status of contractors in this list is that at 1 April 1989.

Source: *Statement on the Defence Estimates 1990*, Vol. II, p. x, CM 1022–I.

capacity via the creation of an, ostensibly, civil–industrial framework. As a final example, India, in the space and nuclear fields, has also followed the path of constructing a civil–industrial sector, with the purpose of enjoying 'reverse' civil–military technological spin-offs should the need ever arise to produce rockets and nuclear energy in a manner that would satisfy military requirements.

Clearly, then, the 'dual-use' nature of engineering production is an obstacle in providing a satisfactory definition of the output of a DIB.

Moreover, this difficulty needs to be addressed from both the output and the input side. For example, is the collaboration between Alfa Romeo and Nissan for a dual-use light 4×4 vehicle to be regarded as a civil or a military good?[6] Of pertinence here is the wide use of Toyota jeeps and similar light 4×4 vehicles among the warring factions of the long-running Western Sahara conflict. The prevalence of such vehicles in this conflict leading it to be labelled the 'Toyota War'.[7] The vagueness of military–industrial activity also affects the input side. Almost none of the factors of production can be regarded as dedicated to defence sector use. Particular pieces of capital equipment may come closest, but the boundaries are not rigid. The forging of Iraq's speculative space-gun, requiring incredibly exacting degrees of precision, did not take place in a military steel shop, but a civil one. This problem of dual-use technology, from the input side, is also strikingly illustrated by reference to the celebrated Toshiba–Kongsberg affair. Here, a Japanese and a Norwegian company were found to be supplying the Soviet Union during the early to mid-1980s with sophisticated milling machine tools and computing equipment. This was a violation of the CoCOM regulations, restricting specified high-technology items from being exported to the USSR as a quick and easy method of boosting the Soviets' military effort. In the event, the US authorities argued that the sales by Toshiba and Kongsberg achieved just that. The equipment these companies sold allowed the Soviets to squeeze the US–USSR military technology gap. It provided them with the means of building more efficient propellers than hitherto possible for their nuclear attack submarines. At a stroke, much of the US submarine detection technology was made redundant, while American submarines themselves had now become vulnerable. The perceived damage done to America's security interests led to calls by the Senate and House of Representatives for punitive damages from the Japanese and Norwegian companies involved. Indeed, the House voted by a 415-to-1 margin to seek damages that were in the view of some Congressmen likely to run to $30 billion (or the cost, generously estimated, of 30 Los Angeles-Class SSNs).[8]

The importance of the dual-use nature of technology relates importantly to policy considerations. For instance, CoCOM's aim to stem the flow of military sensitive technology to the former communist countries centres on the need to identify for embargo purposes, not only sophisticated machine tools, relatively easy to categorise, but also chemical compounds, whose categorisation are fraught with difficulty. Due to these definitional problems, CoCOM membership is presently experiencing internecine strife over its ill-defined technological sanctions. In a similar vein, Japan and India, due to the difficulty of adequately defining the nature of the goods to be included in their self-proclaimed bans on the export of defence equipment are often in practice bound to be breaking them, in spirit if not officially. Furthermore, in the post-1992 commercially liberalised climate of Europe, the policy framework will be inconsistently applied, with some civil producers manufacturing 'civil' goods, which, although serving the needs of defence in some manner, are not eligible for exemption from the removal of protectionist barriers.

Defence Industrial Structure

General Characteristics

For most of the advanced, and also industrialising, countries, there is a positive correlation between defence expenditure and the size of the defence–industrial complex. Although defence procurement is an umbrella term, incorporating off-the-shelf foreign purchases at one extreme and indigenous development and production at the other, it is taken or given, that States with high defence expenditure will also have substantial DIBs. These nations have, for political, economic and strategic reasons, sought to develop local defence production capacity. Although Germany and Britain are both active supporters of armaments collaboration, it should be noted that domestic production still accounts for 80 per cent of the value of procurement expenditure in the former country and 75 per cent in the latter.[9] For Britain, moreover, international collaboration only accounts for 15 per cent of total equipment procurement value, with the remaining 10 per cent taken up by direct foreign sales.[10]

Table 4.3 supports the contention that high defence expenditure is associated with big, diversified DIBs, though to reach this conclusion some cross-referencing is required between countries in Table 4.3 and the nationality of those (European) companies listed in Appendix A. Save for perhaps one or two exceptions, Europe's biggest defence industrial contractors belong to the 'big three' States: France; Germany; and the UK; that is, those having the highest levels of defence expenditure. These same States are also generally regarded as being the most industrially advanced, generating, in absolute terms, the greatest amounts of GDP. Table 4.3 lists the countries in terms of their ranking of defence expenditure. However, it also closely corresponds to their ranking according to defence–industrial advancement. The related classification of these countries into 'tiers' based on their comparative levels of defence expenditure and defence industrialisation, though simplistic, has the advantage of highlighting approximate stages of development. The US,

74

the sole member of the first tier spends, at around $300 bn, almost 9 times as much on defence as the nearest European nation, France. The French, Germans and British, with defence budgets at about $33–35 bn, are NATO's second tier defence–industrial nations, and first rank European countries. At a level of defence expenditure around $14 bn below these States is third tier Italy. The fourth tier defence–industrialising nations are about $12 bn below Italy, at approximately $7 bn. The fifth and final tier of nations included in this categorisation relates to those nations, which, for various reasons, possess only fledgling defence–industrial sectors. In the international policy-making fora, these are familiarly described as the Less Developed Defence Industry (LDDI) nations, though recently this has been deferentially shortened to the Developing Defence Industry (DDI) nations.

A recent SIPRI report on West European Arms Production[11] indicates that three of the region's major arms producing States, France, Germany and the United Kingdom (NATO's Second Tier States) account for almost 80 per cent of the total arms sales (domestic and export) of Western Europe's 100 biggest defence companies. These three Second Tier States also dominate in terms of industrial concentration. Seventy firms in the list of Europe's 100 biggest defence contractors are represented by British (28), German (25) and French (17) companies.[12] Appendix A shows SIPRI's full listing of Western Europe's 100 biggest arms producing companies. The data is for 1988, and under normal circumstances its relatively recent origin would have been reflective of reality. However, given the tremendous market and structural changes affecting the defence sector since 1988, the accuracy of the table in respect to current conditions may be somewhat less than perfect. A sense of Europe's defence–industrial structure should nevertheless be possible.

Major Defence Players

British Aerospace (B.Ae.) is Europe's biggest defence contractor, with US $5,470 mn worth of arms sales. The ranking of the table is according to defence sales and not total sales (civil and defence). This point is worth making because the corporate goal of most defence undertakings is to diversify out of arms production. Interestingly, although the Daimler–Benz conglomerate is ranked four in defence sales, it is the biggest company in respect of total sales, with over four times B.Ae.'s total sales figures. B.Ae.'s exposure to the defence market is 54 per cent, against 40 per cent for Rolls Royce, and only 8 per cent for the Daimler–Benz group. B.Ae. has been aiming to reduce its dependency on defence

Table 4.3: KEY Defence Indicators

	Mil expend (US $ M)	Milex to GDP (%)	Milex per capita (US $)	Defence employment ('000)	Defence exports (US $ M)	Defence imports (US $ M)	GDP (US $ bn)	Popn (Mill)	GDP per capita ('000)	Tiers (Milex)
1st Tier										
US	299,144	5.8	1,214	2,022	9,367		4,839	249	19.4	> $40 bn
2nd Tier										
France	35,085	3.7	628	231	2,881		950.2	55.8	17.0	> $20 bn
FRG	33,638	2.9	550	280	1,455	324	1,206.0	61.2	19.7	
UK	33,436	4.0	581	515	1,586	247				
3rd Tier										
Italy	19,754	2.4	344	92	397		815.3	57.6	14.2	> $10 bn

4th Tier									
Spain	7,700	2.1	196	211	1,362	340.1	39.3	8.7	> $5 bn
Canada	6,820	2.0	261	67	506	494	26.1	18.9	
Netherlands	6,402	2.9	434	756	214	227.5	14.8	15.4	
5th Tier									
Belgium	3,939	2.7	398		1,150	152.5	10.0	15.3	< $5 bn
Greece	3,208	6.0	320			51.8	10.1	5.1	
Norway	3,058	3.3	725			90.4	4.2	21.5	
Turkey	2,879	3.9	51		1,090	62.2	55.5	1.1	
Denmark	2,162	2.1	422			107.6	5.1	21.1	
Portugal	1,319	3.0	128			37.0	10.4	3.6	
Luxembourg	80	1.2	211			6.2	.37	16.8	

Source: *SIPRI 1989 Yearbook*, OUP 1989.

Notes:

Mil. Exp. Data relate to US $M in 1986 prices and exchange rates.

Military Balance 1989–90, 11SS, 1989 – Defence exports and imports relate to US $M in 1985 prices.

SDE 1990, British Government, p. 47 – GDP (current prices) and population relate to 1988.

Hartley, K. 'The European Defence Market and Industry' in (eds) Creasey, P. and May. S., *The European Armaments Market and Procurement Cooperation*, Macmillan (1988), pp. 42–43.

77

business. The company's recent acquisitions of the Rover Automotive group and the Dutch engineering construction firm, Ballast Nedham, support this policy approach, bringing down B.Ae.'s defence to total sales ratio from its previous 60–70 per cent.

Thomson CSF was to be B.Ae.'s partner in the Eurodynamics missile cooperation project before it was terminated in 1991. The company forms part of the Thomson S.A. group. The CSF subsidiary is defence-electronics biased, and 77 per cent dependent on arms sales. It has been aggressive in acquisitions/alliances with other NATO member country firms during the early 1990s, including the purchase of Philip's (NL) defence operations, Pilkington's (UK) optronics, and a cooperative agreement with the US company, Boeing.

Daimler–Dasa represents the aircraft manufacturing element within Germany's Daimler–Benz group. It comprises MBB, Dornier, MTU and TST. Formed in 1989, it accounts for 15 per cent of the holding company's total sales. It is participating in the Airbus, Eurocopter, and EFA projects.

Rolls Royce, discussed later in this chapter, is clearly a world league aviation engine producer, taking around 10 per cent of global market share. The company is the UK's major turbine manufacturer, exporting around 70 per cent of its sales. It is currently involved in a costly 'Trent' engine development programme, and is a major participant in the Tornado (Turbo Union group) and EFA (EJ200) engine projects.

GEC is Britain's foremost defence electronics company. Consolidating its expertise in this field it acquired in the early 1990s Plessy and Ferranti-radar. GEC specialises in system integration, surveillance, radar, and missile guidance. It is second only to Thomson in European defence electronics.

Aerospatiale and Dassault are two formidable French aerospace companies. The former is state-owned, involving itself in aircraft, helicopter and missile production. Aerospatiale participates in the Airbus programme, the Puma anti-sub attack helicopter and the NH90 helicopter; produces the Roland missile, and is assisting in the development of the Hades nuclear ballistic missile system. Dassault, in contrast to Aerospatiale, is a family-owned defence company. It produces the Mirage range of jet fighters, and is developing the Rafale military aircraft.

GIAT is France's major ordnance producer. It acquired the Belgium firm FN in the 1990s to project a European image. GIAT produces the AMX Leclerc MBT and a wide range of armoured vehicles and artillery pieces. This state-owned firm is 100 per cent dependent on defence business.

Kraus–Maffei and Rhein–Metall AG are two German companies involved in the production of Leopard tanks. Kraus–Maffei is the principal manufacturer of Leopard I and II tanks, though it is increasingly attempting to diversify into heavy engineering civil work, such as power plants for rail transportation. Rhein–Metall AG is a manufacturer of all forms of gun, and is the principal subcontractor for the Leopard II.

Italy, NATO's third tier arms producing country, has several important medium size defence companies. Augusta is the country's major helicopter manufacturer, and is currently involved in the production of the EH101 (with Westland–UK) and the NH90 with Franco–German cooperation; Finbreda is a specialist producer of missiles and systems; and, Fiat Aviazone, Italy's only aeroengine manufacturer, is participating in the Tornado, EFA, and AMX aircraft engines.

This brief outline of Europe's major defence undertakings is not intended to be exhaustive. Firms like Vickers (UK), Matra (Fr) and Oto Melara (IT) have not been mentioned. Although they feature well down on the table of Europe's biggest defence contractors, they are nevertheless vital in their area of expertise, i.e. tanks and missile systems. This will also be the case with other specialist defence producers.

Only a minority of defence concerns will be unaffected by the changing market conditions of the 1990s. Many will be those belonging to the defence developing industry nations; a subject which will be discussed further in Chapter Five, while others will belong to the high growth defence areas to be examined in the next section.

Europe's Defence Industry : Engines of Growth

Albeit that the revitalisation of the WEU, IEPG, and the raised interest of the EC in the defence field, has spawned an increasing level of research into Europe's defence industry,[13] data on the subject are sparse. Keeping this in view, this section is concerned with assessing the current economic status of Europe's defence–industrial complex. In particular, the two main driving forces of technological development in the defence field, aerospace and electronics, will be examined, beginning with the former.

Britain, the leading defence aerospace nation in Europe, acts as the departure point for the analysis. Even though its aerospace sector is big, making a valuable contribution to national employment and output, it has still been necessary, as later discussion indicates, for leading firms to enter into transnational collaboration. The size and growth of the sector can be judged from Table 4.4, below. Although the data relate to current

Table 4.4: UK Manufacturers' Production of Aerospace Equipment 1984–87 (£m)

	1984	1985	1986	1987
Aircraft	877.7	930.4	1,399.9	3.377
Aircraft parts	953.8	1,074.6	1,035.7	
Aero-engines (new)	381.0	477.3	585.8	897.4
Aero-engines (re-conditioned)	8.1	15.8	28.1	23.8
Aero-engine parts	796.1	985.9	1,076.5	993.5
Guided weapons	793.7	836.6	895.3	935.8
Development	688.8	857.4	779.2	686.7
Experimental & repairs	236.8	263.5	323.9	359.3
Space	115.5	180.1	237.1	184.3
Others	282	398.8	555.1	674.6
Total	5,133.5	6,020.4	6,916.6	8132.5

NB: Data in current prices
Source: Keynote: Aerospace Report 6th Edn. (1989) p. 22. Original source: Business Monitor PQ 3640.

prices, note the coverage is for a period when levels of inflation were relatively low. Thus the growth in what is high value-added production is impressive. Between 1984 and 1987, according to the Business Monitor, the value of output grew by nearly 60 per cent. Moreover, in 1987 around 61 per cent of aerospace production was sold overseas, making a valuable contribution to the UK's balance of payments. The sector's trading performance is particularly impressive, given the weakness of the UK's manufacturing sector, which since 1984 has been running a deficit on international trade. The value of British aerospace exports, in current prices, has risen by 70 per cent between 1984 and 1988. However, this performance is tempered by the fact that imports have grown even faster. Hence, even though the trade surplus in aerospace products rose from £892.9 mn in 1984 to £1,474,9 mn in 1988 representing a rate of growth of 65 per cent, this is somewhat less than the rate of increase in exports (71 per cent). Table 4.5 shows the trading performance of the UK aerospace industry. British exports have shown buoyancy in all of the major areas and particularly so in aircraft and parts, aero-engines and guided missiles. Many of the exports were to developing countries, such as B.Ae's, 'Al-Yamamah' contract with Saudi Arabia.

B.Ae. is the UK's biggest defence contractor and its second largest exporter of manufacturers (after ICI), selling over 60 per cent of its output overseas.[14] Total sales (civil and defence) for 1989 reached £5.4 bn. Defence sales accounted for approximately 54 per cent of this

Table 4.5: UK Trading Performance of Aerospace Equipment 1984–88 (£m)

Exports	1984	1985	1986	1987	1988
Helicopters	34.6	32.3	20.7	87.1	53.7
Aircraft	678.9	831.3	1,010.0	1,215.7	1,696.4
Aircraft (parts)	1,360.2	1,492.1	1,687.0	1,942.5	1,761.5
Aero-engines	521.1	786.9	889.2	906.5	976.1
Aero-engines (parts)	528.4	605.6	638.8	734.1	813.7
Guided missiles	52.4	54.7	38.8	94.0	113.2
Others	5.4	8.2	9.1	13.0	15.1
	3,181.0	3,811.1	4,293.6	4,992.9	5,429.7
Imports					
Helicopters	64.7	60.7	20.8	20.2	44.8
Aircraft	585.8	879.4	363.3	552.3	1,345.8
Aircraft (parts)	618.1	692.1	748.9	936.6	1,012.5
Aero-engines	521.4	559.4	557.9	567.1	745.6
Aero-engines (parts)	392.3	481.8	551.0	571.0	687.7
Guided missiles	102.3	119.5	175.5	73.1	115.2
Others	3.5	3.4	2.5	3.3	3.2
Total	2,288.1	2,796.3	2,419.9	2,723.6	3,954.8
Trade balance	892.9	1,014.8	1,873.7	2,269.3	1,474.9

Source: *Keynote Aerospace Report* pp. 23–24 (1989).

figure. B.Ae. has been, and continues to be, involved in several major aerospace collaborative projects, including production of the Tornado fighter and development of its successor, the Efa. In addition to these European ventures, B.Ae. has cooperated with the Americans. In particular, Harrier AV-8B fighters have been co-produced with McDonnell Douglas, with co-development taking place in regard to a Harrier II plus version and a variant of the Hawk jet trainer aircraft.

One other very important company in the UK aerospace market is Rolls Royce. Defence accounts for around 40 per cent of the company's work, with exports representing about 70 per cent of its output.[15] In 1987, Rolls had 'over 110 military customers in 87 countries operating over 7,700 aircraft with over 11,600 engines across the spectrum of military aircraft types' and across the Atlantic 'approximately 9 per cent of the combat aircraft in service are powered by engines supplied or designed by Rolls Royce.'[16] In 1988, the company signed a contract to develop and produce the Eurojet EJ200 engine, which will power the Efa. Rolls

Royce estimates that around 1,800 of these European fighters will eventually be produced.[17] In regard to the Efa's predecessor aircraft, the Tornado, Rolls by early 1989, had orders for over 2,400 of these engines, the RB199, of which at that time about 2,000 had been delivered. The company is also currently involved in the production and development of the Spey and Pegasus range of military engines, and the GEM and RTM-322 helicopter engines; the latter being a collaborative venture with TURBOMECA of France. Rolls Royce is also cooperating with this same company and the German engine manufacturer, MTU, to co-produce an engine for the prospective Franco–German battlefield helicopter.

In the field of helicopters, the UK has only one manufacturer, Westland Plc. It has been a troubled company, stemming from the political controversy surrounding its near insolvency in 1985.[18] In March 1986, the US firm, Sikorsky and Italy's Fiat, became minority shareholders in Westland. Two years later, in 1988, the Italian company sold its shareholding to GKN, which is now the major shareholder. Westland's EH 101 Merlin is recognised by many observers to be a superior military and naval helicopter, but even so, the trading position remained uncertain, leading to rationalisation, and over 1,000 job losses in the late 1980s. The UK government's 1991 £1.5 bn anti-submarine helicopter contract for the Royal Navy with an IBM–Westland consortium undertaking the systems integration work on the EH101 looks to have stabilised the firm's medium-term future.

Short Bros. is another UK defence firm specialising in aerospace activities. It is believed to be the oldest civil manufacturing company in this field in the world. Entering the 1990s, Shorts is Northern Ireland's biggest employer, with around 3,500 workers. The company was sold by the British Government in June 1989 to the Canadian company, Bombardier. The intention was for Short Bros. to be merged with the Canadian firm's subsidiary, Canadair, which is involved in the production of business jets. Currently, Short Bros. produces the 330 and 360 range of commuter aircraft, the Tucano military trainer (a Brazilian cooperative venture), and blowpipe and starstreak missile systems.

Although aerospace production enjoys a separate industrial classification it obviously depends vitally on associated engineering and electronic and software manufactures. According to Jane's Information Group, the electronics in aeroplanes accounts for between 5 per cent (for training aircraft and transporters) and 75 per cent (for airborne command and early warning aircraft) of total costs.[19] The success of modern military aircraft and their weapons systems is dependent upon the cross-pollination of ideas and innovation between engineers of the two industries. Table 4.6 lists Britain's 10 principal aerospace and electronics

Table 4.6: Defence Sales of UK Aerospace and Electronics Companies, 1986

	Defence Sales £m	Defence Sales to Total Sales (%)	MOD Sales to Defence Sales (%)	Total employment ('000)	MOD related employment ('000)
B Aerospace	1900	70	33	76	25.7
GEC	1565	30	55	165	–
Rolls Royce	935	58	20	38	9.3
Plessey	495	35	70	–	–
Racal	414	37	40	–	–
Ferranti	340	60	60	–	–
Westland	280	90	50	10.8	3.5
Thorn-EMI	190	6	65	–	–
Short Bros.	150	38	20	7	1
STC	140	7	78	–	–

Source: Taylor et al., *The UK Defence Industrial Base* Brassey's (1989), p. 49, and, *Sector Review on Aerospace*, West Midlands Enterprise Board (February 1989), p. 18.

companies serving the defence sector. The data relate to the 1986 position. Since that year, GEC, the UK's second biggest defence conglomerate has swallowed both Plessey and Ferranti. This concentration of hi-tech electronic expertise is emerging as a powerful industrial force in Europe as evidenced by GEC's capture of the contract for the Efa's radar system. Electronics has become pervasive in the defence sector. From surveillance radar and communications networks to data processing, it plays an ever increasing role in aerospace and wider military production. In World War One, electronics accounted for only one per cent of the American defence budget; after World War Two, six per cent; 20 per cent during the 1970s; and almost 26 per cent in 1986.[20] By 1996, between 35 and 40 per cent of the UK equipment budget is expected to be electronics related.[21]

The IEPG has recognised the significance of the electronics sector in relation to the construction of a viable European defence–industrial complex. However, the sector's strategic importance (in both military and economic terms) is very much shaped by the dynamic quality of its output. Currently, technological innovation is dominated by the Japanese and American civil and defence contractors. From the 1987 report, the IEPG study team stated . . .

'At present, Europe's technology base, taken overall and including space, is encouragingly competitive but shows some critical areas of weakness, particularly in electronics and new materials; both technologies are of first importance and will enable dramatic improvements in capability to be obtained in many types of systems. For the future, massive US efforts stemming *inter alia* from the SDI initiative could pull that nation rapidly ahead in electronics and other high technologies. In development and production, Europe is less competitive than her current technology base would suggest, primarily because of her fragmented markets. The threat from Japan is not direct, since she does not currently export defence products. There is however a significant indirect threat. There are very important transfers of military technology from Japan to the United States. Furthermore, Japan exports large quantities of highly competitive civil high technology products to Europe and this has an undermining effect on the European industrial base which supports both the civil economy and the defence industry.'[22]

The study team are right to be concerned. America's domination and Japan's emerging threat in the microelectronics and telecommunications markets are powerful forces undermining indigenous European defence efforts. The US and Japan enjoy a technological gap over European producers in both the quantity and quality of semi-conductor chips, representing the technological core of the contemporary electronic 'revolution'. A measure of Europe's laggard performance in this field can be sensed by reference to Table 4.7, below.

Even though in value terms semi-conductors do not rank among the most important of the world's manufactured products, in defence terms, they are a critically strategic area of production. Thus, dependency in this field is what sparks the IEPG's anxieties. Paradoxically, perhaps, it is the US defence sector which provides an example of the dangers to be faced. For instance, without the 'chips' to run the F-16 systems this high performance fighter which was one of the mainstays of the Allied air effort during the Gulf war would be neutralised; yet, while the Pentagon accounts for roughly 10 per cent of all US semi-conductor sales, the major suppliers are not American but Japanese.[23] Japan holds nearly a 100 per cent share of the one mega-bit semi-conductors used in the hearts of advanced computers.[24] Indeed, for NATO defence industrialists, in general, the potential development of the Japanese defence–industrial base sets the nerve-ends twitching. There are signs that with the breaking of the self-imposed export embargo of defence equipment, through recent transfers of military technology to the US, the scene is primed for the onslaught of Japanese defence manufacturers into the export market.

Table 4.7: Semi-Conductor Production: Selected Leading National Producers 1985–87 (By Value: billions of US $)

National Producer	1985	1986	1987(a)
US			
Discretes	1,460	1,498	1,642
ICs	8,665	9,327	10,428
Total semiconductor	10,396	11,129	12,418
Japan			
Discretes	2,584	2,394	2,444
ICs	8,070	8,429	9,242
Total semiconductor	11,870	12,224	13,227
West Germany			
Discretes	423	412	434
ICs	1,408	1,255	1,435
Total semiconductor	1,945	1,774	1,984
UK			
Discretes	191	191	209
ICs	737	782	895
Total semiconductor	979	1,027	1,159
Italy			
Discretes	129	136	142
ICs	445	417	468
Total semiconductor	599	577	637

Source: Henderson, J., *The Globalisation of High Technology Production*, Routledge (1989), p. 7. Original source: *Electronics* (January 22, 1987).
NB: (a) Estimates.
ICs = Integrated Circuits.

Following the successful civil–industrial development model of licensed production through to local development and production, Japan remains cautiously poised to expand its export base from 'dual-use' technology to direct military sales.

In facing the competition from the Japanese and US aerospace and electronics corporations, European firms have been encouraged to rationalise, consolidate and concentrate. As a consequence, some very strong commercial organisations have evolved. For instance, the German defence–industrial conglomerate, Daimler Benz, which recently absorbed MBB, is very big. In terms of overall sales in the world aerospace and electronics league it lies third behind Boeing and McDonnell Douglas. B.Ae is the world's fourth biggest aerospace manufacturer, after the aforementioned US and German companies.

This again exemplifies the pyramidal structure of defence industry in NATO and Europe. Its layered nature can be found in all strategic sectors of the military–industrial relation. For example, European output contributions in the technological bow-wave C^3I (Command, control, communication, and information) area are given in Table 4.8, below.

Table 4.8: West Europe: Output Data for the Communications and Military Electronics Industries (1988)

Country	Defence Output ($M)	Civil & Defence Output ($M)	Defence to Total Sales (%)
France	6,339	26,010	24.4
UK	4,313	28,836	15.0
FRG	2,449	40,787	6.0
Italy	1,969	17,277	11.4
Netherlands	590	7,512	7.9
Spain	376	5,170	7.3
Denmark	258	1,635	15.8
Belgium	233	4,395	5.3
Norway	158	1,375	11.5
Ireland	74	4,165	1.8

Source: *Yearbook of World Electronics Data 1990 – West Europe*, Elsevier Science Publishing Company (1989), p. 18.

The table contains the production data of Europe's ten leading country producers of communications and military electronic equipment.[25] Here again, the 'big three' European defence producers, save for Italy, stand apart from the rest of Europe's electronics producers. France is the biggest manufacturer, by sales value, of military electronics, with over $6000 m turnover. This is more than three times Italy's approximately $2000 mn turnover, which, in turn, is over three times the value of its nearest rival, the Netherlands, having a market share of $590 mn. Interestingly, although Norway has a lowly $158 m defence electronics turnover for 1988, having a relatively high defence to civil sales ratio for communications and electronics products appears to suggest defence is being used as a technology-driver for civil expansion in this area.

Just as important as the production position is the trading performance of the communications and military electronics industries. The success of the export drive reflects the productive efficiency, quality and competitiveness of the output. By contrast, the degree of import penetration relative to production denotes the extent of dependence on foreign sources of supply. The data do not permit judgements on the origins of these imports, but it is probable that Japanese and American companies are the principal suppliers. Table 4.9 shows the trading position of ten major European nations in the military-related communications and electronics field. The former West Germany, being Europe's foremost, diversified electronics producer exports a huge $25 bn worth of civil and defence communications and electronics equipment. Only 3.4 per cent of this is related to defence, but the German's strictly controlled export regime, making it very difficult to sell military material to non-NATO States,[26] would be a conditioning factor for this low ratio. The country's defence imports in this field to total communications and electronics imports is relatively low; yet, as a percentage of defence electronics production it exceeds 20 per cent. This would suggest that Germany is still, to some extent, on a learning curve in this area. Ranking the countries according to their balance of trade, Germany heads the league with a surplus of $362 mn. Spain, a defence-industrialising nation which emerged in the 1980s, comes last, with a trading deficit of $130 mn. Both Denmark and Belgium enjoy favourable trading accounts, though from small export value bases. But the Danes' $66 m surplus is not insignificant for a small industrial, let alone defence–industrial NATO member State. A special effort would appear to be being made by Denmark in this hi-tech field judged by the fact that defence exports in 1988 represented over 60 per cent of military communications and electronics output. Several further points are worth mentioning. France's dependency ratio at 8.5 per cent, is after Denmark's ratio, the lowest of all the nations listed. This, of course, is symptomatic of the overall defence–industrial strategy of the French in securing as high a level of self-sufficiency as possible. Britain, by comparison, has three times the dependency ratio of the French, reflecting the UK's more open trading model; note, in this respect, that its imports were more than the combined total of France and former West Germany. Finally, the case of Norway stands out for mention. Only recently easing its strict restrictions on defence exports,[27] Norway has, at 14.2 per cent, the highest defence export to total communications and electronics exports of all the nations shown. The push in this area is possibly a reaction to the export successes of its near neighbours: Sweden, in the defence–electronics area, and Finland, in civil electronics.[28] Yet import-substitution must by necessity always precede export promotion, and Norway's defence-development path provides no exception. Its import dependence of around 109 per cent of domestic output illustrates this point, deriving from the country's licensed production of defence

Table 4.9: West Europe: Trading Performance of the Communications and Military Electronics Industries (1988)

Country	Defence exports ($M)	Civil & Defence exports ($M)	Defence Exp to Total elec. exports (%)	Defence Exports as % of Def. Prodn (%)	Defence imports ($M)	Civil & Defence imports ($M)	Defence Imp to Total Elec. imports (%)	Defence Imp as % of Def prodn. (%)	Balance of Trade ($M)
FRG	867	25,560	3.4	35.4	505	25,231	2.0	20.6	362
France	765	11,701	6.5	12.1	539	17,293	3.1	8.5	226
UK	1393	17,896	7.8	32.3	1186	23,657	5.0	27.5	207
Denmark	163	1,535	10.6	63.2	97	2,169	4.5	3.8	66
Belgium	77	3,550	2.2	33.0	62	4,459	1.4	26.6	15
Italy	333	7,178	4.6	16.9	338	12,976	2.6	17.2	(5)
Ireland	14	4,471	.3	18.9	21	2,661	.8	28.4	(7)
Norway	108	761	14.2	68.4	172	1,959	8.8	108.9	(64)
Netherlands	159	8,000	2.0	26.9	268	10,873	2.5	45.4	(109)
Spain	30	1,579	1.9	8.0	160	6,437	2.5	43.0	(130)

Source: *Yearbook of World Electronics Data 1990 – West Europe*, Elsevier Science Publishing Co. (1989), pp. 16–18.

electronic equipment from fellow NATO countries, especially Britain and the US.[29]

Cultivating Defence–Industrial Capability

There are two aspects to defence–industrial capability. Firstly, there is the capacity to produce. Although this is an obvious requirement, distinctions can be made regarding the degree of difficulty involved in the manufacturing process. Most developing defence nations are able at an early stage to produce small arms and ammunition. The engineering processes are fairly basic, and civil engineers and equipment can easily be transferred to this work. Graduating to artillery pieces and tanks is more difficult. Given time, however, and the host country's willingness to finance the transfer of technology from the advanced supplier countries, there is no reason why a local production base cannot be constructed. Licensed production programmes provide the developmental vehicle for this intermediate phase of defence–industrial evolution to occur. It provides the norm in the Third World countries, with India license-producing Soviet T-72 tanks, and Egypt and Saudi Arabia license-producing American M1-A1 Abrams tanks. Aircraft production is also possible, but much of this takes place through the medium of CKD equipment. A country acquiring this 'productive' capacity may later become involved in manufacturing certain of the components and sub-assemblies, though much of this will be basic activity, and will not include the airframe proper nor the engines, avionics and weapons systems. Thus caution needs to be exercised when discussing arms production capacity. Those Euro NATO States, such as Greece, Turkey and the Benelux countries, involved in cooperative production of the US F-16 fighter gained some related manufacturing expertise but certainly not consumate skills and capacity to indigenously produce a modern fighter aircraft. Thus productionisation does not equate to indigenisation; and for the latter to emerge, high levels of defence R&D are necessary.

Military R&D expenditure is the second aspect of developing defence–industrial capability. This is the difficult stage. The ability to move on from static copying of extant military equipment and weapons systems to the development of new and improved versions of the technology. When this occurs, productive and design dependencies are overcome, and a nation becomes self-sufficient in defence–industrial endeavour. The opportunity costs of achieving self-sufficiency are enormous, and particularly in the R&D area. Currently, the lack of a common or coordinated European research programme compared to the

US' ability to pursue a coherent defence–industrial policy, compounds a situation where NATO Europe is able to afford collectively only one-third the military R&D of the US.[30] Significantly, C^3I functions absorb some \$20.5 bn of the US defence budget; that is, a fifth of US defence investment.[31] The impact of NATO's defence effort is certainly lessened by the degree of national duplication that exists. This problem is particularly pronounced in Europe where it has been estimated that the unit costs of European weapons systems are elevated by about 12 per cent through research and development duplication.[32] Britain and France are the high spenders on defence R&D in Europe, with Germany taking third place. Table 4.10 provides the data on the broad areas of R&D expenditure, by European country, for 1985. In relation to Europe's major defence–industrial nations, total defence R&D spending amounted to over £5000 m; around 26 per cent of European Government R&D spending. Britain accounted for almost 46 per cent of total government defence R&D spending in Europe compared to 13 per cent for former West Germany. If France's share of about 36 per cent of defence R&D is taken into account the big three European NATO nations' dominance becomes evident, representing over 95 per cent of European Government R&D expenditure on defence.

Developing military R&D within the European context is regarded as a priority by NATO observers, generally, and European defence institutions, in particular. Cooperation and harmonisation of initiatives is viewed as the key to the success of policies in this area. For Europe to increase its self-sufficiency, and to cooperate with the US on leading-edge weapons development, then two objectives should become paramount:

- the need to reduce duplication in defence R&D effort, so as to maximise the benefits from a given level of expenditure; and,
- the promotion of 'dual use' R&D programmes through European Cooperative programmes, so providing direct advantages to civil technological development with, at the same time, potential strategic benefits to the defence–industrial base.

The problem with NATO, as currently constituted, is that irrespective of recent cooperative policies such as CAPS, procurement remains very much a national prerogative. The Europeans rightly recognise this as a problem, and, from an R&D perspective, have introduced through the IEPG a programme to raise Euro cooperative defence R&D effort. In June 1989, the European Cooperative Long Term Initiative for Defence (EUCLID) was introduced, with funding aimed at around \$135 m for 1990. Its target R&D areas cover: radar technology; micro electronics; composite materials; avionics; and optronics. As it stands, EUCLID

Table 4.10: Government R&D Expenditure in European Countries, 1985 (£m)

	FRG	France	Italy	Holland	Belgium	UK	Other	Total	EC
Exploration, exploitation of the Earth	118	86	27	6	9	82	7	334	5
Infrastructure, general planning of land use	107	182	24	43	9	55	9	429	2
Control of environmental pollution	175	28	22	28	8	52	6	319	18
Protection, improvement of human health	169	232	99	22	26	167	16	731	14
Production, distribution and rational utilisation of energy	703	458	425	41	27	206	19	1879	188
Agricultural production and technology	110	207	82	42	23	213	54	731	9
Industrial production and technology	787	710	446	94	39	308	76	2460	90
Social structures and relationships	128	150	23	34	18	55	19	427	2
Exploration, exploitation of space	217	330	153	23	23	84	9	840	3
Research financed from 'GUF' (a)	1749	697	469	421	127	670	108	4240	–
Non-oriented research	634	842	163	90	40	299	50	2117	5
Other civil research	5	97	13	39	23	12	1	190	–
Defence	664	1829	215	28	1	2379	3	5118	–
Total	5564	5847	2163	911	373	4582	377	19816	337

(a) General University Funds

Source: *The Times* newspaper (November 26. 1987).

possesses no central authority to allocate funds according to NATO priorities and is thus a diluted form of what most Euro-defence observers see as the primary goal, a common European defence research body. EUCLID is, however, a step in the right direction. In structure, it appears to mirror the civil R&D programmes sponsored by the EEC. The EEC collectively spends about 50 bn European Currency Units (ECU) annually on public and private civil R&D, but only about 10 per cent of this total is devoted to collaborative projects under the auspices of bodies such as the EEC, the European Space Agency, EUREKA (European Research Coordinating Agency), and the *Centre Europeen pour las Researche Nucleaire.*[33] Notwithstanding the low funding of such European cooperative projects, several have nevertheless been successful. The European Space Agency, for instance, with a modest budget of 1.2 bn ECUs per year has captured around 50 per cent of the Western market for commerical satellite launchers. Other EEC civil R&D efforts, operating under the 'Framework Programme' include: the European Strategic Programme for Research in Information Technology (ESPRIT); Basic Research in Industrial Technologies for Europe (BRITE); Research in Advanced Communications-Technology in Europe (RACE); and EUREKA. All these programmes are over-subscribed. They require matching funds from participating nations in the projects entered into, save for EUREKA where each nation devotes an amount deemed appropriate. In an attempt to reduce Europe's dependence on the US and Japan for its supply of microelectronic components, EUREKA has introduced the ambitious Joint European Sub-micron Silicon Initiative (JESSI). The goal of this $4 bn, eight year project is to increase Europe's indigenous development and production capability in this strategically important area, providing valuable civil–military industrial spin-offs.

These civil-oriented EC research programmes may provide the model for ameliorating the European defence research effort. To date, the nearest Europe has come to common research has been the IEPG's Cooperative Technology Projects (CTP) programme, begun during the early 1980s. However, there is no centralised funding for the CTPs, so clearly funds for them will have to be sourced from national defence budgets, taking Europe backwards towards competition rather than forwards to cooperation. EUCLID represents an improvement in this arrangement, even though initial funding for the effort is meagre. EUCLID appears to be adopting an organisational structure closely resembling the commercially-biased EUREKA programme, whose *modus operandi* is specifically geared towards developing saleable products. Francois Heisbourg, by contrast, has long advocated[34] that the IEPG should promote defence research collaboration along the lines of

EEC programmes, such as ESPRIT, where emphasis is far more on cooperation. Moreover, there is need for a distinct focus and strategic direction to be given to the EUCLID programme, rather than leaving it to the *ad hoc* selection of projects based solely on commercial grounds.

During the 1980s, pressure was on Europe to raise R&D funding to close the defence technology gap with the US. Increased Euro R&D spending could be beneficial in several ways. It might reduce US resentment over what is seen as the unfair military burden it shoulders within NATO *viz à viz* its European NATO Allies. Secondly, it could assist in reducing the trading imbalance in military goods between the US and Europe, still heavily in the former country's favour. Finally, raised levels of research funding adds to the technological level of Europe's defence–industrial effort.

The evidence on comparative military R&D spending by major NATO States at the start of the 1990s is that the increase in the Alliance's second and third tier States R&D budgets is outstripping that of the US. Table 4.11 lists the data in this respect. Looking beyond the Euro–US comparison, if these R&D growth figures for one year develop into a

Table 4.11: Percentage Changes in Military R&D Budgets by NATO's 1st, 2nd and 3rd Tier States

Country	Year	Denomination	Amount	% change from previous year
USA[a]	1991	$ billion	38.0	+3.2
UK[b]	1989–90	£ million	2 538	+10.8
FRG[c]	1990	DM million	3 123	+9.8
France[d]	1990	FF billion	16.001	+14.0
Italy[e]	1990	LIT billion	150.0	+13.3
Japan[f]	1990	Y billion	103.2	+12.1

[a] Budget authority for fiscal year 1991; see *Navy International*, June 1990, p. 200.
[b] *Statement on the Defence Estimates*, vol. 2, *Defence Statistics* (HMSO: London, Apr. 1990), p. 18.
[c] *Deutscher Bundestag*, 11. Wahlperiode, Drucksache 11/7373, 12 June 1990, p. 31.
[d] *Europäische Wehrkunde*, no. 4, Apr. 1990, p. 227.
[e] *Jane's Defence Weekly*, 22 Apr. 1989, p. 680 (planned spending as of early 1989).
[f] Defense Agency 1989, *Outline of Japan's Defense Budget Fiscal Year 1990*.
Source: Abstracted from Table 3.5, p. 11, *West European Arms Protection* SIPRI Research Report (October 1990).

trend, then real declines in NATO procurement expenditure will be moving in the opposite direction to the defence R&D spend. SIPRI describes this development as a 'double-track' strategy, in which serious negotiations are being undertaken in conventional arms reduction at the same time as ever more sophisticated weapons technology is being developed unabated.[35] The streamlined nature of NATO's Armed Forces which this process connotes fits comfortably into the changed strategic and defence–industrial environment of the 1990s. For Europe, this new defence environment will also be conducive for partial emulation of Japan's approach to defence technology development where high-tech 'dual-use' industries have been encouraged to grow, providing the necessary technological foundations, infrastructure, and cross-over for parallel defence–industrial advancement.

Conclusion

NATO's second tier nations, i.e. France, Britain and Germany, have been shown to be Europe's premier defence-industrialising nations. They have the region's biggest defence budgets, Armed Forces, and defence contractors. More importantly, these countries also lead Europe in terms of their dual-use aerospace, communications and electronics output. The growth and development characteristics of these strategic industries have been recognised by the smaller defence developing nations, which have been attempting to employ tham as technology drivers in the advancement of their civil sectors.

It is clear that policies aimed at increasing R&D as well as its non-duplication will raise the salience of European specialisation in these high tech areas. Significantly, early indications appear to suggest that overall reductions in defence outlays are being correlated to rising R&D expenditures. In the 1990s, R&D almost by definition relates to sophisticated aerospace, telecommunications and electronics applications. The implication therefore has to be that the increasing focus of defence R&D towards dual-use products and activities is already taking place.

5 EUROPEAN DEFENCE–INDUSTRIAL STRUCTURE

Introduction

Controlling rather than overtly encouraging, European governments have had little influence in shaping the emerging macro defence–industrial structure. Instead, corporate pressures have provided the impulse. The search has been for bigness. This goal being pursued through acquisition, merger, technical relationships, and, indirectly, collaborative programmes. But what are the reasons lying behind this rash of consolidation moves? Are they desirable in the economic sense? Do the arguments concerning synergy and military-to-civil spin-offs stand-up to empirical investigation? Is the restructuring of Europe's defence–industrial base likely to lead to a "hollow triangle" effect, whereby middle-ranking defence contractors are squeezed out of the market? Is there a role for Europe's defence developing nations in the increasingly sophisticated scale conscious European defence market?

These are the questions this chapter attempts to address. Underpinning most if not all the discussion is the conflict of forces between competition and scale. To assist in an appreciation of the finer points of this trade-off, a theoretical overview of the economic tenets of smallness vs bigness opens the chapter. It soon becomes clear, however, that the real world represents an amalgam of both theoretical models: competition at the sub-contractor level through institutionally imposed market pressures and, scale, achieved through market forces at the prime contractor level. Strategic considerations make it unlikely that defence activity can be left totally to the vagaries of the market place. Profit ensures survival, but without it private organisations will choose to diversify or exit from the market. Governments will continue to have an important micro role in influencing these choices through such mediums as the profit-formula, R&D sponsorship, and collaborative programmes. Just as likely, though, in light of future dramatic shortfalls in demand for Europe's defence industry in the 1990s, will be the raised profile of supra-national bodies orchestrating the rationalisation, coordination and integration of defence development and procurement through cooperative frameworks.

Primary Issues

The mature armaments producers believe that a major justification for international industrial collaboration in an era of declining defence budgets and heightened competition is that it manages through rationalisation to preserve viable local defence–industrial capacity. For the DDI nations, by contrast, the objective has been more to trigger and then nurture defence–industrial activity. International industrial cooperation is a dynamic process, stimulating the restructuring of national and, increasingly, transnational defence-industry. And even though the consequences of this restructuring process have not been given a high profile in the US–Euro/Intra-Euro defence collaboration debate, it is, nevertheless, a policy-issue of some importance, being a crucial determining factor in the cost-price relationship of final output.

Conflicting Conceptual Approaches

Economic theory suggests that a competitive philosophy provides a preferable form of market structure compared with the opposite extreme of monopoly. In explanation, economists emphasise the differing market pressures bearing upon the cost structure and price. In the case of monopoly, where the demand faced is inelastic (few, if any substitute goods), the profit-maximising monopolist is aware that price increases raise profitability, even though excess capacity may occur as a result. This cannot happen in a liberated market scenario where there are: lots of firms competing; comprehensive information flows on prices and product-attributes; and freedom of entry and exit into the market as dictated by cost-price-profit signals. If these conditions operate, economic theory postulates that the demand faced by firms will be elastic (an abundance of substitute goods) so that through competitive pressures, costs and prices are forced to some minimum point. When this is reached, the market stabilises. If, in particular markets, the goods produced are reasonably similar, then the ability of a firm to increase profits can only come from reducing costs through process innovations, because the alternative of price increases leads to reduced demand, sales, and thus profits. If prices cannot be lowered because costs are too high, then the market solution is for the firm to voluntarily (or ultimately, involuntarily) exit from production. The pristine quality of this competitive theoretical model is that, for those firms sufficiently efficient to compete and remain in the market:

(i) prices charged are the lowest possible (maximising the benefit to the consumer);

(ii) costs are at a minimum (maximising the welfare of society); while,

(iii) firms still earn the highest, "normal", profit possible (satisfying the goal of profit maximisation).

Reality: the Pre-eminence of Scale

If this conceptual framework is related to contemporary reality, it becomes clear that the competitive philosophy is far removed from reality. Especially since the Second World War, the market trend has been in the direction of industrial 'bigness'. In the defence area, this concentration achieved by a combination of organic growth, mergers and acquisition, was initially promoted through institutional mechanisms. With the onset of international industrial collaboration, pressures to increase market share, capacity, and thus growth, have meant that much of the structural change has been market-driven. The rationale behind industrial concentration has been based on the by now familiar motivations of, firstly, economies of scale through lengthening of production runs, and, secondly, cost-savings deriving from non-duplication of R&D. The search for bigness, organically, by merger and takeover, and also through industrial collaboration, relates to the monopoly model. The issue at stake is, which of the economic models of contestable markets or monopoly is more efficient in reducing costs, and thus, potentially prices. In defence production, as in civil manufacturing, it is reasonable to expect an inverse relationship between local production of military equipment and costs and prices. Collaborative experience suggests, however, that the extent of this trade-off is tempered. History reveals a pragmatic benefit of collaboration in that it possesses the politically attractive attribute of conserving large slices of national defence capacity; and although this is at the cost of not maximising efficiency through international specialisation, the widely accepted evidence (see Chapter Seven) is that cost savings do exist if the yardstick of comparison is national production. This despite the fact that separate

Table 5.1: Choices of Weapons Procurement, for Selected European Countries, 1985–89 (%)

Country	Domestic	Co-development	Co-production	Imports
France	80	15	–	5
UK	75	15	–	10
FRG	45	25	20	10

Source: Moravcsik, A., 'The European Armaments Industry at the Crossroads', *Survival*, IISS, Vol. XXXII, No. 1 (Jan/Feb 1990), p. 66.

national production facilities in each of the participating countries in cooperative ventures is normal practice. This occurred in the multi-national Tornado project, and is planned to happen in the Efa programme. These are essentially co-development projects. Only Germany of the 'big three' European States involves itself to any extent in co-production. Table 5.1 above shows the data on the nature of arms procurement sourcing by the major European nations. Germany has more keenly embraced collaboration than either of the other two countries, and political considerations more than anything else are what have led to this situation. France and Britain continue to maintain 90–95 per cent of 'productive' capacity and between 75–80 per cent of military equipment continues to be indigenously developed.

The primary collaborative impulse for the major European arms producing nations would thus appear to emphasise non-duplication of R&D rather than seeking to exploit economies of scale. Clearly, there are reductions in cost through lengthened production runs serving an expanded captive market, but these tend to be eaten up through duplicated assembly lines. By contrast, the US does enjoy economies of scale in production, though bearing the full cost of R&D expenditure. For the US arms producers, therefore, high demand is essential. In comparison with European scales of production, the US does in fact enjoy a much bigger internal market. Thus, for combat aircraft, the UK, France and Germany produce around 175–400 each, while the US produces 4–6 times as many; for battle tanks, the output range is from 700 to 3,600 for the European countries, with the US from 10–12 times as many; for frigates/destroyers the variation for the largest three countries is from 2–25, though mostly at the lower end of this bracket, while for the US it is typically 2–4 times greater.[1] These scale advantages confer favourable cost differentials on the US of between 20–50 per cent when compared with European production.[2]

Eschewing the benefits of buying off-the-shelf from the US, the European countries have sought to effect cost savings instead by entering into intra-European collaboration. France's Rafale aircraft is a striking exception, however. It is currently a single-country venture, with naval and airforce requirements running just short of 600 planes. This makes its unit cost slightly over $50 million compared to $32 million for the McDonnell Douglas F/A 18, the closest comparable aircraft to the Rafale.[3] With 4–5,000 aircraft outside of Europe and the US falling due for replacement at the beginning of the 21st century, Dassault, the company in charge of the Rafale project, is projecting demand at around the 1200 mark. Depending on your viewpoint, Dassault's strategy is either commercially courageous or financially suicidal, given the: depressed state of world arms sales; the competition of the international market; the emergence of third world producers; and the increasing emphasis given to modernising aircraft.

Taking into account the substantial cost advantages the US enjoys in defence production, it is hard to understand why the American Administration is supportive of US–European collaboration efforts. Yet even big companies can operate inefficiently, and the US defence industry is not immune to the ill-effects of a declining defence market. For the past five consecutive years the real value (1988 constant prices) of the US defence budget culminating in FY89 has declined.[4] Compounding the problem is the fact that between 1983 and 1986, American defence exports to Europe fell from $9.8 billion to $4.5 billion.[5] This has recently prompted expressions of concern, such as contained in Section 821 of the 1989 Defence Authorisation Act, in which . . . 'a series of studies over a 10 year period showed a steady, unchecked erosion of the defense–industrial base of the United States', and Thomas A. Callaghan's observation that . . . 'During the past five years, weapons have been produced at just 50 per cent of efficient production capacity',[6] . . . predicting that . . . 'one-third of the American defense industry will not see it through to the 21st century'.[7] Evidence to this effect is already emerging: US defence contractors such as Hughes, Northrop, Lockheed, General Dynamics, Litton Industries, TRW, and others, have announced substantial lay-offs since the beginning of the 1990s . . . 'to be in a competitive position when future cuts start coming'.[8] The US defence industry's slackening pace, with reduced monies available for new products and technologies, has led to European teaming arrangements becoming more competitive and therefore more attractive, thus precipitating movement towards trans-Atlantic collaboration.

The apparent appeal of international industrial cooperation to the US defence industry is mirrored by internal reforms providing possible portents for increased American industrial concentration. In 1984, Congress revised the nation's anti-trust legislation, making it easier for competing companies to engage in joint research. It is estimated that 125 such cooperative ventures now exist in the US.[9] The mood is such that bills are currently in Congress seeking similar Anti-trust protection for joint *manufacturing* ventures. Agglomeration, however, is already occurring. The acquisition by General Motors Corporation of Hughes aircraft and Chrysler Corporation's purchase of Gulf Stream Aerospace are evidence of this.[10]

Similar developments are taking place in the US defence sector. Here, consolidation and rationalisation is presaged by the recent surge in US–Euro industrial collaboration. Numerous major international co-operative programmes now exist. For instance, Lockheed has recently signed a long-term MoU with the French state-owned aerospace group, Aerospatiale, to explore wide-ranging cooperative opportunities.[11] Westinghouse Electric has signed a similar agreement with MEL, since January 1991 part of the UK Thorn-EMI group, encompassing electronic warfare and military radio equipment; the two will combine research, development, production and marketing in these areas.[12] AT&T, the huge US telecommunications company is reported to be having talks with the UK's MoD about joint R&D in a number of high technology defence projects.[13] Consolidation has occurred through the number two UK electronics company, Plessy, recently acquiring Sippican, which specialises in anti-submarine warfare,[14] and Lucas industries taking over Zeta laboratories, an advanced US electronics company.[15] These collaborative agreements indicate a trend, but overall their significance in the US is small compared to corporate relationships in Europe. Figure 5.1 contrasts US–Euro collaborative arrangements.

The Trend Towards Euro Defence–Industrial Concentration

The US corporate sector's push for industrial concentration and rationalisation lags similar developments in Europe. Market concentration in Europe is endemic across all sectors of Europe's defence industrial base, affecting weapons systems output for all three of the Armed Services as well as logistical equipment, such as trucks, naval dockyards, and land-based military platforms. Although France, Germany, Italy and the UK each continue to produce MBTs, the pressure will be on in the medium term for rationalisation through collaboration,[16] if not by market contraction.

100

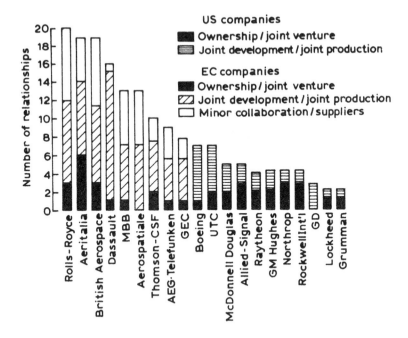

Figure 5.1: Comparison of US–Euro Aerospace/Defence Company Relationships

Source: Roos, J. G., 'Lots of Talk, Little Action in US; Europe Forging New Order', *AFJI* (December 1989), p. 48.

Characterising the concentrated structure of European defence production is the aerospace sector. Daimler–Benz dominates German aerospace production; Aerospatiale and Dassault dominate the French; while in Britain, B.Ae. and Rolls Royce are the major players, with Westland and Shorts being specialist manufacturers. B.Ae., is one of only a few European defence undertaking in this field to approach the size of the American companies. B.Ae. is big, but its growth did not come organically. Rather, it derived from a long period of acquisition. Figure 5.2 below illustrates the lineage of B.Ae.

B.Ae. stands at the pinnacle of a triangular structure representing the UK's aerospace industry. It manufactures airframes and integrates the various components, including the essential engines, avionics and related electronics systems into the aircraft. This equipment is supplied from upstream defence contractors; their numbers increasing the less sophisticated the items to be produced. Figure 5.3 shows the pyramidal

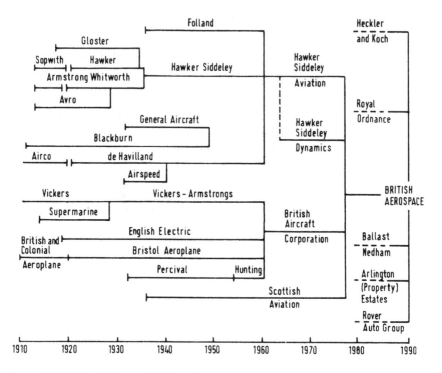

Figure 5.2: B.Ae.'s Inorganic Growth

Source: Adapted from *Sector Review – Aerospace*, West Midlands Enterprise Board (February 1989), p. 4.

structure of the UK aerospace industry. Although there is only one major airframe producer in the country, there are 288 equipment suppliers, and a myriad of smaller subcontracting enterprises.

The process of concentration has not been isolated to the aerospace sector, but has been a characteristic of industrial restructuring affecting most sectors of military, and, indeed, civil production. Note, for example, the European truck industry: in 1950 there were 55 commercial vehicle manufacturers in Western Europe; by 1988, this was down to 11.[17] In the UK there is now only one publically quoted independent truck producer, ERF (Holdings) Plc.[18]

In Europe, the push towards industrial concentration has been driven by: the '1992' phenomenon; the unrelenting search for scale; the need to secure the affordability of high cost, advanced R&D programmes; and the search for overseas sales. The pace of restructuring has been

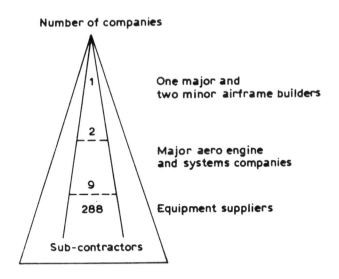

Number of companies

One major and
two minor airframe builders

Major aero engine
and systems companies

Equipment suppliers

Sub-contractors

Figure 5.3: Structure of the UK Aerospace Industry

Source: *Aerospace* (April 1988), p. 12.

frenetic. This may be examined by reference to particular defence-related sectors.

Electronics

GEC and Siemens' combined assault on Plessey represents one of the more glamourous examples in this context. There are others, and not least GEC's capture of parts of the troubled UK company, Ferranti. Here, after Ferranti International was allegedly defrauded of £215 million, GEC reinforced its domination of what hitherto had been a dispersed UK electronics sector by purchasing the former company's core radar and electro-optics operations. France has merged much of its defence-electronics activity into Thomson–CSF, which, in turn, has for some time been on the verge of consumating a merger with Aerospatiale. Moreover, the move from solely intra-national mergers and acquisitions to transnational European collaboration has quickened. Plessey now owns 49 per cent of Italy's Electronica.[19] The joint venture between Britain's GEC and the French electrical group, CGE, boasts Europe's second biggest electrical and power engineering company. Also, Thomson–

CSF's ambitions of becoming Europe's leading defence electronics company were strengthened following its purchased control of the Dutch Philips Group's defence interests: an approximately 80 per cent stake in the Dutch defence company, Hollandse Signaalapparaten, and a 40 per cent stake in the defence side of Philips' French affiliate, TRT.[20] Philips' Swedish defence off-shoot was picked-up by Bofors.[21] Semicon-ductor production, already identified as one of Europe's weakest areas of electronics activity, has undergone a radical shakeout, mainly through the creation of the SGS–Thomson–Inmos group, a company bringing together assets in Italy, France and the US; but there is a belief that further restructuring may be advantageous between Philips, Siemans and the SGS activities.[22] This adjustment to European scales of activity is also taking place in smaller, but no less significant ways, through greater transnational procurement of electronic, optical and other sub-systems. For instance, Vickers' Challenger II tank will have a French sight; the first time such equipment has not been supplied by local sources.[23] International procurement of defence equipment is also an increasing feature of the European aerospace sector.

Aerospace

In this context, B.Ae. recently agreed, for the first time, to use a French guidance system for an air-to-air weapon, and GEC–Marconi made a parallel agreement in the same sector with Thomson–CSF's rival, Electronique Serge Dassault.[24] B.Ae.'s decision was possibly associated with its abortive attempt to merge its missile division with that of Thomson–CSF, which was to be called Eurodynamics. The Franco–Belgium link-up between Thomson–Brandt Armaments and Forger de Zeebrugge to develop and service air-to-ground rockets provides yet another example of Pan European defence cooperation. Moreover, Matra, the French missile manufacturing concern, has also indicated that in its search to reinforce its market position in France, Europe and the US, it is willing to develop cooperative links with the three European groups; that is, GEC/Marconi (UK); Wallenberg/Ericsson, Saab and ASEA (Sweden); and Daimler–Benz (Ger), which own 10 per cent of Matra's capital[25] 'Cross-participation' is what is being planned, with Matra's Space-Defence Division being spun-off as an affiliate organisation in which 20 per cent stakes go to GEC, Wallenberg and Daimler–Benz, while Matra takes 20 per cent holdings in GEC Marconi and Deutsche Aerospace.[26]

The Chairman of Daimler–Benz argued in 1988 that corporate links through a network of cross-shareholdings is the way forward for improving cooperation between European defence and aerospace companies. There may be related significance, therefore, in the fact that the British government raised the ceiling in 1989 on foreign shareholdings in B.Ae. and Rolls Royce from 15 to 29.5 per cent.[27] Finally, of course, there is the merger between two of Germany's biggest defence contracting companies, Daimler–Benz and MBB. In September 1989, the West German Economics Minister, Mr H. Haussmann, casting aside the objections of the Federal Cartel Office, approved the merger in which Daimler absorbed the State-controlled aerospace company, MBB, along with its loss-making civilian aircraft programme. The merged company is now Germany's biggest aerospace company, absorbing about one-third of Germany's defence spending, and one of the biggest in Europe. The firm now accounts for all German military aircraft production, as Daimler had already garnered Dornier GmbH some years previously, putting it in control of two other big military contractors, the AEG electronics group and the MTU Motoren-und-Turbinen Union GmbH engine producer. However, one of the conditions which the German Government imposed on Daimler for the merger to go through was that it sell MBB's 12.5 per cent shareholding in Krauss Maffei AG (the manufacturer of Leopard tanks) and the naval warfare, torpedo, and drone technology divisions of AEG and MBB.

Aerospace and Associated Technology: Synergy and Spin-Offs

In a bid to exploit the synergies from joint engineering and aerospace production, vehicle and defence conglomerates are blossoming. Apart from the archetype models in Sweden and Italy, Saab–Scania and Fiat, respectively, there is now the German conglomerate of Daimler–Benz–Mercedes–MBB, and also the B.Ae.–Rover Group. The motivation for creating such military–civil aerospace and engineering conglomerates stems from the uncertain nature of military markets. Although MBB and B.Ae. military aircraft production activities have been successful, and civil programmes have suffered losses, the following factors: defence expenditure cuts; reductions in government sponsored military R&D; greater market competitiveness; and contracting overseas sales, have led to precautionary strategies of diversification.

Improvements in efficiency through engineering cross-fertilisation will not emerge automatically, but such opportunities do exist, especially through the interchange and application of technical, managerial, production and marketing expertise between the aerospace and vehicle sectors of activity. Economies can be exploited between, for instance, B.Ae. and Rover's heavy R&D bias in advanced high technologies at the

105

product-end and also through complementarities in robotics and com-
puterised manufacturing systems at the process level.

The problem, however, is that there is little in the way of hard evidence
to suggest that the significance of military–civil technology spillovers is
anything like that commonly supposed. Several points need to be raised
in this respect. Firstly, many of the arguments in favour of spin-offs
compensating for the 'crowding out' of civil resources by military R&D
have been based on anecdote rather than scientific study. The infamous
'teflon pan' is a prime example in this respect. Rather than being a spin-
off from a high tech space programme, which is the widespread
perception encouraged by commercial advertising, its origins are more
humble. The teflon pan was granted a patent in Germany in 1938 when
butter, for frying, became scarce. The advertising slogan at that time
was "frying without butter", though this was changed in the post-war
years when butter supply returned to normal levels to "make it a space
pan".[28]

A second point which needs emphasising is the difficulty surrounding
the methodology of spill-overs. The innovational nexus between military
and civil application is complex. The technologies transferable are often
not defence-specific, but generic to both the military and civil domain. In
the defence sector, generic or 'dual-use' technologies will clearly not
feature prominently as end-products. Weapons systems have limited use
in the civil sector. However, at the materials, sub-systems and
components level, dual-use technologies do have a significant military to
civil spin-off potential. This issue has already been addressed in the
previous chapter. It should be noted, however, that although the civil
sector may appear to be in a position to exploit some of the underlying
processes and sub-systems developed within, say, the Star Wars Defence
Initiative, the sophisticated military demands in product design and
manufacture may lead to them being cost ineffective in a civil commercial
environment. This signifies the basic difference between the military and
the commercial context: while there is limited sensitivity to cost in the
former, it is of vital concern in the latter. Sectorally, aerospace and
electronics, the two fields where much of the spin-offs are held to occur,
have defence R&D profiles that support this thesis. The key issue here is
that government defence funds have helped to stimulate the aerospace
and electronic industries' technological growth by acting as a 'creative
first user' of their products. Thus, not only were efforts to improve
quality and reliability subsidized by the defence authorities but high risk
innovations were purchased before they became commercially market-
able. There are few systems that have been originally designed for the
military that have later found civilian application. Navigational radar

provides a notable exception, but substantial and costly redesign was required to make it appropriate for the less refined needs of the civil market. Generally, however, defence R&D has not led directly to technology adoption by the civil sector. For example, although the military, dominated R&D spending on semi-conductors during the early decades of their development, the consensus view is that few of the patents registered in the West, that did result from military R&D, found commercial application. This judgement is supported by research at Germany's Karlsruhe Systems Technology and Innovation Institute, which found that civil application from several thousand government-financed projects, including military R&D, was close to nil. This finding led the research director, Professor Krupp, to conclude that 'Assumptions about a massive transfer of technology to areas such as . . . micro-electronics and computer hard- and soft-ware have been found greatly exaggerated.'[29]

However, albeit that few spin-offs derive directly from military research, the defence sector's 'indirect' sponsorship may be profoundly important. The fact is that many new dual-use technologies developed by the civil sector have been heavily subsidized by the military through substantial early purchases. Interestingly, this was the case in the discovery of the transistor at the US' Bell Laboratories. The transistor was developed by Bell in 1947 for civil application, but the US military requiring smaller, quicker and less power-consuming electrical components, soon became the largest purchaser of transistor devices. This approach is clearly the appropriate strategy NATO defence industries need to adopt for the future: civil activities supporting (and being sponsored by) the defence sector. In other words, civil-to-military spin-off rather than the reverse.

A third issue of military to civil spin-offs relates to the measurement problem. Specifically, is it possible for the output of defence R&D effort to be accurately quantified? Unpredictabilities, uncertainties and time delays all combine to obfuscate the ability to identify the diffusion process of particular defence R&D inputs to civil applications. The fact is that the fruits of R&D are often not reflected through major innovations, but rather via incremental problem-solving and learning effects carried over on numerous research projects, including those deemed 'unsuccessful'.

The generalised view that military R&D possesses a simple and convenient conduit to civil application is now being widely recognised as false. The Maddock Report,[30] examining the civil exploitation of defence electronics technology, represented the first serious UK study to expose the deficiencies of the military–civil R&D link. This was followed in 1989 by another official report which found that in 1986–87 less than 20 per cent of governmental defence R&D was aimed at technologies which have potential for application in both defence and civil sectors.[31] One result of the greater institutional awareness surrounding the problems of effecting spin-off has been the British government's attempts to encourage innovational flows from the demand-side. The primary vehicle for this has been the Defence Technology Enterprise (DTE) initiative. The DTEs are funded by private capital, but are uniquely allowed access to government research bodies. The purpose of the DTEs is to tap the research establishments' R&D, modifying it to meet the needs of civil companies subscribing to the DTE's associate membership scheme.

From the aforesaid the scope for spin-offs from defence to civil companies in the aerospace and engineering conglomerates appears to be limited. Indeed, only isolated evidence concerning corporate efforts to induce innovational flows and synergy between the military and civil domain can be found. For instance, Saab–Scania has been investigating the 'transfer-use' of composite materials already employed in aircraft for possible use in cars. Composite materials are strong but lightweight, so enhancing fuel consumption. Emmission controls and other devices are also expected to affect volume car manufacture after incorporation into the premier range of motor cars. Perhaps the most important breakthrough, though, has been Saab's innovative 'direct ignition system', having no cables or distributors, and according to Saab, tripling the life of a spark plug.[32]

Besides potential military spin-offs to civil automotive production, there are possible opportunities to be gained from widening international engineering linkages. B.Ae., for instance, has acquired the capacity not only to produce motor cars, but importantly to access an established engineering relationship between Rover and the big and successful Japanese concern, Honda. Honda's links with Rover and, indeed, B.Ae. can be expected to increase. Japan makes no secret of its ambitions to develop a military and civil aerospace sector. Several of the country's leading consumer electronics firms are already involved in the development of systems for the hybrid FSX – F-16 US–Japanese sophisticated fighter aircraft. However, the political friction generated from this controversial collaboration may lead Japan to look to Europe for future cooperative partners in the development of its aerospace activities.

A link between Germany's Daimler–Benz and Japan's Mitsubishi Group (of 160 engineering companies)[33] may be a forerunner of this transcontinental European–Oriental collaboration. After the German company's cooperative agreement with the US firm, United Technologies (the holding company of Pratt & Whitney), to seek joint venture projects on commercial jet engines, and its agreement to merge helicopter development and production with Aerospatiale of France, forming the world's second biggest helicopter manufacturer after Sikorsky of America, Daimler–Benz has been exploring the possibilities with Mitsubishi of cooperation in aerospace and electronics programmes. Although these two huge business groups have tried to cooperate before, in the abortive coproduction of commercial vehicles in Spain in 1988, the aerospace field could provide more fertile ground to cultivate German–Japanese collaborative endeavour. Mitsubishi's already heavy participation in the FSX – F-16 project, and the Japanese Government's belief that aerospace will be the technological sector propelling Japan's economy towards the 21st century provides the incentive from the Japanese side. An equally important benefit from Japanese–German cooperation is that it would assist the Japanese in getting behind Europe's Common External Tariff, so as to enjoy post-1992 competitive benefits. While for Daimler–Benz there is: the added stimulus for diversification into the civil aerospace market; the controversial possibilities of increased military technology-sharing in aerospace if Japan continues to expand defence production as it has done during the late 1980s; and economies in the wider engineering arena.

Changing Market Structures

The major implication from the convulsive corporate acquisition and merger activities in Europe's defence industry is that middle-level military contractors are being squeezed out of the market, leaving a small number of powerful primary defence contractors rooted on to a competitive structure of defence subcontractors. Intended or otherwise, this has been the result of EC and IEPG competition policies.

To 'compete and cooperate' effectively with the US defence industries, Europe has been obliged to build-up and develop its defence manufacturing entities. The manner in which this has evolved in the run-up to '1992' is for primary defence contractors to merge their businesses, such that the synergies derived make for a more efficient joint undertaking. But although 'bigness' is being achieved at the primary contractor level, competition remains at the subcontracting level. This is because there tends to be numerous producers operating in the less technologically demanding component-supplier branches. As with individual primary contractors, such as B.Ae. in the UK aerospace industry, the European defence industry is progressively becoming characterised by a 'pyramid' industrial structure. This competition and concentration (created through merger and collaboration) approach stems from the IEPG's policy thrust of the Vredeling report. Subsequently at its Luxembourg meeting in the late 1980s, 'Ministers affirmed that border-crossing competition and comprehensive cooperation in research and technology are essential for the creation of a European armaments market.'[34] From the competition perspective, cross-border business in both procurement and maintenance contracts will be encouraged. This is to be done through: standardising across Europe, IEPG procurement requirements and procedural processes; the establishment of 'focal points' so that companies can register as potential suppliers to the wider market; international compatibility of 'tender and contract placement' requirements and conditions; and the distribution to IEPG member countries of bulletins of bidding opportunities together with lists of potential supplying companies from a centralised and permanent IEPG secretariat.

Note also that collaboration has been emphasised in relation to defence R&D. An initiative has begun through a French chaired IEPG Panel, directed towards developing a European Technology Programme. Here, the aim is to create a framework for pre-competitive military research based on a common defence research fund. Rather than relying on the *ad hoc* Cooperative Technology Projects, it was felt that a more coordinated and structured approach would be less duplicative and more efficient. The nature of this defence research organisation would be similar to the US Defence Advanced Research Projects Agency (DARPA).

This model, based on a step-by-step gradual approach to securing the benefits of both 'bigness' (through concentration and collaboration) at the primary contractor level, and 'smallness' (through competition) at the subcontractor level, appears as a relevant and pragmatic solution to the theoretical trade-off described at the beginning of this chapter. Indeed, the model could even be refined further by advocating competing industrial consortia (as the IEPG does in its *Towards a Stronger Europe* report) either at the primary contractor level for, say, the Efa project as a whole, and/or for the electronics and avionics sub-systems which go into the aircraft. Supply of the less sophisticated components and sub-assemblies could be decided on the basis of cross-border competitive pricing.[35] Although the approach has much to commend it, its deficiencies need to be recognised. The problems essentially fall under two rubrics. The first is at the micro level, dealing with the efficiency-pressures defence contractors now have to operate under, while the second relates to the difficulties faced by the policy-makers at the macro level in incorporating the DDI nations equitably into Europe's evolving defence–industrial pillar.

110

Micro-Management Anomalies

Problems with Bigness

The search for efficient scales of production has already led big defence contractors like B.Ae. and Thomson–CSF to consider merging their separate missile making activities. Other defence contractors have entered into similar arrangements, with the trend very clearly towards perhaps only three or four principal producers of defence equipment in Europe. It has been the corporate sector that has driven the restructuring taking place. The paradox associated with this degree of consolidation is that although some scale economies may be enjoyed through rationalisation of production and, particularly, the non-duplication of R&D, the question is, whether, as James Heitz Jackson puts it, . . . 'the creation of essentially anti-competitive behemoths will support initiative or drive the defence industry into a technological backwater.'[36] Commenting on how progressive industrial consolidation and cooperation may impact upon the vitality of technological development, the writer continues by making the following perceptive point:

> 'Far from answering the prayers of the Vredeling report on preserving the technology base and encouraging a broad-band technological strategy, predatory monoliths can lack focus and complacently fail to stimulate research in key areas.
>
> 'Perhaps in the future it is to the Japanese, and second and third tier producers, that Europe and the United States will have to turn for competitive prices and technically leading subsystems and components. The traditional contractors may become integration specialists, relying on international sources for their "nuts and bolts". This has already occurred with semiconductors.'[37]

Interestingly, B.Ae. and GEC have already signalled their intentions to specialise in the systems integration field through their joint bid to become the consortium to supply and fit the complex electronic systems for Westland's EH101 Merlin helicopter, but failing to win what would have been the UK's first prime contractorship award, GEC subsequently announced the reorganisation of its Naval activities so that increased specialisation in systems integration will stand it in a better position to compete for future contracts.

Another flaw in the European defence industry's push towards industrial concentration is the problem associated with earning a reasonable return on investment. With the downturn taking place on the demand side during the 1990s, the corporate and institutional pressures working against profitability are likely to get worse, thereby reducing still further innovational flair in defence activities. This is a real concern on both sides of the Atlantic.

Problems with Competitive Markets

Europe's defence industry in the latter half of the 1980s has begun to emphasise competition in its procurement practices. Britain has led the way in this approach, spurred on by MoD fears that defence contractors were prone to 'gold-plating'. Concern over gross overcharging on government contracts led in the 1970s and, increasingly, in the 1980s, to an aggressive regime of measures designed to monitor, control and stem cost excesses in the manufacture of defence equipment. Economy, efficiency and effectiveness became the bywords of the MoD's Procurement Executive (PE), especially after the arrival of Sir Peter Levene as the Branch's Head in 1985. On taking office he announced potential savings in defence procurement of up to 10 per cent by a greater commitment to increased competition. Much of this heightened competitiveness occurring at the component-end of the market as numerous contractors were obliged to enter into competitive tendering for contracts. It was also planned to raise the primary contractor and systems supplier end by opening up the national market to international competition. At a meeting of the Committee of Public Accounts in November 1988 Sir Peter justified his initial assertion of an average 10 per cent saving by reference to a MoD study of 17 major programmes let in the previous two-year period. The original estimated value of these projects was £2.5 billion, with real savings achieved in practice amounting to £400 million. Some of the savings were as low as 6 per cent, while others were as high as 70 per cent on particular programmes. But if the 10 per cent average saving is a reasonable benchmark then over £800 million is currently being saved on Britain's defence procurement budget through greater efficiency.

In achieving this level of saving the government's policy approach has been to introduce privatisation and 'contracting out' in selected parts and activities of the UK defence industry. There has also been emphasis on competitive 'fixed price' contracts, which accounted in 1988–89 for around 50 per cent of all MoD contracts compared to below 40 per cent in the mid-1980s. Official encouragement of competitive sub-contracting now occurs. Thus, even where a prime contractor of a major defence contract possesses the capability to produce given components, it is now MoD policy that the prime contractor invites bids so as to ensure, through competition, that prices are at their lowest level. Moreover, the quickening pace of transnational mergers and acquisitions has spurred bi-lateral and multi-lateral reciprocal purchasing initiatives. Increased competition of this nature has already begun. At the bi-lateral level, the 1987 reciprocal purchasing agreement between Britain and France, was established to foster cross-channel defence contracting through the free circulation of bulletins advertising defence contracting opportunities. British and French companies tendering in each other's home markets have been assured equal consideration for production contracts valued in the range £1–50 million, and development work between £1–10 million. Since the Gleneagles IEPG meeting in early 1990, this approach, emphasising the 'transparency' of national procurement practices and requirements, has been widened to incorporate cross-border competition with all IEPG countries.

The raised level of competition, which these measures have cultivated has a downside, however. Mr Peter Sachs, Director of the UK Electronics and Business Equipment Association (EEA) whose 200 members account for combined sales of £5 billion in the defence field, has identified several practical difficulties from the push for greater competi-tiveness which are not obvious from the economist's competitive markets model. He argues that the PE's competitive bidding policy has reached such extremes that for many companies 'bidding costs are equal to any profit they may make.'[38] This stems from the fact that several rounds of bids may be required by PE, continually paring contractors' costs to the bone. An inherent problem in this process is that defence electronics firms may fail to maximise profits when compared to civil work. In the short run, then, shareholders will become unhappy as the growth in profits falls. The directors in turn feel threatened, and not solely from the short-run contraction in profitability but from the erosion of long-run corporate viability caused by the lack of investment funding. Of course, these deficiencies are mitigated to some extent if an electronics firm's ratio of military to civil work is small. However, in certain cases, defence contractors are so big, specialised and leading-edge, that no competition exists. Thus, on the supply-side, in a number of important areas, e.g. tank production, only one firm (e.g. Vickers) can be contracted to produce; often, because of the contract size, it will account for a substantial portion of that contract. In such instances, non-price competition occurs. Prime and overhead costs have to be evaluated and agreed by accountancy and technical costs experts at PE, and, in addition, a profit element has to be institutionally agreed. The 'Profit Formula', which, according to the 1990 Statement on the Defence Estimates, accounted for 47 per cent of all the contracts placed by the MoD, has been the mechanism for calculating this. The technicalities of the formula are involved, but stripped to the barest essentials, profit has been based on the average, civil industry can earn during a specified time period. Historically, the results of such government interference have, according to Professor Gavin Kennedy, led to the predictable negative economic consequence that Britain's high technology industries have had to operate with rates of return that might be suitable for fast moving consumer goods, mature industries of declining relevance to Britain's future, and to the average performance of British firms, which by most standards performed worse than their competitors abroad.[39]

The UK's MoD policy of allowing foreign incursions into the ownership of Britain's defence–industrial complex has also been criticised on the grounds that R&D and technical work done in the UK will be diluted, perhaps reducing manufacturing, and even exports from this country. Hence, if transnational consolidation continues, there are anxieties similar to those expressed previously that the UK (as, indeed, Europe's) defence industrial base will lose its middle rank companies, being left with a few 'first rank' ones, and 'third rank' niche manufacture specialists and subcontractors.[40]

Similar reservations concerning the encouragement of competitive defence countracting procedures have been voiced in the US. American defence industrialists have directed criticism at fixed price development contracts for high risk programmes; increased second-sourcing of production, often for the sake of competition and not economically justified; separate development and production competitions; competitive teaming; and excessive regulations, audits, and inspections.[41] The last of these was evaluated in 1987 by Georgetown University's Center for Strategic and International Affairs, noting that: defence procurement regulations ran to more than 30,000 pages, were issued by 70 different offices; with nearly 25,000 DoD auditors and inspectors monitoring the acquisition process, such that to comply with the regulations adds an estimated 20–30 per cent to the cost of acquisition programmes.[42]

These US procurement regulations have grown during the 1980s to counter contractor opportunities of 'gold-plating' and to increase efficiency. However, the opposite effect is being realised, in that the maze of regulations and excessive micro-management has led to increased risk and reduced profits. In a recent US study by Vollmer,[43] a list of the major financial risks and burdens imposed by government involvement in the market included the following items:

– The percentage of bid, proposal and independent R&D expenditures which US industry can now recoup from the government has dropped from its 1985 level of 90 per cent to 70 per cent. Remarkably, the

Vollmer analysis suggests that the US defence industry is now spending as much money on bid and proposal as on 'independent' R&D;
- Shifts away from 'cost-plus' to 'firm fixed price' contracts increase corporate risk when break-even points are often decades distant;
- Cost-sharing rules have changed, such that the defence industry is now responsible for 20 per cent of pre-full scale development expenses, and 50 per cent of special tooling and test equipment;
- Progress payment (to ease the financial burden of long development times) rates have fallen from 90 per cent in 1985 to 75 per cent at the beginning of the 1990s.
- Finally, the requirement to second-source has been criticised for its negative influence on investment. Government second-sourcing, by infringing on what defence contractors see as their proprietory rights, has created a corporate strategy whereby contractors wait for second-source opportunities to avoid the high initial development costs of new equipment.

Taken together, these considerations have acted to depress the US defence sector's profitability. A recent study,[44] entitled: *The Impact on Defense Industrial Capability of Changes in Procurement and Tax Policy, 1984–87*, with nine defence contractors collectively accounting for 25 per cent of DoD's prime contract awards, concluded that, had the acquisition policy changes introduced by the US Government been in place at the beginning of each programme, 'there would have been no financial reason to bid the programs'. Discussing the basis for this finding, an article in the *Armed Forces Journal International* developed the point further by stating: . . .

'All but two of the programs would have lost money, and the firms' after-tax profits would have been reduced by an average of 23%. Moreover, cash flows to industry from the programs would have decreased an average of 27%, and the additional financing needed by the nine companies would have exceeded $8.5 billion – equivalent to 50% of their total 1985 equity' . . . moreover . . . 'Defense industry profits, contrary to some perceptions, have been low in recent years. As a percentage of sales, for example, the after-tax profit rate for the aerospace segment of the defense industry was 4.1% in 1984, 3.7% in 1985, 2.8% in 1986 (artificially low due to write-offs prior to a new tax law) and 3.8% in 1987, according to the Aerospace Industries Association. The 1986 and 1987 figures were far below the average for all US manufacturing industries in those years, which were 3.7% and 4.9%, respectively.[45]

Two issues arise from this discussion of micro-management anomalies. Firstly, that while initial consolidation, rationalisation and international collaboration accommodate the requirement for economies of scale, there may be costs involved. It is obvious that the bigger a firm's market share, then the lower the level of competition. This is a cost directly affecting choice. But beyond this, the debate suggests that as firms grow, corporate dynamism and technological innovation retards. The theoretical models have little to say on this additional cost, and no evidence, either way, is offered here, but it is an area for future research.

The second issue is entwined with the first. The European defence market's inexorable movement towards monopoly does not, in a sense, inhibit the consumer because only govenments do the purchasing, and it funds its choice. The ability of the monopoly, either nationally or through Pan-European and NATO-wide collaboration, to maximise profits is impinged, however. National and supra-national monitoring, control and regulation may act against corporate interests. Conceptually, a benefit of monopoly is that sufficiently high levels of profit are earned to fund R&D expenditure. The debate has highlighted the fact that the institutionalised push for more and more efficiency in defence manufacture harbours the danger that profits will be squeezed to the point where it becomes uneconomic for industry to remain in production. Here, low profits act as the market signal for firms to exit the market. Combined, of course, with the declining trend in defence budgets, a growing number of defence businesses are considering this option. All these developments have not gone unnoticed in the financial markets but at the broader international level, it is ominous to note that while US defence industry shares have performed badly since 1985,[46] the performance of Japanese defence contractor equity has been strong.[47]

Weaving DDI Nations into the Collaborative Framework

In appraising progress towards an integrated European, indeed NATO-wide, defence–industrial base the role of the developing military–industrial States needs to be considered. The metaphor of twin defence–industrial pillars supporting a bridge of transatlantic military trade was surely not a concept based solely around Europe's 'big three' representing the eastern Pillar, but rather on a composite of all Europe's defence industries and markets. Here lies one of the formidable challenges in achieving progress in international industrial collaboration.

Defining DDI Nations

Although Mr Vredeling's IEPG report discussed the DDI nations, no attempt was made to name particular NATO States. The British Government in its 1990 Statement on the Defence Estimates does name names in the DDI category, including Greece, Portugal and Turkey. But no methodology has been introduced to justify this categorisation, save for descriptive interpretations, such as that contained in the IEPG document . . .

'While the [DDI] nations spend a relatively high percentage of their GDPs on defence, these GDPs are lower than average for Europe and, since their national economic capabilities are limited, they cannot invest heavily in defence industries. Typically, their defence industries are relatively new, have a limited but increasing technological capability, have very limited experience and only a few products which are known in other nations. In consequence, their markets, with the exception of a few items, are mostly restricted to their own nations, their production quantities are low and their unit costs high. Since production output is low and their technological base limited, it is only possible to maintain a limited programme of research and development despite the existence of a great number of excellent and experienced scientists most of whom have trained or worked in foreign R&D establishments.'[48]

This description is appropriate to the defence–industrial circumstances of Greece, Portugal and Turkey. Their inclusion into the DDI category is reinforced by reference to Table 4.3, Chapter Four. Here data were given for the NATO nations, listed according to tiers of defence expenditure. The fifth and lowest tier includes Belgium, Denmark, Luxembourg, Norway, Greece, Portugal and Turkey, with the latter three also having the lowest per capita incomes in NATO. Although unsatisfactory in a number of ways, GDP per person is the World Bank's official indicator of underdevelopment. Thus, according to this criterion, and the other indicators in Table 4.3, the three Southern European NATO countries can rightly be described as DDI nations.

This categorisation is further supported in respect to what the IEPG describes as 'limited . . . technological capacity'. Table 5.2 provides the evidence here. The data relate to what is termed the Potential Defence Capacity (PDC). This is a proxy indicator, given that precise defence manufacturing data are unavailable, for gauging an economy's capability for arms production. The technique was first introduced by Professor

Kennedy during the early 1970s.[49] His definition includes in its scope the following industries: iron and steel; non-ferrous metals; metal products; nonelectrical machinery; electrical machinery; transport equipment, including repair and also motor vehicles. These strategic or PDC industries are essential for arms production, and if compared to total manufacturing capacity then a sense can be gained regarding the viability of defence industrialisation in particular economies. The higher the PDC ratio, the greater the weapons production capability.

Kennedy employed the PDC technique to assess the potential for defence industrialisation in the Third World context. Caution must be exercised in interpretating the results of the PDC analysis for NATO nations, however. Thus, from Table 5.2 even though between 1976 and 1986 particular countries' PDC ratios may be declining such as in France, Italy and Spain, this does not mean their ability to produce weapons is being weakened. It is more a reflection of deindustrialisation in the traditional sectors not yet being compensated by the growth in electronics and other high technology industries. Equally, although Luxembourg, a fifth tier military industrial power, has an exceptionally high PDC ratio for 1986, at 64.6 per cent, investigation of the data reveals that there is a low value of output in all strategic industries save for iron and steel, which clearly has a distorting influence on the size of the PDC. The analysis, however, confirms the notion that Greece (PDC of 19.8 per cent), Portugal (21.5 per cent) and Turkey (28.4 per cent) possess limited technological capacity. For policy-making purposes it is important to be definitive regarding the nature of developing defence industrial nations, because the Netherlands, which is a small and in a relative sense, seemingly poorly endowed defence nation across the spectrum of strategic industries, has a lower PDC ratio than Turkey. The Netherlands, however, would be an unlikely beneficiary of a Vredeling report recommendation that the IEPG recognise the plight of the DDI nations by providing interproject compensation in support of their defence industrialisation drive.[50]

Impact of Arms Collaboration on DDI Nations

For the DDI countries the goal is to lay a foundation for defence industrialisation, initially to compensate, if not economise, on the high costs of procuring foreign military equipment. At a later stage there may also be the possibility of earning foreign exchange through exports. Studies of Third World development refer to this cycle as import substitution leading to export promotion. The initial import substitution phase conventionally moving from off-the-shelf purchases to licensed production (primarily assembly prior to local manufacture of components and sub-assemblies), and finally to indigenous production.[51] There is no reason to believe that the sequence for acquiring defence manufacturing expertise will be any different for Europe's DDI countries. Licensing arrangements for the F-16 fighter encompassed several of the fifth tier countries and also, interestingly, the Netherlands in the third tier.

The participation of DDI nations in collaborative procurement, whether by comprehensive project involvement or via licensing, enables not only access to modern engineering and electronics technology, but also to markets. Through collaboration with the big NATO defence–industrial States, the DDI countries, particularly Greece and Turkey, have benefitted from co-production programmes. The road to defence–industrial competence can, however, be long and arduous. Professor Taylor argues that European licensed production of US equipment leads to dependence on the US because proprietory knowledge regarding leading-edge technology is not released, thus making indigenous design and development that much harder to achieve.[52]

Technology-sharing in collaborative weapons programmes depends on the comparative industrial size and technological sophistication of the countries and companies involved. M. de Donnea, the Belgian Minister of Defence, has argued that the only easy collaboration is between industries of comparable technological levels and production capacity. Assymmetrical capacity and capability may lead to a perception on the part of the bigger nation that there will be an automatic transfer of free technology to the smaller less advanced industry, thus stifling arms cooperation between advanced defence–industrial nations and the DDIs.[53] A further obstacle constraining the smaller military–industrial nations from enjoying the full benefits of collaboration arises from the work-sharing arrangements. For example, at the production stage, the big military nations, based on the *juste retour* principle of relating the level of production input on the size of output take-up, will attract more 'credits', thereby standing a greater chance of winning the development contracts for the major project technologies. The limitations imposed on the smaller nations are even greater because of the paucity of funds available for sponsoring high cost weapons design and development. In support of this point, de Donnea notes that the typical arrangement adopted for international arms collaboration is for the participating nations to equally share expenses during pre-feasibility and feasibility stages on the assumption that technology developed will be shared and exploited equally. Compounding the situation for the DDI States is that their immature DIBs hinder them in exploiting any technology gained.[54]

Discussion of the weaknesses of collaboration in relation to small

Table 5.2: PDC Analysis of NATO States, 1976 Against 1986, Based on Gross Output

Countries		371 (Iron & Steel)		372 (non-ferrous metals)		ISIC 381 (Metal products)		382 (non-elect machinery)		383 (electrical machinery)		384 (Transport Equipment)		Total Manufacturing		PDC Ratio (%)	
Year		1976	1986	1976	1986	1976	1986	1976	1986	1976	1986	1976	1986	1976	1986	1976	1986
1st Tier																	
US		58.9	56.9	30.3	39.6	69.4	124	111	218	77.7	199	263	549.6	1188	2245	51.4	52.9
(Japan)		12.7	14.5	3.8	4.0	7.8	14.3	12.8	28.9	14.4	37.6	32.7	680	147.9	253.6	56.9	66.0
2nd Tier																	
France		73.0	129	24.2	56.8	40.2	89.0	113	287	70.0	181	133	312.1	1119	2799	40.5	37.7
FRG		66.7	59.0	15.8	26.1	42.8	90.7	94.1	179	79.1	157	92.0	205.0	797.2	1416	49.0	50.6
UK		6.5	9.4	2.8	4.6	6.8	11.8	10.7	24.3	7.6	20.0	19.2	41.0	112.2	236.1	47.8	47.1
3rd Tier																	
Italy		10.3	31.3	1.3	8.0	5.2	16.8	8.6	29.5	7.5	27.0	11.0	34.4	107.0	406.5	41.0	36.2

4th Tier															
Spain 63.0	99.2	1.5	46.8	29.4	75.2	11.1	76.6	19.9	79.2	68.3	292.3	444.0	1652	46.6	40.5
Canada 4.6	10.0	3.4	7.7	7.2	13.8	5.1	14.2	6.2	12.6	35.6	110.1	114.5	288.3	54.2	58.4
Netherlands 12.6	11.8 →	→	→	9.3	13.0	9.5	14.6	13.1	20.7	12.8	19.6	189.7	311.4	30.2	25.6
5th Tier															
Belgium 37.8	55.8	10.9	22.5	208.2 →	→	→	317 →	→	→	654.2 →	1031.3	39.3	38.3		
Greece 19.2	60.5	13.3	50.3	16.8	80.3	7.2	20.3	15.0	60.4	26.8	80.0	358.6	1776.0	27.4	19.8
Norway 4.9	8.8	5.9	14.7	5.0	11.6	10.9	40.9	5.1	12.7	29.5	25.7	108.0	253.8	56.8	45.1
Turkey 2.3	157	0.6	36.8	0.9	43	1.4	74.6	1.1	7.65	2.3	162	30.4	1695.0	27.9	28.4
Denmark 1.4	2.9	0.8	1.4	5.5	19.6	10.4	29.1	4.9	14.0	13.7	24.6	103.6	281.3	35.4	32.6
Portugal 6.6	71.3	1.5	16.3	11.4	91.6	5.0	58.0	10.0	122	33.7	219.8	260.4	2691	26.2	21.5
Luxembourg 41.4	71.4	2.2	3.4	1.1	6.5	5.4	9.2	.8	1.7	1.3	1.5	81.9	152.9	63.7	64.6

Source: *Industrial Statistics Yearbook* UN, New York (various years).

Notes: Data in local currencies: US $ bn; Japan, ('000) Y bn; France, Frs bn (1985); UK. £ bn (1985); FRG, Marks bn; Italy. ('000) lire bn (1985); Canada, $ bn (1985), Spain, (10) Pesatas bn (1984); Netherlands, Guilders bn (1984), Belgium, Frs, bn (of value-added) (1985); Greece, Dracmas bn (1983); Norway, Kroner bn; Turkey (10) Lire bn; Denmark, Kroner bn; Portugal, Escudos bn (1985); Luxembourg ('000) Frs bn (1984).

For the Netherlands: ISIC data for industries 371 and 372 are not disaggregated.

For Belgium: ISIC data for industries 381, 382, 383 and 384 are not disaggregated.

defence countries should not ignore two significant points. Firstly, if these States wish to develop defence–industrial platforms as quickly as possible there is in practical terms no alternative but to enter into some form of international cooperative arrangements. Secondly, it should be recognised that both fourth and fifth tier countries have for long been active participants in such programmes, irrespective of the various pitfalls highlighted. Spain participates in over 20 cooperative agreements; Norway contributes to the ASRAAM project; Belgium's defence sector has several cooperative links with other NATO countries; and Greece and Turkey are involved in numerous licensed production projects. None of this hides the real problem, however, which is that as specialisation increases, the big powerful defence conglomerates will increasingly dominate the defence–industrial map of NATO. There is no easy answer to this. Second-source suppliers and competing consortia for some of the intermediate technologies could be suggested as partial solutions, but the high cost and severe practical problems associated with such policies make them infeasible. Thus, even allowing for the IEPG proposal for interproject assistance for the DDI nations, there exists the real possibility that a static international division of labour will evolve whereby DDI nations will predominantly be involved in low skilled and therefore low value-added activities. At the present time, with the DDI countries possessing such small markets for major items of defence equipment, and there being little alternative to the application of *juste retour* allocation, the consequent determination of a proportionately small share of the development and production activity for these States is unavoidable. At the level of the collaborative venture itself, the incorporation of DDI States into the production network implies sacrificing efficiency for equity; a further cost to be included in the premium to be paid for international industrial collaboration endeavour.

Conclusion

This chapter has offered a discussion of the main features associated with Europe's defence–industrial dilemma: the mix between competition and collaboration. Transcontinental economic threats rather than military threats have encouraged the search for scale at the major systems and manufacturing level. Corporate acquisition, however, has not always been prompted on the basis of deepening defence specialisation but often for the purpose of diversification, thus lowering dependency levels on defence activity. Europe's aerospace and automotive conglomerates appear to have been created on this premise. Possibilities for synergies, particularly technological cross-threading of products and processes from the military core to civil subsidiaries seems, with one or two exceptions, to be limited. Nevertheless, the agglomeration of aerospace and probably also land and maritime equipment manufacture seems certain to continue. The trend is likely to include link-ups with companies in North America, as well as those in Japan and Eastern Europe. NATO's DDI nations, Greece, Portugal and Turkey, will be peripheral to this process, continuing to develop their defence–industrial bases through licensing programmes with NATO's first and second tier defence–industrial nations. With the support of such supra-national bodies as the IEPG and possibly EC, assistance may be forthcoming for their endeavours to promote domestic arms production capacity, especially as the DDI States are located in the Mediterranean region, being the southerly starting point of NATO's re-focused strategic concern.

6 US ATTITUDES

Introduction

The US is the world's most powerful military nation. Its defence spending in relation to the European nations is striking. The US government spends more than twice as much on the procurement of major weapons systems ($71.8 bn in 1989) than all the European NATO countries together ($32.4 bn), including France.[1] Defence–industrial comparisons are just as stark. The combined arms sales of the 100 largest West European companies amounted to roughly $66 bn in 1988, which was only slightly more than the combined arms sales of the 10 largest US arms-producing companies.[2]

Such comparisons call into question the reasoning behind US involvement in transatlantic arms cooperation. Can collaboration provide anything more than marginal benefit to the Americans when their scales of production and procurement are so very much greater than those in Europe? This is an important issue, representing the focus of attention for this chapter. US collaborative policy is reviewed, and implicit contradictions in approach are revealed. Although progress is clearly being made towards encouraging transatlantic arms cooperation, especially in the R&D field, there are numerous obstacles including what appear to be conflicting commitments in the US stance. For the Americans, nationalism is still an important influence on defence–industrial sovereignty some 60 years after the Buy American Act was introduced. Transatlantic friction, real and potential, continues to arise over technology-transfer, third country sales and joint R&D funding. These and related topics are all considered in this chapter.

US Collaborative Policy

The NATO position has been one continuously in favour of defence cooperation among member States, but it would be surprising if this were otherwise. After all, the basis of the Alliance is cooperation; it would be illogical if this did not extend backwards into equipment production, development and procurement. However, policies aimed at raising the consensus in economic as well as political and military matters does not mean they necessarily find expression in practice. As Ambassador William H. Taft IV, US Permanent Representative on NATO's North Atlantic Council remarked in early 1990 . . .

'NATO has experimented with a range of mechanisms to promote cooperation . . . [and] . . . these have all been valuable in their way but, in the end, many have fallen short of expectations.'[3]

Often the enthusiasm and rhetoric heralding the drive towards arms collaboration is tempered in practice by political asymmetries. Indeed, it has been this revealed contradiction between NATO consensus and plurality (collaboration and competition) that has led the US to introduce a series of additional measures to stimulate transatlantic arms cooperation. In the early stages, most of these initiatives emerged institutionally through NATO; more recently they have not.

The US' conversion to the philosophy of weapons collaboration occurred during the early to mid-1970s. The Americans' greater predisposition to consider arms cooperation was tied to the emerging NATO policy of Rationalisation, Standardisation and Interoperability (RSI). NATO RSI became part of a policy to combat the estimated 30 to 40 per cent loss of combat effectiveness and the $10–15 billion wasted by NATO each year due to its failure to standardise production.[4] In addition, there were two other pressures adding force to the cooperative logic, especially from the US standpoint. Firstly, NATO–Europe was becoming increasingly strident in its calls for reducing its reliance on 'foreign' arms suppliers, restraining the growth of the European defence industry. Secondly, there were growing anxieties over the build-up and modernisation of WP forces which began in the 1970s and gathered speed over the latter part of the decade. As this build-up was associated with the military and economic benefits ascribed to the Soviet's monopoly of arms production, this influenced the positive light in which armaments standardisation and cooperation was perceived by NATO over the following decade. The eminent US defence observer, A. H. Cordesman provides the flavour of this enormous military build-up:

'During 1978–87, and despite the rise in real defence spending that occurred under the Reagan Administration the Soviet Union produced 3.2 times as many tanks, 8.7 times as many artillery weapons, 4.3 times as many tactical combat aircraft, 2.1 times as many military helicopters,

5.3 times as many surface-to-air missiles, 1.8 times as many submarines, and twice as many attack submarines.'[5]

The extent of Soviet defence production led to over 50 Department of Defence Directives being issued from the mid-1970s for guidance in the implementation of RSI. In the US Defence Appropriation Authorisation Acts of 1975 and 1976 explicit reference was made regarding the need for the Secretary of Defence to both investigate the costs of not standardising NATO equipment and to identify, wherever possible, common research, development and procurement opportunities among NATO Allies. Also, in 1976, President Ford espoused the virtues of a 'Two-Way Street' leading to a US–Euro common market in defence equipment. To secure this goal, the US President recognised that the European nations would need to develop their domestic armaments producing sectors. The US Government was in favour of this. Not only was US support forthcoming when the IEPG was created in 1976, but the US in its policy statements since that time has been consistent in its support of European defence industrialisation. To aid this goal, President Carter in 1977 indicated that his new Administration would work towards increasing the flow of arms trading traffic from the eastern end of the 'Two-Way Street'. This positive US policy response was represented in an RSI Directive prepared by President Carter's Undersecretary of Defence for Research and Engineering, William Perry. The document, entitled *Standardisation and Interoperability of Weapons Systems and Equipment Within NATO* was important in the manner in which it added greater definition and purposefulness in the US' approach to transatlantic arms cooperation.

The Triad of Initiatives

The new policy was to be tripolar in character, often being described as the 'Triad of Initiatives', it covered the following:

(i) General Memoranda of Understanding;
(ii) Dual Production;
(iii) Family of Weapons Concept.

Although the Americans had indicated that the viability of the 'Two-Way Street' depended on the pooling of European resources to compete on an equal footing with US defence firms, this new three-pronged framework was a tacit acknowledgement by Washington of the increased strength of Europe's defence industry. The policy measures were not an act of benevolence from the free world's most powerful defence–industrial nation, rather they were the first grudging steps towards the acceptance that self-sufficiency, whether economic or military, was no longer a rational goal even for the US. The growing European preference for locally developed and produced weapons had stirred US administrators into positive action. This can best be illustrated by citing the comments made to Congress by William Perry, in 1979, when justifying the Triad of Initiatives . . .

'The cooperative programmes which we recommend will produce no net loss of jobs for US industry. But, the key question here is loss with respect to what. If the frame of reference is the 1960s in the midst of the "Buy American" program, then there already has been a loss of jobs – not from our efforts to improve cooperation, but from the isolationist "go-it-alone" approach that is beginning to develop in Europe. If instead, the frame of reference is established by the level of defence activity already underway in Europe, then the programs we recommend will not involve a loss of US jobs.

'Europe is no longer content to proceed with one-sided purchases from the US. They [sic] are proceeding to successfully develop their defence industry. The inherent disadvantages of small size are being overcome by formation of consortium and various multinational corporations. The Europeans will continue this trend towards exclusive dependence on their own defence industry if they are not offered a reasonable opportunity to participate in a competitive program.

'The programs we are pursuing will cause no loss of jobs given these facts of life. At this point, we have but two alternatives. We can participate with our Allies in a broad NATO defence market, expecting our fair share. Or we can go it alone, and our Allies will increasingly do the same. If we go it alone, there will be no benefit to US jobs, and there will be incredible duplication of effort and waste. The net result would be reduced effectiveness of our NATO forces, higher defence costs, or both.'[6]

The three prongs to the Triad were thus introduced with the aim of sharing transatlantic defence resources. The main features of each of these cooperative policies are detailed below:

(i) Memoranda of Understanding (MOUs)
MOUs in reciprocal purchasing are the first leg of the Triad. They represent a mechanism that is claimed to facilitate competition in NATO's defence industry by freeing trade barriers between those

countries in which MOUs apply. MOUs are able to do this through their waiving of 'buy national' and other restrictive provisions inhibiting international trade in defence equipment. These restrictions include tariffs, duties and other protectionist legislation. Furthermore, as the MOUs lie outside the bureaucratic machinery of NATO and the IEPG, they can be negotiated quickly and easily by the participants to the Agreement.

The first MOU to be signed was the UK–US Accord in 1975. The Agreement aimed to secure a balance in defence sales between the two countries as well as . . . 'making the most rational use of industrial, economic, and technological resources so as to achieve maximum military capability at the lowest possible cost and greater standardisation and interoperability of weapon systems.'[7] Since then, there have been numerous other MOUs signed by countries such as Belgium, Denmark, France, Germany, Italy, the Netherlands, Norway, Portugal and Canada. Examples of MOUs in operation with the US include: the Vought Multiple-Launch Rocket System (MLRS), which is an all-weather, rapid-fire, non-nuclear system, arising from a 1979 MOU with the UK, Germany and France; there is also a MOU with Germany and Denmark (though this latter State ceased financial participation in 1985) to develop a Rolling Airframe Missile (RAM), which is a high-firepower, lightweight system designed to engage and defeat anti-ship missiles, now in full scale engineering development; a UK MOU for technical support during the McDonnell Douglas AV-8B development progamme; a MOU with France and Germany for the establishment and operation of a multi-national Aircrew Electronic Warfare Tactics Facility (AEWTF) in Central Europe; and a MOU with Germany, Italy, Spain and the UK in the Modular Stand-Off Weapons (MSOW) programme, incorporating short and long range systems against fixed targets and a short range system against mobile targets. The greatest momentum sustained by the MOUs was at the end of the 1970s and the beginning of the 1980s.

(ii) Dual Production
The main aim of this second leg of the Triad, aside from standardisation, has been to secure the savings of research and development funds that would otherwise have been spent developing similar systems. The US Department of Defence and America's defence contractors have a preference for dual production because it emphasises competitive research and development leading to licensed or co-production. A benefit of this approach is that the proprietory nature of US innovations could be safeguarded. In 1978, the US submitted a list of 17 systems to the IEPG for consideration as dual production projects. After lengthy deliberations,

the European body informed the US authorities that it had unanimous interest in only the STINGER System, though intimating that it might be possible to conclude bi-lateral or multi-lateral agreements for some of the other weapons projects. This seemingly negative response from the Europeans diminished the US' early enthusiasm in this area, tending to confirm suspicions that the IEPG, with French participation, was intended more as an institution for the unreserved promotion of European armaments collaboration rather than as a stepping stone for intensifying transatlantic cooperative effort.

Notwithstanding this initial set back, several coproduction projects have been undertaken. The most notable examples of US licensing include: the multinational General Dynamics F-16 fighter programme; the production of the M-113 personnel carrier involving Italy, the Netherlands and Belgium, and the German-led consortium producing the AIM-9L air-to-air missile. European countries, on the other hand, have initiated joint production schemes with the US, such as: the UK's VSTOL Harrier fighter; Belgium's MAG-5 armoured vehicle machine gun; the French DURANDAL runway-busting bomb; and the Franco–German ROLAND short-range, surface-to-air missile system.

(iii) Family of Weapons Concept (FoW)

This initiative, the final element of the US' Triad policy approach, represents a bold attempt at reducing, through Alliance collaboration, the duplication of development programmes. When the FoW concept was introduced, it was suggested that the $16–17 billion then spent by NATO on R&D would yield results that were complementary rather than duplicative in nature. The new division of labour was planned to save hundreds of millions of dollars eliminating duplication.[8] The methodology through which a 'Family' would be established is based on identifying the aggregate future weapons development plans of NATO countries, and then dividing the development responsibility where a plurality of similar missions cross-match. The intention was that the division of programme responsibility would be between North American and European consortia. There are variations to the approach, but the general theme was that the lead company in any family in the US designates a portion of the development work to counterpart defence industries on the other side of the Atlantic. Corresponding action would occur in relation to that part of the family of weapons that the consortium in Europe is responsible for. In this way, transatlantic teaming would be encouraged, ensuring through the transfer of information, the optimal development of weapons technology at the lowest possible cost.

Early NATO weapons packages were established in the following four

129

areas: anti-ship missiles; air-to-surface missiles; anti-tank guided missiles; and, air-to-air missiles. Examples of these include the British-developed JP-233 airfield attack bomb; the French Atlis II Laser designator (illuminating a target with laser radiation); and the US Copperhead laser-guided artillery shell, intended to be compatible with the 155 mm Howitzers of at least ten NATO States. Perhaps the best known of the 'Family of Weapons' projects is in the air-to-air category. An ambitious programme was begun during the early 1980s, with European partners in the project agreeing to develop the Advanced Short-Range Air-to-Air Missile (ASRAAM) while the US took responsibility for developing the Advanced Medium-Range Air-to-Air Missile (AMRAAM). On the European side, Germany and the UK took lead responsibility with each having 42.5 per cent share of the total cost. The other active partners were Canada and Norway. France and the US are signatories to the ASRAAM Agreement, but are not active participants. The plan was that the US would purchase ASRAAM from the European consortium while the European signatories would procure the AMRAAM from the US.

The 'Family of Weapons' model of allocating the development of weapons packages among NATO countries is on the face of it a creative step towards securing weapons commonality. The concept has not found easy acceptance, however. There were numerous criticisms. The view was expressed that by eliminating competition the result would be higher than normal costs and second-best results. There was scepticism on the European side that, given the extremely strong US R&D base, American defence interests would be loathe to forego investment in European-designated areas of responsibility. The US, for its part, was concerned about the lowered threshold of failure with the major portion of the development work taking place at a single industrial source. There were some US policy-makers, however, who believed that this third leg of the Triad would not serve to restrain innovatory progress. In fact, they took the opposite view: that by spreading available funds across the spectrum of weapons development, there would be greater resources available to devote to additional projects. An approach that one US author metaphorically described as . . . the Alliance slicing the cake rather than collaborating to bake it together.[9]

Increasing the Cooperative Momentum

Senator S. Nunn has established a reputation for being an ardent supporter of NATO arms collaboration. He was the sponsor of an important piece of legislation, paving the way for the entry of the Triad initiatives. The Senator won official US acknowledgement that NATO arms cooperation was a primary objective. This was expressed in Section 803 of the Culver–Nunn Amendment to the Department of Defence Appropriation Authorisation Act of 1976. The Act approved of cooperation in weapons production among NATO States, albeit with the proviso that licensing and dual production arrangements must be properly constructed . . . 'so as to preserve the efficiencies associated with the economies of scale'. The Section stated . . .

'It is the sense of the Congress that progress toward the realisation of the objectives of standardisation and inter-operability would be enhanced by expanded inter-Allied procurement of arms and equipment within the North Atlantic Treaty Organisation. It is further the sense of Congress that expanded inter-Allied procurement would be facilitated by greater reliance on licensing and coproduction agreements among the signatories of the North Atlantic Treaty.'

Furthermore, paragraph (c) of Section 803 made it plain that the US welcomed the progress that was taking place in intra-European collaborative schemes . . .

'It is the sense of the Congress that standardisation of weapons and equipment within the North Atlantic Alliance on the basis of a "Two-Way Street" concept of cooperation in defence procurement between Europe and North America could only work in a realistic sense if the European nations operated on a united and collective basis. Accordingly, the Congress encourages the governments of Europe to accelerate their present efforts to achieve European armaments collaboration among all European members of the Alliance.'

These two Amendments highlighted US authorities' recognition concerning the importance of transatlantic cooperation as a means of countering the reduced scale and increased unit costs of US produced military equipment. Table 6.1 illustrates this trade-off between scale and cost by reference to the US Air Force. The table shows the number of combat aircraft in 1985 was only 57 per cent of what it was in 1970; which was a much greater decline than that experienced by other NATO Air Forces. Moreover, the fall in the numbers of combat aircraft being produced by the US defence industry coincided with rising military expenditure.

Thus the force of collaborative pressures was not solely being felt by the European nations but also by the US defence sector. A major

Table 6.1: Evolution of Total Military Expenditure and the Number of Combat Aircraft, 1970–85

	Number of combat aircraft		Evolution of overall military expenditure	
	1970	1985	1970–82	1982–5
US Air Force	6500	3700	8%	19%
French Armée de l'Air	500	485	40%	0%
Royal Air Force	720	599	28%	7%
Luftwaffe	980	586	29%	3%

Source: Heisbourg, F., 'Public Policy and the Creation of A European Arms Market', (eds) Creasey, P. and May, S., *The European Armaments Market and Procurement Cooperation*, Macmillan (1988), Table 3.1, p. 62.

expression of these pressures is, of course, falling demand, and this came to the fore in the 1980s. The Senate Armed Services Committee reported in May 1987 that:

- During the past five years, weapons have been produced at just 50 per cent of efficient production capacity; and,
- a fourth of the major acquisition programmes during the past five years were manufactured at a rate below the minimum economic rate for those systems.[10]

Thomas Callaghan in a recent report to the US Department of Defence argues along similar lines, stating that . . .

. . . 'declining US foreign military sales credits, greatly reduces the range of foreign sales possibilities for US industry while raising the cost of equipment for DoD. Add to these pressures a spate of increased expenses and risks for US industry in dealings with the DoD, and joint ventures with European Allies are fast becoming the most promising avenue open to domestic defence manufacturers.'[11]

The focus of US cooperation measures introduced during the 1980s was on reducing the high costs of R&D incurred by the US defence establishment. Escalation of R&D costs had been rapid. In relation to combat aircraft, for example, the proportion of R&D on weapons programmes had practically doubled within a quarter of a century, from 15 per cent during the early 1960s to around 30 per cent by the end of the 1980s.[12] Clearly, then, with the burden of R&D becoming difficult to sustain, collaborative R&D programmes made sense. This is especially so, given that the US and, indeed, most other NATO States demand that local production capability is a *sine qua non* of international collaborative ventures. In very few instances has cooperation led to the fullest exploitation of economies of scale. Countries have grouped to collaborate, but maximum economies have generally not derived from the production phase because final assembly has been duplicated among project members. Much of the cost savings have thus been achieved from research, development, design and testing activities.

However, if one country spends substantially more on R&D than any of its potential project partners, then there is little incentive for that country to engage in collaboration. This is the problem facing US defence contractors enjoying heavy R&D support in comparison with their European counterparts. Thomson–CSF, for instance, obtains only 35 per cent of its R&D spending from the French Government, whereas the proportion in the US is often 80 per cent.[13] Even though the differential between US and European R&D is narrowing, the difference in money terms remains significant. Overall, the US spends seven to eight times more on R&D than Europe: in Fiscal Year 1985, US expenditure on military R&D amounted to $27 billion, while all of Western Europe only spent about $4 billion; and more than 80 per cent of this came from two States, Britain and France.[14] Partly as an attempt to ease the R&D burden in relation to its Allies, the US initiated a series of policy measures to encourage US–European R&D and ultimately production endeavour:

(i) Foreign Weapons Evaluation (FWE)
This programme was introduced in 1979, its purpose being to provide funds for testing and evaluation of foreign weapons systems in a bid to avoid the high cost of domestic R&D efforts when US Allies already have systems that meet recognised US requirements. The claimed benefits are several. The US Armed Forces gain by being able to field equipment more quickly and with the possibility of cost savings also. European (and other foreign) defence contractors benefit from extra sales. This, in turn, leads to benefits for the Alliance through cost savings derived from more efficient rates of production, which will be accompanied by the higher degree of equipment standardisation achieved. Up to 1989, the FWE programme cost the US about $2 billion for 29 foreign systems, and about $75 million evaluating all candidate programmes.[15] The following countries, listed in order of contracts received, have been involved in the FWE programme: the UK, France, Germany and Israel. Funding for the programme amounted to $19.8 million in FY 88.

(ii) Cooperative R&D (CR&D)

A further Amendment was introduced by Senator Nunn in 1985 as a partial panacea to the problem of declining scale and rising costs. This Nunn Amendment secured authorisation to provide up to $200 million for NATO weapons research to reduce duplicative development. The authorisation annually 'fenced off' $50 million each for Army, Navy and Air Force R&D projects shared with other NATO Allies.[16]. Congress also authorised $50 million for side-by-side cooperative tests of US–European armaments before the US puts a major new system into production.[17]

(iii) Balanced Technology Initiatives

This measure, established in May 1987, concentrates on advanced conventional force multiplier technologies, such as 'smart' and high-powered micro-wave weapons systems. The US plans to spend $1.5 billion on joint US–European ventures in this field by 1993.

In aggregate, these policies have led to US collaborative commitment being stepped up. In solely the CR&D area, 82 programmes have been certified since 1986, leading to 28 contracts; 8 of these are the subject of signed MOUs, and 11 are close to contract (with a further 21 programmes deleted from participation).[18] Through the Nunn Amendment, and other efforts, the US is spending about 20 times more now on cooperative R&D than it did in 1980.[19]

Transatlantic Cooperation: Some Obstacles

Although the US policy framework for fostering NATO arms collaboration appears impressive, numerous obstacles to effective transatlantic defence cooperation have been identified in the literature. These are described below:

Nationalism

There remain anxieties in almost all NATO States that international arms collaboration denudes their domestic defence–industrial bases of expertise and capacity. This may be in part due to economic and political reasons, but a major cause continues to be the desire to avoid dependency on foreign sources for defence needs. The procurement of equipment through collaboration for even the two main proponents of cooperative programmes, Britain and France, only accounts for around 15 per cent of their respective expenditure on military equipment. Moreover, it is instructive that no other Alliance State has gone as far as the Germans in formalising collaboration as an integral and unqualified part of policy. Germany was the first, and continues to be the only, Alliance country pledging itself (1971–72 Defence White Paper) to always collaborating with NATO partners in the development of new weapons systems. Even so, in particular fields of procurement, Europe does appear much less reticent to cooperate than does the US. While all combat aircraft being produced or developed in Europe, except the French *Mirage* 2000 and *Rafale*, as well as close to 75 per cent of European missiles, are already co-developed or co-produced, the US, since World War I, has imported only two major systems from abroad – the initial order by the Marine Corps for the UK *Harrier* V/STOL fighter, and the US Navy's T-45 Goshawk (B.Ae. Hawk) trainer. An argument put forward by the Americans explaining their reticance to cooperate has regard to not wanting to sacrifice the quality of equipment that cooperation might invite. The fear that we might 'standardise to the point of the lowest common denominator' was expressed by Alexander Haig in testimony before the House Armed Services Committee in 1978.[20]

Protectionism

In essence, this problem is identical to that of nationalism, save that it provides the means through which self-sufficiency in defence production is safeguarded. In several respects, US policy in connection with arms collaboration is enigmatic. While it has been promoting a series of cooperative funding programmes, legislation exists which represents the antithesis of international cooperation. Although the conditions can be waived for MOUs, the 'Buy America' Act of 1933 poses, at the very least, a psychological barrier to US–European trade. With its built-in discrimination in favour of domestically produced defence equipment, it suggests potential problems for European penetration of the American market. The Act enables the Department of Defence to buy American even when the US product costs 50 per cent or, exceptionally, 90 per cent more than the European competitor. In addition to this measure, there is the 'Speciality Metals' rider to the Department of Defence Appropriations Act, introduced in each of the years since Fiscal Year 1973. This bans the import of exotic metals, such as Titanium, which are key elements in defence equipment. Thus, cooperative ventures involving US procurement of foreign components containing speciality metals, again have to rely on the Department of Defence obtaining special waivers for these to be imported from NATO countries. An unsatisfactory state of affairs for prospective partners in a collaboration involving the US because the rider can be reinstated at any time.

Moreover, protectionist sentiments are rising in Congress. In this respect, Thomas Callaghan cites the following points: firstly, since the MOU with the UK was renewed in 1985, no other bilateral General MOU with a NATO ally has been extended. Secondly, legislation has been introduced that would abolish bilateral MOUs in five years. Other legislation would give the Secretary of Commerce the right to appeal to the President to overturn any MOU that affects the competitiveness of the US. Finally, and paradoxically, given that the subject of this section is US Protectionism, is the report that the US Trade Representative was requested to make to the President (and Congress) in the early 1990s concerning the procurement practices of the US' NATO Allies. Quoting Callaghan directly on this point, he states . . .

'Government procurement markets have long been the largest and last frontiers of world trade. They are also the most protected, and the most technologically dynamic. But whereas markets in the United States for communications, aircraft, power plants and electronics are open competitive markets largely in the private sector – these same markets in Europe are cozy national preserves in the public sector. The Congress wants European government procurement markets opened' . . .[21]

Military 'Black Boxes'

The US recalcitrance in sharing 'openly' its technology with European Allies has irritated European governments, and acted to suppress the transatlantic collaboration process. This was well illustrated when the Americans were seeking a share in the EFa venture. US Defence Secretary Weinberger's offer of American cooperation on the fighter aircraft was received with considerable suspicion by NATO Europe when the Defence Secretary emphasised that the Europeans had to appreciate that 'some sensitive technologies can only be shared under unique arrangements while a very few very sensitive technologies may not be eligible for release'.[22] The European authorities found this negotiating posture unacceptable. Reversing a trend of reliance on US science and technology that had been built-up over several decades, it is evident that US technological input into Efa is being minimalised (see Figure 6.1). Missiles remain the exception, with around 50 per cent of the missiles procured by European governments being US designs. Compared to Efa, about 10–30 per cent of the components in the Tornado (depending on the model) are American in origin,

Figure 6.1: Artists impression of the EFA in pale grey air defence camoflage. Grateful thanks to British Aerospace Military Aircraft Division, Warton, UK.

incorporating 146 essential technologies, including the Texas Instruments terrain-following radar and the essential swing-wing box technology from the F-111.[23] Although the US encourages such exports, it remains sensitive about what it perceives as an erosion of the US defence industry's technological advantage. The Europeans, for their part, are anxious to avoid over-dependence on the supply of defence equipment, and the associated restrictions on third-country sales.

Technological Hemorrhaging

The US concern over the loss, through exports, of its defence technological superiority has influenced policy since the Second World War. Limitations on technological transfer were imposed in 1949 through the Export Control Act (ECA), and during the 1950s and 1960s the list of controlled technologies grew. The scope of US military export controls is extensive . . .

'Under US law – specifically, the Mutual Security Act of 1951, the Foreign Assistance Act of 1961 and the Arms Export Control Act of 1976 – all exports of military goods are subject to government supervision and control. US law also distinguishes between two categories of arms transfer: government-to-government transactions administered by the Defense Security Assistance Agency (DSAA) through the Foreign Military Sales (FMS) programme; and "commercial sales" of military goods by private US firms to foreign governments, firms and individuals. FMS sales, which account for approximately 80–90 per cent of US military exports, are entirely controlled by the Federal Government. Commercial sales, which account for the remaining 20–30 per cent, are regulated through the licensing function of the State Department's Office of Munitions Control (OMC).'[24]

At the end of the 1960s, US policy-emphasis temporarily changed. In the 1969 ECA, trade was seen as a means of breaking down the cold-war barrier. But policy soon reverted back to its original restrictive thrust following the far from benign Soviet inspired military events in Africa and Soviet direct military action in Afghanistan.

Ironically, while the 1969 Act emphasised the promotion of trade, it also introduced a list of specified technologies and manufacturing processes, the export of which was to be carefully monitored. This Militarily Critical Technologies List (MCTL) was intended to cover the grey area of 'dual-user' technology escaping the scrutiny of the US Arms

Export Control Act (AECA). The purpose of the MCTL was to restrict the supply of militarily critical technologies reaching WP countries. Since 1949 the US' Allies have been subscribing to a similar set of technology transfer restrictions. The Coordinating Committee for Multilateral Export Controls (CoCOM), as it is called, has grown to include all NATO countries (save Iceland) plus Australia and Japan. In 1973, a revised list of embargoed exports to communist States was drawn up. But enforcement of the CoCOM controls is a contentious business. An example of this was the abrasive Toshiba/Kongsberg affair in 1987, discussed in Chapter Four. The principal problem relates to the vagueness of the 'dual-user' label; that is, the possible use of particular technologies in both civil and military contexts, means that effective control of prohibited technologies to the WP States was very difficult to achieve in practice. Indeed, it is a nettle that still remains to be grasped in regard to Europe's 1992 legislation.

Assuming that the US will require CoCOM to continue to function in some limited form in the future in light of Soviet and East European liberalisation, the EC's position will require clarification. The fact is that CoCOM is not based on any formal treaty. The EC Commission does not have representation in CoCOM, nor does CoCOM possess any legal influence over the EC. Thus, with the easing of trading restrictions between EC States in 1992, the ability of European countries to control the trade of sophisticated military-related technology will be impaired. As it stands, the EC insists that the Community be treated as a single entity from 1992, with US complaints addressed to Brussels. The US, in response, believes that the power of CoCOM will be diluted as a result. Washington fears that sanctions against individuals exporting, primarily US, CoCOM prohibited technologies to former communist regimes will be difficult to apply, for two interconnected reasons: firstly, in the light of German reunification and the absorption of greater Germany into the EEC; and secondly, due to the liberalisation of trade between Eastern and Western Europe.

Aside from the ECA and AECA, the US Department of Defence has additional powers inhibiting technological transfer. In January 1984, Defence Secretary Weinberger signed Directive 2040.2 imposing export restrictions on 'sensitive' technology as well as that which is 'military critical'.[25] Of course, none of these technology control measures are intended for use against fellow NATO countries. However, for the purposes of arms collaboration, it does concern European nations. Historically, Europe has not viewed export constraints on technology transfer with the same degree of seriousness as the Americans. Cooperative arms agreements with US participation would thus take on the risk of US–European friction in the event of equipment sales to States regarded as unacceptable to the US. It is not impossible to consider, for instance, that East–West European trade in defence equipment will develop in the 1990s. The well-worn anecdote regarding the purchase by Britain's tank manufacturer, Vickers, of ball-bearings from an East European country is well-known. But, surprisingly, this is not an isolated phenomenon: between 1982 and 1987 the value of arms sold by NATO countries to the WP was $35 million, while the value of arms bought from the WP by NATO was $165 million.[26]

The US now accepts that its strict technology transfer controls could have acted to inhibit transatlantic arms collaboration. Accordingly, reforms have been instituted to liberalise these controls. In early 1990, the Pentagon relinquished its role in the licensing of US technology for export to what were the WP countries, with the Commerce Department instead taking over the controls. In addition, the US is working within the CoCOM framework to reform export controls on machine tool exports, and truck manufacturing technology destined for the Soviet Union. Small beginnings, but it is a start.

Third-Country Sales

US restrictions on technology transfer not only apply on sales to, and collaboration with, Allied States but extend also to third-country sales. This will play a key part in European nations' considerations to cooperate in arms production with the US, not least because Europe exports around 40 per cent of its defence output compared with 15 per cent for the US.[27] Thus, due to Europe's defence export dependency, third-country sales is not a frictionless issue in US–Euro relations. For example, having already refused Saudi Arabia's bids in the late 1980s to procure American fighter planes, it is unlikely the US would have agreed to the Tornado sale if the Americans had collaborated directly on that aircraft. European sensitivities over US export restrictions did surface in relation to the Efa programme. The aircraft's radar system was the bone-of-contention until the Ferranti system proved successful. Up to that point, Germany preferred a system produced by Hughes of the US, because it could be adapted for use in the Luftwaffe's American-designed F-4 Phantoms. By contrast, the UK preferred the more sophisticated Ferranti system, not least because it would not be based on a US license, potentially meaning export curbs on third-country sales.

Not surprisingly, then, these export restraints have led to hesitancy among European firms to team with their US counterparts because of the uncertainty over whether the Americans would allow the jointly

140

developed defence technologies to be sold on the world market. As with the easing of the CoCOM restrictions, the US is now liberalising its constraints on exports to third countries. In early 1990, the US lifted restrictions on re-exports to most countries on products that contain less than 25 per cent (previously the threshold had been 10 per cent) in value of US-controlled high technology parts and components; it has removed controls altogether on a majority of lower-level technology goods, but this has not stopped the acrimony.[28] Evidence of this is the State Department's initial ban on political and commercial grounds of the $450 mn sale of Britain's B.Ae. 146 aircraft to Iran. The 1991 US veto was activated because the plane contains around 40 per cent American-made components on the US 'sensitive' technology list.

Europeanism: 1992

Traditional European fears over US domination of the transatlantic arms trade are now increasingly being countered by American concern over '1992', and the consolidation of Europeanism which it represents. American defence contractors are worried about being squeezed out of Europe's single market, and several see that the only way of overcoming the SEA is to either establish EC-based subsidiaries or to invest into the EC defence–industrial base to acquire 'insider' status.

American anxieties have come about in response to expressions of 'Europe first' by European statesmen. Note the comments by the Dutch IEPG representative, Mr Ab Sligting, who stated at the end of 1988 . . . 'what we [the Europeans] don't want any longer is to be sub-contractors of the United States . . . what sense is there to spend more money on European defence if the benefits go to American firms?'[29] As has already been quoted in previous chapters, such sentiments were not new. European resentment over American technological superiority and the challenge it poses for the development of Europe's technological base were forcefully expressed by the British Prime Minister, Mr Wilson, as long ago as 1967. He stated . . .

'there is no future for Europe, or for Britain, if we allow American business and American industry so to dominate the strategic growth-industries of our individual countries that they, and not we, are able to determine the pace and direction of Europe's industrial advance, that we are left in industrial terms as the hewers of wood and drawers of water while they, because of the scale of research, development and production which they can deploy, based on the vast size of their single

141

market, come to enjoy a growing monopoly in the production of the technological instruments of industrial advance . . . this is the road not to partnership but to an industrial helotry.'[30]

A major issue raising the hackles of the US authorities is the protectionist nature of the 1992 arrangements. Associated with the Europeans' calls for a 'fair return' from US–European cooperation (as a counter to the 'burden-sharing' criticisms the Americans direct at Europe) was the threat to impose import tariffs on the import of defence materials. This serves, of course, to raise US apprehension over the emergence of a European preference in arms procurement. The threat was delivered by the French Defence Minister, M. Jean Pierre Chevenement, who in 1988, brandishing the same protectionist stick he obliquely accused the US of wielding, alluded to current European Community studies on "the advisability of imposing customs duties on the import of defence materials."[31] Until the end of 1991 the Council of Ministers was prepared to exempt tanks, helicopters, military aircraft, warships, bombs, grenades, torpedoes, mines, and missiles, but the situation is to be reviewed in 1992.[32]

Washington responded to this French-sponsored move to extend the EEC's common external tariff (CET) to cover military as well as civil imports by conveying the warning to the Commission in the Summer of 1988 that 'if enacted it would seriously weaken NATO'. A statement that perhaps lacks weight with the French, though taken seriously by other countries, such as Britain. The Commission's proposal is based on its interpretation of the Treaty of Rome's Articles relating to defence, discussed in Chapter Two. For the past three decades, EC member countries have viewed the legal exemptions for defence as allowing them to freely import military equipment duty-free. The Commission's interpretation is that the Treaty only exempts the defence sector from EC internal regulations, such as those relating to competition policy. Defence, it claims, is not exempted from the CET. While the Commission argues there could be special exemptions, for instance on major defence platforms such as aircraft or tanks, its view is that the community budget is being weakened by the loss of revenue from military import tariffs, potentially ranging from 3.5 to 12 per cent.

The Commission may be attempting to use '1992' as a vehicle for clarifying the ambiguity of its constitutional position, by resolving a number of outstanding legal disputes on the subject. Since the early 1980s around six legal suits brought by the Commission against member States have been stalled over the corect interpretation the Treaty of Rome placed on defence. Complaints against Greece, Spain, Portugal and the

UK have been levied.[33] Not all EC States have attracted the criticism of the Commission in this matter. Germany has not provoked its ire, because it applies a flat 3 per cent import duty on military imports, a portion of which it then pays into the EC budget, while France alone, according to the Commission's officials, has always levied the CET on its military imports.[34]

The Commission's 1985 Action Plan called explicitly for the EC internal market to include defence, but if the same community-wide deregulation, already affecting the civil economy is to be applied to the highly-fragmented European defence industry then the argument is that the defence sector should first be granted the same degree of external protection which the CET already extends to Europe's civil industry. Britain, in particular, is against this proposal, believing that the development of Europe's defence industry would not be assisted by the imposition of customs duties. On this point, Mr. T. Sainsbury, Britain's Junior Defence Procurement Minister, has recently stated . . . "It is the Government's policy to encourage the free flow of defence trade with all friendly countries, and in particular with members of NATO."[35] The CET issue may have subsided from media comment since 1988, but to the consternation of the US authorities the problem has not been resolved. Thus only time will tell whether the Commission's vision that the imposition of the CET on imports of military equipment will facilitate an historic extension of community competence can be reconciled with the US view that it heralds the weakening of NATO.

Reversing Down the Cooperative Channel?

The liberalisation of trading flows as a result of 1992 cannot but affect Europe's defence–industrial activities. The fact that many of the component inputs into military production are of a 'dual-use' nature means it is unavoidable that efficiencies from deregulation will seep into the military–industrial sphere. While the Europeans may welcome this benefit and other associated 1992 spin-offs as a means of strengthening Europe's common defence industry, the Americans remain cautious. They are nervous on two counts: firstly, as has just been observed, there is anxiety over the possibility that the EC will extend the CET to cover military as well as civil imports; and secondly, there is concern over the unregulated flow of US defence technology to States with unpredictable rather than unfriendly relations with the US. The Commission is aware that the defence industry will not be untouched by the '1992' programme and, as a consequence, has established an advisory team to examine its

143

impact on the defence sector. This is unlikely to impress Washington as the US authorities believe that whatever the team advises, it will be difficult, perhaps impossible in practical terms, not to make civil technologies, such as computers, laser equipment, optronics, and nuclear and space technologies imported from third countries, including the US, subject to the general rule. In other words, US technologies defined as 'sensitive' by Washington will leak into countries on the US authorities' proscribed list.

Given these difficulties, both Europe and the US nevertheless concur that cooperative international arms development and production arrangements are essential. Yet recent practice is struggling to reflect this common position. At a time of shrinking defence budgets and declining international arms demand, when collaborative effort ought to be at a premium, the opposite appears to be happening. The beginning of the 1990s has witnessed an unmistakable reversal in the fortunes of armaments collaboration (see also the comments in Chapter Seven). Germany, for instance, has pulled out of the joint-venture to produce the ASRAAM. This leaves Canada, Norway and the UK the remaining participants in a programme financially weakened by the loss of Germany's 42.5 per cent share of the costs. The ASRAAM was intended to be the follow-on for the US-designed Sidewinder missile. Thus, Germany's withdrawal adds strength to the US Senate Appropriation Committee's recent recommendation that the US should cease participation in ASRAAM, and opt instead for a national Sidewinder-plus project. Note also that the Rockwell(US)-led multinational consortium, which was awarded the MSOW development contract in June 1989, suffered the withdrawal shortly afterwards of the UK and the US. Canada and France withdrew earlier. Also, the UK, France and Italy were the first of numerous withdrawals from the NFR-90 project to develop a replacement frigate for the 1990s. The project's eventual abandonment led to the cancellation of the related NATO anti-Air Warfare System (AAWS) for the ship's hull. Further, the UK Government has withdrawn from the Advanced Sea Mine and the 155 mm Autonomous Precision guided Munitions (APGM) Programmes.

This is a disturbing trend, but there is a further development which is calling into question the stamina and, indeed, commitment of specifically the US to transatlantic cooperation. Over recent years the supply of funding to support US–European cooperative programmes has been under attack. In 1989 the US House Appropriations Committee proposed ending funding for the APGM, AAWS, and the UK–US Surface Ship Torpedo Defence System.[36] More profound is the apparent down-grading in the priority given to funding of cooperative R&D. Although these

144

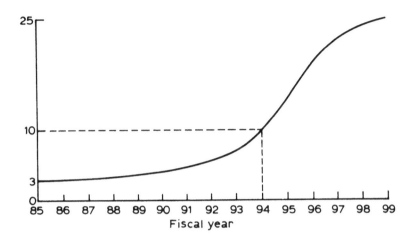

Figure 6.2: US Cooperative Research and Development (per cent of Total
Research, Development, Testing and Evaluation Budget)

Source: *AFJI* (December 1989), p. 52. Original source: DoD FY89 *Annual Report to the
Congress.*

efforts, described earlier in this chapter, appear impressive, the US
Department of Defence currently spends only 3 per cent of the
Pentagon's $37 billion research, development, test and evaluation funds
on cooperative programmes.[37] The Secretary of Defence, F. Carlucci, in
the DoD's FY89 Annual Report, indicated that . . . 'this ratio will rise by
the end of the century to 25 per cent, while in the mid-term these funds
would rise from the present $154 million to $300 million.[38] Thus, by 1994,
as Figure 6.2 shows, 10 per cent of all defence R&D will be on a
collaborative basis.[39] Two cautionary points need to be made, however:

Firstly, the amount of CR&D funding requested by DoD for FY89 was
$201 million, but the actual appropriation was $154 million.[40] This meant
that in real terms, there had been no growth over the previous year's
($150 million) figures, stemming the strong upward funding trend of this
programme during its early life. The trend in CR&D funding is now
actually declining. The US FY90 defence authorisation budget agreed by
Congress approved $126 million in funds for NATO cooperative R&D
programmes, representing a compromise between the $97 million
authorised by the House and the $200 million authorised by the Senate.
Thus, this was the second consecutive year that cooperative funds had

been reduced, but within this, while the FWE programme has obtained a constant $15 million, the NATO comparative test programme had its funds reduced from $43 million in FY88 to about $26 million.[41] This lowered financial contribution is now beginning to affect the goal of 25 per cent of US R&D expenditure being given over to cooperative effort by the year 2000. This goal was retained by Mr Richard Cheney, the successor to Secretary of Defence, Carlucci, but the 22 per cent decline in cooperative R&D funding from $154 to $126 million means US–European programmes now account for only 2–3 per cent of the overall defence R&D effort. Furthermore, items being tested under both schemes fell from 32 in FY89 to 18 in FY90; similarly, 'new starts' fell from 11 to 6.[42] The US sees this fall as being due to more careful screening procedures to ensure that both the FWE and NCT programmes, fund evaluations of Allies' equipment being *seriously considered* by a Service as a procurement option.[43]

The second reservation regarding US CR&D funding has to do with the allocation of the funds. Egypt, Israel, South Korea, Australia and Japan are covered under the Nunn provisions as non-NATO cooperative development nations. However, while in FY88 cooperative projects with these countries were limited to only $15 million of that year's $150 million, for 1989 no limitation on the distribution of funds for CR&D was imposed, suggesting that NATO Europe no longer represents a priority for CR&D funds. Thus, as the US Assistant Under Secretary of Defence for International Development and Production, Mr F. Cevasco, states . . . 'These monies can be divided any way that suits us . . . so we now can focus on programme merit, instead of worrying about geographical distribution.'[44]

In summary, then, armaments cooperation in NATO, which was a vibrant activity during the mid-1980s, has begun to falter at the start of the nineties. As defence budgets contract, this is just the time when the benefits of cooperation are important, and most needed. Ambassador Taft argues that the weakening of transatlantic collaborative effort has been caused more by CR&D monies being used inappropriately by European NATO States than falling defence expenditures *per se*. He makes the pointed criticism that NATO Allies have not . . .

'. . . always used Nunn money for their top priority weapons systems; these they have generally preferred to fund separately without cooperation with others. Nunn money has been more frequently used for programs whose funding would have been uncertain. Where the choice for a service was no program or a Nunn program, the Services chose the latter – despite bureaucratic complexities and extra time involved in an international program. The result has been that Nunn programs have tended to be those projects of lower priority to the different countries. This was not a problem during periods of rising budgets; but as defence budgets have begun to shrink, these Nunn programs have been among the first to be sacrificed to the budget axe.[45]

Although the 1990s provide the conditions for defence collaboration to be the relevant course of action for NATO States, early indications are that US–Euro cooperative programmes do not have a high priority. Early adjustments of defence expenditure to reflect the more peaceful international climate will affect intra-European and transatlantic cooperation programmes alike. Once defence budgets have stabilised at a lower level, then arms collaboration will continue to evolve as the primary procurement option. Given the disappointments and psychological damage, caused by the recent collapse of transatlantic cooperation programmes, the likelihood is that Europe will continue, progressively, to go its own way.

Conclusion

This chapter has evaluated US attitudes towards NATO collaboration. It has identified US policies in this area, and from this there is no doubt that the 1980s witnessed a trend of rising American policy endeavour towards encouraging defence cooperation with NATO Europe. However, results have fallen short of expectations. The purchase of major European defence systems for co-development and production in the US is minimal. Moreover, although various R&D cooperative mechanisms have been American-sponsored, results of these measures have been questionable. Also, joint efforts have not been helped by the obstacles to be found in the collaborative penumbra of technology transfer and third country sales.

At the same time that the role of CoCOM, following the democratisation of the Soviet Union and Eastern Europe, is being debated, the US continues to show hesitancy in limiting the scope of its 'sensitive' list of technologies and the countries to which it applies. The US' veto on the sale to Iran of British aircraft containing US restricted technologies did little to enhance the prospects of increased levels of US–Euro collaborative effort. But the real issue, stemming from the discussion in this and previous chapters, is whether the corporate merger, acquisition and technical-sharing arrangements at the transatlantic level will raise the US' commitment to collaborate. In the more stable international climate of the 1990s, even the US defence–industrial base is feeling the chill wind of declining arms demand. Falling scale and rising costs will be powerful friends in advancing the ideal of transnational defence collaboration.

7 PRACTICE

Introduction

One of the problems facing academic study of arms collaboration is the dearth of empirical evidence attesting to the validity of the cost savings thesis. A major difficulty in obtaining data has regard to the counter-factual element in the comparative framework; that is, once a decision has been taken to collaboratively develop and produce a weapons system then cost data on the alternative national production option automatically becomes unavailable. Under such conditions evaluation of collaborative cost-savings have necessarily to be reduced to rough approximations of national production costs of 'similar' equipment types. A clearly hazardous exercise.

One result of the arms collaboration model's theoretical precision, but empirical impreciseness, has been the growth of critical comment concerning the costs that can be identified when contrasted with original estimates. Invariably such costs do increase, leading to a groundswell of opinion that collaboration can incur costs as well as providing for the often mooted savings.

Collaborative costs arise from delays, compromise, withdrawal and other considerations such as *juste retour*. This chapter examines these issues. It adopts a dispassionate stance, suggesting that a cost-benefit approach to collaboration is required. The reality of collaboration is that there are flaws in the fabric, and these should be recognised. Even the much vaunted WP collaborative model, discussed in the latter part of the chapter, is not the icon it was once commonly held to be.

Economics and the Demagogy of Cost-Savings

Collaboration means different things to different people. It is an umbrella term, covering licensing, codevelopment and coproduction of particular bits of weapons systems, as well as fully integrated design and production of joint ventures.[1] However defined, the economic arguments advocating joint weapons production are the familiar textbook ones of economies of scale, standardisation, and specialisation. Combine these with non-duplication of research and development expenditure, and considerable

149

opportunities exist for exploiting cost reductions. Since the 1950s when the Americans through a 'one-way street' trading arrangement engineered NATO arms standardisation by default, most observers have agreed that international arms cooperation represents the most equitable, cost effective method of 'balancing' NATO defence production. Yet, the reality does not quite match the rhetoric.

Due to the scarcity, sensitivity and non-comparability of the data involved, verification of the oft-cited economies enjoyed from collaboration represents an elusive field of empirical analysis. But the recognition of this lacuna is not novel. Note the trenchant comments made in 1980 by the American defence and political analyst, Robert Dean: . . .

'To the best of the writer's knowledge, no successful efforts have been made thus far . . . to specify actual savings derived from past or current European collaborative programmes. The paucity of detailed comparative cost data means that it is difficult, if not impossible, to verify the economies which might result from greater collaboration'.[2]

Several years later Professor Hartley, an expert on NATO collaboration, made a similar remark:

'What is interesting about the cost saving argument is that whilst it is often used by governments, there is little publicly-available information on the *magnitude* of cost savings from collaboration'.[3]

Appreciation of the opportunity-costs involved in collaborative projects has not increased significantly since these statements were made. This is remarkable, given the enormous scarce resources invested by NATO nations in pursuance of this goal: it is also perhaps inevitable. Attempting to unearth cost and related data for comparative evaluation would be a heroic exercise, necessiting data on research, design, development and production of identical weapons systems for both single-country projects and multi-country collaborative ventures. This empirical inability to provide substantive evidence of cost savings has led to suspicions that collaboration may involve cost premiums. A rather precise, though empirically unproven, expression of this view surfaced in the 1970s by a French observer who postulated that the unit cost of a weapons system increases by the square-root of the number of countries participating in its development, and that the length of the programme increases by the cube-root of the participants.[4] Supporting the supposition of collaborative cost premiums, is some crude and fragmentary information. One source indicates that development costs may be twenty per cent more if the project is divided conventionally, or up to fifty per cent more if several versions of the equipment are produced to meet differing national 'requirements'.[5] This percentage cost differential is calculated by comparison with what the equipment would have cost if bought direct from an existing supplier, usually meaning the US.

For American weapons built in Europe, some 25 per cent co-production might raise costs by 10 per cent.[6] Note that the early German–American projects, such as the F-104 G Starfighter; the Hawk surface-to-air missile; the Bullpup air-to-surface missile; and the side-winder air-to-air missile, have all been held to demonstrate that licensed production is more expensive than buying the same item off-the-shelf.[7] This trend was also evident in the licensing agreements between the US and the Benelux/Scandinavian countries, adding $1 million to the cost of each F-16 built in Europe.[8] These arrangements are estimated to have involved a 34 per cent cost penalty compared with buying directly from the US, whilst the UK Phantoms cost an extra 23–43 per cent per unit compared again with buying directly from the US.[9] Cost increases through transatlantic licensing also run counter to popular conception: the cost of the US made Roland II, doubling, with over $250 million being spent on redesigning the system for use by the American army.[10]

Intra-European collaborative development and production also suffers the malady of rapidly escalating costs. Without accounting for inflation, the price of the Anglo–French Jaguar was estimated to have risen 475 per cent above original estimates.[11] Similarly with the classic example of Europe's multi-national collaborative development and production project, the Tornado fighter: it was initially costed at around $3.5 million in 1970; the unit price 10 years later rose to $16 million, including spares and pilot training; and, in the late eighties, the cost of the fighter was estimated to have increased over the 1970 figure by a factor of almost three.[12] Again, these figures have not been adjusted for the effects of inflation but an approximate, though nevertheless revealing comparison with a similar aircraft produced under a national programme can be made in this instance. The Interceptor and Attack versions of the Tornado are comparable to the American Grumman F-14 and the Grumman A-6, respectively. Although the British government has never released R&D costs of the Tornado, the *Economist* magazine estimated indirectly that the inclusive cost of each Tornado fighter is about $45 million. It then went on to state:

'This price includes spare parts, training aids and the rest of it, which could run as high as $7 m–8 m per aircraft: call the aeroplanes alone $37 m. Today the F-14 costs around $36 m and the A-6 around $23 m. Thus 165 F-14s and 220 A-6s (the respective numbers of Tornado interceptors and Tornado attack aircraft that Britain has bought) would average $29 m per machine'.[13]

Similar comparisons can also be made concerning missiles. When the American TOW anti-tank missile was competing against the Franco–German Euro-missile consortium's HOT missile in 1977 for sales to the British army, 7,500 of the TOW missiles were reportedly offered for £25 million, almost half of HOT's price.[14]

Professor Hartley, in a 1983 seminal study, attempted to construct a framework in which such cost increases can be reconciled with the conventional cost-savings rationale of collaboration. Noting the comments of one UK official who concluded that collaboration results in only marginal savings on production, while the main savings were to be found on R&D costs, Professor Hartley's empirical research indicated production savings of between 10 and 30 per cent against cost premiums of 30–35 per cent on research and 20 per cent on development work.[15] From this he argues that even with a collaboration premium of 30–50 per cent, equal sharing on a two-nation project will still lead to savings of 25–35 per cent on each partner's R&D bill – compared with a national venture.[16] According to this study, then, the *net* effect of collaboration on costs is favourable when compared with a national venture.

Increased Costs Through:

Delays

International arms collaboration inevitably causes delays, and this is a major reason for the increased cost of collaborative ventures *viz-à-viz* the costs of production by the cheapest supplier. Collaborators must iron out differing requirements; translate technical documents; agree on production facilities and work-sharing arrangements, ensuring that production schedules harmonise with replacement requirements in each of the project's member states; and, finally, there is a need to establish management responsibility, control and coordination procedures. The President of one large Italian arms manufacturing firm estimates that joint projects between two States take over 25 per cent more time to complete than a project developed by a single nation; for three party efforts his figure is 50 per cent.[17] Examples of such delays abound, having become almost an inherent feature of armaments cooperation. For instance, in the case of the four countries (UK, Italy, the Netherlands and Spain) collaborating on the Light Attack Helicopter (LAH) project, the venture is stalling before it has even begun. After two years of discussions there is still no consensus on a design or agreement for a go-ahead on a detailed definition and cost study for the LAH.[18] The Franco–German (Aerospatiale and MBB) anti-tank helicopter got further, but in the mid-1980s it became stalled for three years. In 1987 the project was revived, but with the French warning that there must be cost savings. Here, significantly, the French indicated that collaboration costs *can* rise above national production, when in their statement they asserted that the project would be cancelled if the joint-venture threatened to exceed the price of France building the helicopter alone.[19]

The big multinational collaborative programmes are particularly prone to delay, possibly, according to some commentators, because difficulties increase in direct relation to the number of project partners. The European Fighter Aircraft (EFa), involving the UK, Germany, Italy and Spain, is destined to be a hugely expensive venture, costing around £20–22 billion, to develop and produce around 800 EFa. However, Germany has already shown signs of nervousness in funding its share of the bill; the costs of reunification taking priority in a more benign Central European strategic environment. Germany's vacillation has been criticised by other consortium members because indecision causes delay in development and production deadlines, placing increasing pressure on costs. At the beginning of the 1990s there was already a seven month delay in the fighter's development phase, being incurred through what has been described as 'equipment selection delays'.[20] Another big collaborative programme was the NFR-90 frigate project, which was scrapped in 1990. Originally expected to reduce the costs of acquiring such ships by 15 to 20 per cent under normal national procurement costs,[21] the project made tortuous progress. When it was participating in the venture, the UK was held to be partly responsible for delays in the schedule, being reticent to endorse agreement for work on hull design without matching-specifications for the required weapons systems.[22] Such technical problems led to the first industrial contracts for the frigate project costing up to twice the £60–£70 million originally thought necessary.[23]

In the area of missiles, the Franco–German HOT took nine years from development to production against the seven taken for the American TOW.[24] Notwithstanding this, the Euro-missile consortium has in fact proved to be a successful example of international armaments collaboration, capturing a high market share in anti-tank and point-defence missiles through sales of HOT, MILAN and ROLAND. The US–ROLAND license manufacturing programme, however, was not so successful. The US Army selected ROLAND in 1974 for its Short Range Air-Defence Needs. Modification of the ROLAND system to fit US strategic requirements led to the contract being awarded to Hughes and Boeing for a US version mounted on a M109 tracked platform. Delays and cost overruns characterised the project; the first US missiles not being delivered until 1977. From an original 184 fire units, the programme was later reduced first to 95, and then in 1982 to the 27 systems which by then had been completed. These were then deployed with a single light battalion of the US National Guard, which meant that because of the small numbers built, and the costs associated with licensed production and subsequent modification, the unit cost of each system approximated to a staggering $10 million.[25]

The endemic nature of delays has also affected the 'Family of Weapons' collaborative concept. The most notable example has occurred in the air-to-air missiles project, in which the US agreed to develop a medium range version (AMRAAM) while Europe concentrated on the short range version (ASRAAM). The two sets of developers could each then freely procure or license-produce whatever they sought from both sources. Although the US AMRAAM has begun limited production, it has encountered horrendous problems in the US, running into sky-high costs and technical troubles; and while Europe's ASRAAM has proceeded more cautiously, it has yet to reach full-scale development.[26]

The US-license production of Britain's Harrier V/STOL fighter jet was also reportedly affected by delays. These were allegedly caused by tardiness in the UK supplying spare parts, and the use of manuals not geared to the skill levels of US marine mechanics. As a consequence, the US Harrier force at one stage stood at only 20–40 per cent of operational readiness – well below the US navy's minimum requirement of 60 per cent.[27]

Compromise

A further factor contributing to the cost escalation of collaborative programmes has regard to the differing national strategic requirements of the weapons systems being co-produced. Varied national requirements can cause management difficulties, delays, and cost overruns. For instance, in 1962 the US agreed with the West Germans to collaborate on the development and production of a Main Battle Tank, called the MBT-

70. The joint venture suffered because of disssonance in military need. The Germans wanted a vehicle with high mobility, conventional gun armament, and high nuclear protection against conventional attack; the US, on the other hand, sought a vehicle with more modest mobility, missile type armament, low nuclear protection and high protection against attack from conventional projectiles.[28] The result was a compromise satisfying neither party: a tank with high mobility, both gun and missile firepower, high nuclear protection, and high protection against conventional attack; it proved enormously costly, heavy and required a much longer than estimated development time.[29]

The same difficulties have been encountered in aerospace and naval projects. In 1959 a Franco–German collaboration venture was begun with the purpose of developing and producing the Transall transport aircraft. The French wanted a long-range, large capacity transport designed for maximum performance in a desert environment to support their commitments in North Africa; the Germans sought a short-to-medium range, medium capacity transport with STOL capability for Central European climatic conditions.[30] As with the MBT-70, the eventual compromise satisfied neither party. This problem occurred again in the 1970s joint venture between the French and Germans to co-develop and produce the Alpha jet. Disagreement over the type of aircraft sought was only resolved through expensive compromise: the French producing a trainer, while the Luftewaffe produced a close support aircraft. Similarly, two versions of the Tornado fighter emerged from the several roles the participating nations to the project sought for the aircraft. The Italians wanted a single-seat air superiority fighter; the Germans wanted a single-seat close air-support aircraft; the British wanted a two-seat, air defence and long-range interdiction/strike fighter bomber.[31] Again the result was compromise, but with the radar system's avionic software and submunitions different between the two versions of the Tornado.[32] Moreover, one of the reasons the current EFa project lost the participation of the French was over national differences regarding the aircraft's design. This incompatibility was allegedly caused by French insistence that the plane should be light and small so increasing the possibilities for exploitation of the lucrative Third World markets. Here, the differences proved to be irreconcilable, and France went its own way to develop the Rafale fighter.

Compromise has also characterised naval joint-ventures. Considering the initially large number of countries that participated in the NFR-90 project, it was inevitable that there would be deviation from the original timetable. In terms of strategic requirements, some nations saw a need for a ship designed primarily for anti-submarine warfare; others were concentrating on an anti-air warfare ship.[33]

Cancellation and Withdrawal

Until recently it was claimed that one of the advantages for international defence collaboration is that it makes cancellation of the project difficult. Although this claim may no longer hold, it should be noted that delays in cancellation can be a major disadvantage associated with international cooperation. The saga of the SP-70 provides a sorry example of this point. In 1968, West Germany and the UK decided to cooperatively develop and produce a 155 mm howitzer called the SP-70. Delays were caused by the need to compromise: Germany sought an economic close support weapon; while the UK wanted a general service weapon; the later entry of the Italians into the programme also leading to further operational modifications. Development began in 1973, with the MoU specifying that if any partner withdraws from the venture unilaterally then it would have to bear the cancellation costs. In late 1979 the West German Ministry of Defence reported that the SP-70 had become one-third more expensive within two years.[34] Although eight prototypes incorporating numerous design changes were built from 1980, the basic configuration remained essentially the same. While the SP-70 partners were locked into this system specification, developments elsewhere were rendering the gun obsolete. Eventually, in January 1987, the project was cancelled. At that time its total cost exceeded $400 million, with the partners long having been faced with the dilemma that they could neither proceed nor cancel.[35]

The US–German MBT-70 mentioned previously provides another example of costly cancellation delays. Begun in 1962, with the first prototype appearing in 1967, cost overruns and technical difficulties led to the project's termination in 1979. A major flaw in this instance was the management structure. A committee of US and German military, government and industry representatives drew up and voted on technical and military requirements; tied votes were often resolved by developing or incorporating both options, so that two main armaments systems and three engines were developed in this manner.[36]

Withdrawals from collaborative ventures are now becoming common practice. Britain's withdrawal from the NFR-90 programme was the first of a number of other country withdrawals, leading eventually to the scrapping of the project in 1990. Germany recently became the third nation to withdraw from the secure data communication link project (MIDS), originally destined for all NATO fighter aircraft in the early to mid-1990s. For budgetary reasons, the UK and Norway have also withdrawn from this programme, with Canada expected to withdraw, and Italy and Spain considering their positions.[37] Note also that France has

156

pulled out of the multi-nation (Canada, UK, US, Germany, Spain and Italy) MSOW-project, and the UK has withdrawn from the NH-90 helicopter project.[38]

Other Considerations

Operational inefficiency and rising costs also derive from work-sharing arrangements. Collaborative production is allocated according to equity, normally based on national take-up of output. *Juste retour*, as this work allocation is conventionally termed, is acceptable to the collaborative partners because its logic is difficult to fault. The criterion, however, is not in the best interests of efficiency, squeezing out established expertise to accommodate, for example, the technological aspirations of DDI participants.

A common thread in typical joint venture work-sharing arrangements has also been duplication; this encompasses design and development work, testing facilities, and production and assembly lines. Duplication is, of course, the antithesis of specialisation, negating one of the core benefits attributable to arms collaboration. This less appetizing feature of joint-ventures occurred in the MBT-70 project, with the Germans developing their own version of any component for which the US had responsibility.[39] In the European licensing of the US F-16 fighter, two final assembly lines were established in Europe. In the Anglo–French co-production arrangement for the Jaguar ground-attack fighter both British Aerospace and Breguet (later Dassault) maintained their own design teams; and although none of the parts for the aircraft and engine were duplicatively manufactured in Britain and France, separate assembly lines were nevertheless established in both countries.[40] Similarly, with the Tornado project: Britain, Germany and Italy each insisted on domestic final assembly lines.

Work-sharing and duplication require organisation, coordination and monitoring mechanisms. In other words, a sizeable supra-national bureaucracy adding to the total costs of collaborative defence ventures. The Jaguar and Tornado programmes both involved extensive bureaucracies incurring costs of salaries, office accommodation, travel, meetings and associated expenses. The additional cost can reach 30 per cent of the cost of the aircraft produced.[41]

Finally, there is the impact on costs of export restrictions. While the general presumption is that collaborative programmes strengthen the political unity of NATO, the licensed production of the US F-16 by Belgium, Norway, Denmark and the Netherlands caused ill-feeling and dissention in the European Community because the American plane was chosen instead of the French Mirage 5. This was only part of the problem: after the deal was agreed, the EEC placed a duty on imported US parts for the F-16, adding $100 million to the cost of the aircraft.[42]

In every major defence collaboration a primary objective is to seek export orders to reduce total unit costs of the project, but close European collaboration could result in giving a European partner a veto on proposed exports on political grounds alone.[43] The problem lies with German law, prohibiting the sale of war equipment to sensitive areas.[44] As international collaboration accounts for 50–60 per cent of German expenditure on equipment,[45] it is clear that Germany's restrictive export policy stance could seriously hinder export prospects of collaborative production. A case in point relates to the 1970s Franco–German Alpha jet project. The Germans wanted to restrict sales to NATO allies, whereas the French sought a much wider market. In 1975 a compromise agreement was reached whereby the French were given unrestricted export of *only* the Alpha jet trainer.[46] In B.Ae.'s (abortive) efforts to sell Tornados to Jordan in 1990, the German Government encountered criticism, both domestically and in Israel, over the country's role in financing the deal. The political discomfort to West Germany and, indeed, other members of the Panavia consortium, occurred even though the Germans had no right of veto in this deal.[47]

As exports become scarcer in a tighter world arms market, production costs will rise for those countries specialising in defence equipment exports. When this happens the incentive to collaborate to reduce, in particular, the very high R&D costs, will increase. To some extent this explains the recent French predilection for cooperation in armaments production. France has traditionally been an aggressive and highly successful exporter of defence equipment. However, estimated exports of French military equipment in 1988 were 33 per cent of total exports, down from 42 per cent in 1987; and this decrease was no aberration: it capped a seven year pattern of decline.[48]

Warsaw Pact Defence Market: Disentangling Fact From Fiction

There is an idealised view of arms production in the erstwhile WP. Standardisation of equipment was obtained by edict, with the Soviet Union acting as the monopoly supplier of military goods to the Eastern Bloc countries. The benefits that accrued to the WP forces were those associated with international specialisation in arms manufacture. Among these benefits, the economic ones predominated, such as long production runs leading to reductions in the unit costs of production and development; but the military considerations of commonality in weaponry and logistics were also significant. Although this represents the common perception of the WP's arms procurement model, is it an accurate view?

In practice, the Eastern Bloc States did possess a greater degree of armaments conformity than was the case for the Western Alliance, but the extent of this standardisation has been exaggerated. The Soviet Union would perhaps wish to supply all defence equipment at one extreme; however, it did recognise that other WP States sought local arms production capacity. There are a number of reasons why the Eastern Bloc States wished to build-up defence–industrial capacity:

- There was the incentive to compete in the international arms export markets, including those of India, Syria, Iraq, Libya and other parts of the world, to earn the scarce foreign exchange to support the domestic industrialisation push. The need for foreign exchange applies *a fiortiori* in the 1990s, with the massive programmes of economic reconstruction being introduced by the East European States.

- Escalating armaments costs are not a uniquely NATO malady; they were also a characteristic of weapons production in the WP. A major problem was always Soviet pressures for the East European States to modernise equipment by procuring new high-cost Soviet developments. This acquisition of Soviet military equipment imposed costs which WP States believed could be reduced through local production.

- There was, furthermore, much complexity and unpredictability in the supply and cost of Soviet-sourced equipment. Although weapons development planning was, in theory, conducted through the Military Industrial Committee of the Council for Mutual Economic Aid (COMECON), the procedures of Central Planning in the Soviet Union meant that decision making was often secretive, protracted, and lacking proper consultation with client States. Communication often only effectively took place when the Soviets sought to pressure sales to the WP countries.

- East European countries also recognised that 'off-the-shelf' purchases of weapons systems from the Soviet Union added little to the development of defence–industrial capabilities, which they believed could act as a catalyst for wider civil technological development. The acquisition of engineering skills; an industrially disciplined work force; dissemination of innovation; and the extra utilisation of capacity from civil subcontractors servicing the needs of the defence sector, are held to be significant industrial benefits associated with promoting local military–industrial activities. Moreover, these are in addition to the more direct (short-term) economic benefits of higher employment, investment and savings from multiplier effects. For all these reasons, the WP countries sought to establish a military–aerospace R&D base. As with NATO States, the changed strategic environment is lending the former WP countries emphasising the development of a military–civil nexus through the fostering of dual-use aerospace and electronics industries.

Due to the conflicting positions of the Soviet Union and its WP Allies regarding procurement policy, the former adopted an ecletic stance: coercing the East European States to procure major weapons platforms, while allowing national development and production in other equipment areas. The pursuance of this policy led to disparate items of military equipment being deployed by several of the WP States. This led, in turn, to a process of de-standardisation, because little of the equipment was compatible, either between the Soviet Union and the WP countries, or even between the WP nations themselves. More revealing was that numerous of the major weapons platforms procured from the Soviet Union did not, with the elapse of time, remain standardised.

Local Defence Production[49]

(i) Logistics Equipment
Combat support equipment was the main area where the non-Soviet WP States nurtured productive capabilities. The Czechs and Poles, for instance, jointly developed a wheeled armoured troop transporter, the OT-64 SKOT, which was preferred to the inferior Soviet BTR-60 APC. Hungary successfully developed the FUG and PSZH-IV armoured scout vehicles in place of the Soviet BRDM-2 for its own forces, and some of the Hungarian vehicles were sold to Poland and Czechoslovakia. In addition, Romania was producing nearly all its light armoured vehicle requirements. Remarkably, even Bulgaria was doing the same, including a domestically-designed armoured vehicle version, acting as a replacement for the Soviet BMP-2 MICV. Moreover, nearly all the WP States possessed truck manufacturing industries, and hence little commonality existed between the different national military trucks of Eastern Europe. This could have had serious strategic implications if the generally held assumption is accepted that for every tank or APC three or four trucks are needed in support. Note also that the bridging equipment and radios carried by these vehicles were often different and incompatible.

(ii) Basic Armaments
While all the ammunition used by the WP was standardised, local adaption had taken place in respect of small arms, and de-standardisation was also being experienced in missile deployment. For example, much of

the Romanian ground equipment was either Soviet weaponry modified to meet local requirements or designed specifically to meet the requirements of the Romanian Army.[50] A case in point was the latest Romanian Multiple Rocket System (MRS) to enter service before the collapse of the WP. A 122 mm system mounted on a Romanian DAC 665T (6×6) truck, while another was the local development of a 40 mm automatic grenade launcher (the Soviet equipment was the 30 mm AGS-17).[51]

(iii) Weapons Systems De-Standardisation
Even before the East European democratisation process got fully under way, and with it the prospect of significant arms production diversification, it was becoming clear that WP arms standardisation in practice bore little semblance to the conceptual appreciation of the term. There were three principal reasons for this differing perception:

– Firstly, the different pace of modernisation between the Soviet Union and its Allies meant that the equipment of the various national Armed Forces had often been out-of-sink;
– Secondly, several of the East Bloc States, such as Poland, East Germany and Czechoslovakia, possessed relatively mature defence–industrial bases, having been actively engaged in adapting, modifying and upgrading Soviet-supplied weapons systems during the 1980s. Tanks provide a good example. Until the 1970s, the Soviets only allowed two of the six East European countries, Czechoslovakia and Poland, to produce tanks. Both of these States manufactured the T-55 tank before graduating onto the T-72. In addition to supplying their own armies with these tanks, they were also exported to neighbouring East Germany and Hungary. Such standardisation came to be flawed when the Soviets capriciously refused to allow Czechoslovakia and Poland to produce new generations of tanks. Neither country, for instance, being allowed to produce either the T-64 or the T-80.
– Finally, because of the impoverished state of the WP economies, the Soviet Union had been obliged to enter into countertrade arrangements to facilitate arms trading agreements. Moreover, the tentacles of de-standardisation even permeated into the Soviet Union itself, due to the Soviets being forced to agree to 'offset' purchases of 'modified' military equipment from East European States as a means of payment by the latter for Soviet-produced armaments.

Standardisation also suffered due to local adaption taking place. Indigenous production tends to encourage local development initiatives, like the Czechoslovak decision to modernise its ageing fleet of T-55 tanks with a new indigenous fire control system rather than adopt the much cruder Soviet upgrade package.[52] During the 1980s other WP States also began de-standardising their tank inventories. One such case was Romania. The country graduated to producing its own version of the T-72 MBT, known as the TR-125. There were a number of significant differences to the original Soviet tank, which entered production as long ago as 1971–2. The authoritative journal *Jane's Defence Weekly* has detailed several of these differences: compared to the T-72's weight of 41 tonnes the TR-125 weighs 48 tonnes, the increased weight possibly due to additional armour protection over the frontal area; the TR-125 also has seven road wheels of a different design, a new one piece skirt and is powered by a more powerful 880 hp diesal engine.[53]

The Soviets restricted unhelpful competition from their European Allies, but rarely by dictate, rather through exhorbitant licensing fees for access to blueprints and other documentation data, and the withholding of high precision machine tools, without which local production could not take place. Thus, the requirement to procure equipment from the Soviet Union led to some anomalous situations. In this context, Steven Zaloga has chronicled the example of the Poles who . . .

. . . 'finally managed to acquire enough SA-6 Gainful missiles to equip a majority of their divisional air defense regiments. They have not been able to afford the more expensive SA-8 Gecko which is more common with Soviet air defense regiments in the region. Furthermore, the Soviets have already fielded a replacement for the SA-6 Gainful, the SA-11 Gadfly, and are on the verge of fielding a third-generation system, the SA-17, when the Poles can hardly afford the first-generation system.'[54]

The notion, then, that the WP States enjoyed consumate commonality in armaments relates more to myth than reality. Certainly, standardisation was more prevalent in the Eastern Bloc than among NATO countries, but this advantage was dissipated as the non-Soviet Warsaw Pact countries increasingly took the initiative to build-up their own stylised arms manufacturing capacity, customising and tailoring designs to merge with needs of overseas defence markets.

Conclusion

The purpose of this chapter has been to examine the substance of criticisms that collaboration can impose cost premia on arms procurement programmes. The recognition that collaboration can raise costs is not surprising given the increased levels of planning, coordination and administrative bureaucracy involved. The appropriate judgement as to the 'worth' of a particular cooperative venture ought to embrace both 'estimated' savings and costs between collaborative vs national programmes. In calculating the net effect some of the qualitative benefits of collaboration may need to be taken into consideration, such as political consensus, long-term access to markets, and technological learning effects. However, these factors will be almost impossible to quantify. Scientific exactitude in assessing collaborative value is in any case no longer vital. The undeniable fact is that the stupendously high costs of major weapons systems development work in the 1990s almost certainly negates the possibility of national endeavour in NATO Europe. In aerospace, France's Rafale project is probably the last single-nation major aerospace defence project to be undertaken. In the land equipment field, national tank production programmes appear increasingly anacronistic and extravagant. Only the maritime area continues to buck the collaborative trend, but for how long? Unquestionably, then, arms collaboration, warts and all, looks set to increase its role certainly in European NATO procurement, and possibly in transatlantic activity, too.

8 REVIEW AND PROGNOSIS

The difficulty about reaching firm conclusions concerning the worth of international armaments collaboration is that the absence of empirical data inhibits rigorous scientific analysis. This is not surprising, given that a fundamental obstacle to evaluating the benefits and costs of collaboration relative to national programmes is the non-availability of counterfactual data. Lacking a comparative framework for measuring collaborative performance means that serious debate is hindered. The danger with this is that anecdotal evidence and journalistic cliches evolve, and are perhaps relied upon, as though they represented 'iron-laws' on the subject. It is not possible to say with certainty that a collaborative project is less expensive than a national programme aimed at developing and producing an identical piece of equipment. Given the cost premium associated with defence cooperative projects, it may not be far-fetched to conceive that in certain less advanced equipment areas, national programmes could well prove a viable alternative; but the exceedingly high costs of R&D involved in major weapons systems would almost always preclude their consideration for solely domestic production. Thus, European collaboration in advanced, especially aerospace, military platforms are now *de rigueur*, even though the basis for this course of action leans more towards supposition than scientific analysis. For this reason, this book has taken a broad qualitative approach to the subject matter in the belief that it will prove more useful in spotlighting and assessing general trends of long-run policy importance than narrowly focussing on the meticulous investigation of one or two specific joint-ventures.

Complicating the identification of even general trends has been the turbulent politico-economic sequence of events of the early 1990s. The break-up of the Soviet Union and the liberalisation of the East European States has occurred at the same time as the rise in Western Europe's political stature, supported by the increasing maturity of its industrial and technological base. From NATO's perspective the EC countries are at the centre of future defence–industrial developments. In particular, there is the 1992 SEA. In the early 1990s its imminence, perhaps more than its intended impact, has heralded revolutionary restructuring of the European defence industry. The ripples of this structural change: rationalisation, consolidation and cooperation, have also been felt across the Atlantic.

The irony of these developments is that the energising of international arms collaboration has occurred at just the time when a prolonged period of declining defence budgets is imminent. Although, rationally, this ought to reinforce collaborative effort, the danger might be that 'peace dividend' expectations weaken NATO member countries commitment to this goal. Even NATO itself has been under threat, with the belief in some quarters that it represents an anacronism in the changed circumstances of the 1990s.

Thus the genie is out of the bottle: the disparate though interlocking events of the late 1980s have unhinged the ordered economic, political and military networking between foe and friend, such that relationships will never be the same again. The question is, how will arms collaboration emerge from the capricious and challenging process that lies ahead?

Arms Collaboration in a Changing Strategic Environment

Unpredictability breeds insecurity. The 1990s will provide great opportunities for consolidating international peace, but it is important not to become blasé about the continuing dangers. The 'Commonwealth' of (hitherto) Socialist Republics continues to have a powerful military core. For example, in 1988–89, nine nuclear submarines were under construction in the USSR, twice as many as in the US.[1] There may be significance here. After all, it is in the naval area where the CFE discussions will have no impact, and with the speculated growing importance of 'out-of-area' operations, the maritime role of 'Great' powers is likely to increase.

Moreover, in the wider military context, it should not go unnoticed that in a relatively short space of time the erstwhile Soviet Union has come close to achieving many of the strategic goals it has sought for the past 40 years; it is on the verge of considerable economic and technological aid from the West; in a military sense, Central Europe may soon be neutralised; and American forces in Continental Europe are to be dramatically reduced. This is perhaps rather a cynical view to take, given the courageous and often unilateral peace initiatives introduced by former President Gorbachev over the last few years, but, Yugoslavia's internecine strife is a reminder of the tension's that can arise from too rapid a rate of democratisation.

A possible benefit, however, of the apparent waning threat from the East is the lifting of the veil shrouding emerging threats elsewhere. In the 1990s there is an increasing recognition of the military dangers facing NATO Europe's Southern flank. Islamic fundamentalism is on the ascendency, which the Gulf crisis has not diminished. Islamic fervour has

165

engulfed Iran and more recently Algeria. There are also dangerous new spirals in the Middle East's arms race. Several of the States in this region are suspected of possessing chemical, biological and even nuclear weapons. The means of delivering such weapons are also at their disposal. An indication of the serious manner in which NATO views developments in the Middle East is the fact that a huge portion of Turkey's land mass, covered by its South East Military Command has been exempted from the CFE arms reduction discussions in Geneva.

Thus, for the reasons outlined, the demilitarisation process should be a measured and balanced response to defence equipment cuts elsewhere. Given that the need for adequate or 'legitimate' defence will not evaporate, how will this affect the need for collaboration? Logically, arms collaboration should strengthen rather than weaken in the 1990s. With reductions in the demand for equipment leading to shortened production runs, the benefit from technology-sharing ought to increase not diminish. The nature of product technology will not remain constant, however. Structurally defence production will be obliged to change to adapt to changing military tactics, laying greater emphasis on defensive rather than offensive weapons systems.

Demand: Emerging Collaborative Opportunities

In the years leading to the 21st century, there will be growth in collaborative opportunities in the following areas:

Electronics and Communications

This subject has been discussed in detail in Chapters Four and Five. These, and related industries, will be high-growth areas in the 1990s. Production will be undertaken by firms that have an increasing cross-over relation, but from civil to military activities. A major characteristic of future military systems will be their defensive orientation. Examples of this form of military-related equipment include: reconnaissance, surveillance, and verification systems. With Strategic Arms Limitation (SALT) and Intermediate Nuclear Force Reduction Treaties already in the bag, and CFE, Short-Range Nuclear Force reductions, Chemical Weapons Convention, Conventional Forces II, SALT II, 'open-skies' (aerial overflights), and a Comprehensive Nuclear Test Ban Treaty, all on the horizon, there will be a surge in the demand for sophisticated electronic monitoring systems.

The Germans are already working on unmanned drones, such as the CL-289. However, the biggest proportion of NATO country efforts will be directed towards research, development and construction of verification satellites. Investment into associated launching systems will also be a consideration. In terms of expenditure, the US leads the way in these new technologies. To date, the total value of US investment into satellite verification systems has been estimated at around $10–15 billion.[2] US defence firms, such as TRW and Lockheed, are becoming increasingly involved in optic, synthetic, and X-ray sensors, as well as in electronic and signals intelligence. The US government budget for verification was around $170 million in US FY91; this can be expected to rise in the years to come. Moreover, the INF Treaty's verification budget can also be expected to rise from around its $200–300 million level at the beginning of the decade.[3]

Europe is now making efforts to become involved in the satellite verification area. IEPG's EUCLID research programme involves an input into a satellite surveillance project. In addition, it now seems possible that the European Space Agency (ESA) will become involved in satellite verification activities. The ESA used to view this area as being in the military arena, and so was disinterested. Its interpretation of satellite verification is now moving towards acceptability, based on the shifting view that the activity is civil-oriented. Aside from these multilateral programmes, France has assigned a high priority to satellite work. The French have already successfully developed the SPOT satellite. Significantly, the current project to develop a verification satellite system, called HELIOS, is being undertaken with collaboration from Spain. The French benefit through sharing the R&D costs, while the Spanish gain primarily through access to civil-related telecommunications satellite technology, and also in the civil 'technology-driver' aspects relevant to defence work.

Enhanced Mobility of Military Systems

The re-direction in NATO's military tactics will be towards greater mobility. In an era when frontline forces will be considerably reduced, timely warning of potential future hostilities will become paramount. In such circumstances, the ability to respond in a strategic environment where flexibility, speed and ability to change points of main effort over great distances requires the development of relevant platforms. Air mobile forces employing combat helicopters will help to regenerate NATO's ailing helicopter industries. Industrial collaboration is now a dominant characteristic in NATO helicopter production. In fact, it has reached the point where all NATO helicopters are cooperatively produced. Within the US, Bell and McDonnell Douglas cooperate, as do Boeing and Sikorsky; spanning the Atlantic, Sikorsky (US) and recently

IBM (US) have teamed with Westland (UK); and on the European side, France, Italy and the Netherlands are involved in the NH-90 project. There is also the Franco–German HAP/HAC attack and support helicopter project, and the EH101 is a bilateral helicopter venture between Westland and Augusta (It). Thus, particularly in Europe, there is now an interlinking web of helicopter cooperative alliances involving France, Germany, Britain and Italy. The Netherlands (through Fokker) and Spain (CASA) are also collaborating, but in none of the European ventures are the partnerships the same.

Although future military platforms will have to be produced to designs emphasising greater mobility, possibly serving the requirements of 'out-of-area' tasks also, there will be generally less importance attached to platforms and more to the electronics that are strapped on to them. Here, the requirement will be for rapid communications, command and control systems, and also comprehensive electronic warfare capabilities.

Logistics

In pre-unification days, the West Germans had a saying . . . 'the Atlantic Ocean is wider than the Vistula River'. In the event of sudden hostilities in Europe, NATO will be dependent on sea and air transport for supplies. In the post-CFE strategic context there will thus be an increased need for a rapid logistical capability. Air transport in particular will be important. 1990s NATO versions of the European 'Transall' air transport collaborative venture could well attract consideration. Furthermore, the emergence of NATO's Armed Services collaboration; that is the 100,000 strong multi-national rapid reaction force will bring strong pressures to bear to ensure that logistics are fully compatible. Interoperability will be crucial.

Supply: the 1990s Defence–Industrial Scene

In reviewing prospective change from the supply-side, it is evident that declines in NATO defence budgets will lead to falls in military equipment production. Public expectations will ensure that NATO States have difficulty avoiding the realisation of peace dividends. One of the more extreme predictions, in relation to US defence spending, has come from Robert McNamara, former US Defence Secretary and former President of the World Bank, who stated . . . 'I believe that within six to eight years we, in the US, could cut our defence budget about in half in relation to GNP, from 6 per cent to 3 per cent . . . That would free up in

1989 dollars, $15 billion per year'.[4] Cuts of this dimension, if effected, will be far from painless for defence–industrial contractors. In the US over 2 million jobs are defence-related, in Britain half a million, and although NATO countries such as Germany spend relatively smaller amounts on defence, in key sectors, there is a high proportion of workers involved in the defence field. In MBB, for instance, 40 per cent of the workforce is trained in military production. Regions specialising in defence work will be more badly hit than others. One example of such islands of prosperity created through high levels of defence spending is South-East Britain, where 41 per cent of UK defence–industrial employment is generated.[5] Unless Third World defence sales expand, which is unlikely, exports will continue to suffer too. This could have serious implications for output and employment. Statistics for the UK show that jobs supported by military exports as a percentage of jobs generated by MoD expenditure was 31 per cent in 1988 compared to 21 per cent in 1979.[6] The country's military exports earned a staggering £15 billion between 1985 and 1988, making Britain the world's second largest arms exporter in 1986, behind the US but ahead of the USSR and France; accounting in 1988 for about 12 per cent of the world market.[7]

Based on the fact that defence represents a significant proportion of manufacturing activity in the US, UK, France, Italy, and is not insignificant in Germany, extensive restructuring of production and industry will be required. Supply will need to adjust to the changing demands of the military. In the post-CFE defence–industrial arena, there will be a smaller number of programmes, reduced production runs, and, as a consequence, R&D will become proportionately more important.

To assist firms in this transitionary process governmental support and direction will prove helpful. For those defence contractors wishing to reduce their exposure to military production, diversification into civil activities will be disruptive and costly. The trend in this direction has begun. Given that the cross-over from military to civil effort may be lengthy, and that defence funding for certain project areas is curtailed, NATO as well as national defence authorities should, wherever possible, establish clear financial guidelines, encourage harmonisation of military requirements, and invite earlier industrial involvement. To enable these goals to be met, it is incumbent on NATO that armaments planning be better coordinated.

'Jewel' Military–Civil Industries

These will be the growth defence-industries of the future. Market forces will determine industries' division of labour between defence and civil work. Although in the immediate future defence production will continue

169

to be undertaken, its importance will diminish. Increasingly, technological spin-offs will be sought, moving from the civil to the defence area. In this new industrial order, defence work will be seen as supplementing civil operations rather than the other way around. Combine this with the progressively sophisticated nature of the electronics systems required for weapons systems, implying escalating costs with the smaller volumes of production required, and it is evident that industrial collaboration will continue to play an important role in NATO defence production. The dual-purpose integrative technologies, such as semiconductors, along with verification techniques, electronic warfare, C^3I systems and battlefield automatic data processing, will all be prime candidate areas for cooperation.

In terms of the structure of NATO's evolving defence–industrial base, the determining factor will be market forces. A considerable amount of rationalisation and consolidation of the defence electronics industries has already been undertaken. It is likely that the pace of mergers and acquisitions will tend to slow. Boundaries do exist: much of the German defence sector is government-owned or in the case of Daimler–Benz, its very size provides a formidable barrier to takeovers; the same applies to French defence interests; and in the case of France and Britain, limitations exist on foreign shareholdings. This appears to suggest that collaborative arms ventures will continue between the big three European countries, also including Italy and Spain on the technological fringes. Although collaboration will be at its most intense in the growth areas of electronics and aerospace, by necessity it will also prove attractive to the military platform builders. Note, in this context, that preparatory discussions between Krauss–Maffei, the German manufacturer of Leopard II tanks and Britain's MoD had meant that an offset deal was already in place if the German tank had won the tank competition for supply of replacement tanks to the British Army. Vickers (Challenger II tank) was awarded the contract, but in the longer-term, the only sensible course, given the shrinking demand is for cooperative ventures between some or all of Europe's tank manufacturers, and possibly also General Dynamics, the manufacturer of the US M1-A2 MBT. Tank production in all NATO nations is in a parlous state. Krauss–Maffei's situation is representative; this 150 year old tank producer is rapidly diversifying out of the armaments business. The firm is barely profitable, with the last order of tanks for the German Army completed in 1991. Turnover on the military side of the business has now been overtaken by sales from its five civil divisions – plastics production machinery, process engineering, transport systems, castings and automation. Of course, a tank will always be a tank, but here is a good example of military conversion where the 'dual-use' concept applies to the vertical processes of production rather than its more normal horizontal application. For example, Krauss–Maffei is successfully resourcing its military capacity and expertise to similar, technologically convergent work in the civil field. A case in point is its mechanical and electrical engineering work on locomotive power units for the Federal Railways.

Policy Implications: *'Plus ça Change. Tout est la Même Chose'*

This French proverb encapsulates the state of affairs relating to NATO arms collaboration. The radical political and military changes currently affecting NATO and its defence industries have failed to alter the underlying pressures for collaboration: limited budgets; rising weapons costs; the increasing costs of independence; and the desire to protect jobs and technology. The same pressures and challenges remain as before. Although Germany remains the only NATO country that looks to possibilities of international arms collaboration before considering domestic development and production of military equipment, most Alliance members now do the same, even though not enshrined in policy. Twenty-five per cent of Britain's £8 billion plus, defence equipment budget is not indigenous, with 15 per cent sourced collaboratively. Importantly, the French are now warming to both European and, significantly, NATO-wide arms collaboration.

The DDI nations will, as before, need to be accommodated in major collaborative programmes, but two general points in regard to these countries should be raised. Firstly, their defence–industrial efforts may be enhanced through cooperation with countries outside Europe's big three 'core' defence–industrial nations. In this respect, cooperative projects such as that between the Netherlands and Spain in submarines and fleet replenishment ships, provide a step in the right direction. Secondly, an agenda and funding of research into small nations defence–industrial development, e.g. Sweden and Israel, could prove useful here in providing a suitable policy framework for developing NATO's DDI nations.

Moreover, the process of harmonisation and syncronisation of needs and intentions could be improved by effort in the following areas:

Identification. There is now an urgent need for NATO States to identify the direction that the Alliance should take: in particular, a consensus is required regarding the roles that key policy-making institutions, such as the WEU, IEPG and CNADs, should assume in the encouragement of collaboration. This will not be easy, especially as the EC is now claiming

171

competence in the defence area, but any progress towards consensus would be preferable to the *ad hoc* nature of collaboration programmes and policies taking place at present.

Implementation. The process of collaboration and, indeed, movement towards a 'NATO' common defence market will be assisted by a centralist organisation with responsibility for R&D work. The IEPG; the French, and M. Francois Heisbourg, have all suggested the creation of such an institution. Its rationale would be similar to that of the US' Defense Advanced Research Programs Agency, seeking to avoid duplication of military R&D by pooling some portion of the resources involved. In the long-term, the more ambitious goal of a centralised Procurement Agency could be sought, whereby defence work would be allocated according to open competition without regard to national borders. However, this development will probably have to await progress in European political unity first.[8]

Structural. There needs to be increased awareness of the important structural changes taking place within NATO's defence–industrial market. The trend is towards further concentration. Although politically it should bind the Alliance more tightly, from an economic stance it may have negative repercussions on competition. There is a growing school of thought that reducing competition through transnational mergers and acquisitions may narrow the corporate arteries that source technological dynamism.[9] Defence may be a 'special case' at the primary contractor level, but there is less and less justification for rationalisation lower down the defence– industrial hierarchy. As the essence of competitive advantage is to compete then competition policy at national, EC and US (anti-trust) levels should be framed in cognisance of this fact. Therefore, there exists a compensatory need to encourage competitive pressures. Transnational competitive bidding at the sub-contractor level provides a useful starting point.

The imponderable in this discussion is whether international collaboration will act as the vehicle for the progressive integration of European *and* US defence industries. In the US, as in Europe, economic, industrial and technological market forces will be the driving force. Clearly, intra-European defence–industrialisation is accelerating. This may be a necessary prologue to closer US–European cooperation, because for all the hype and fears of European parochialism, the experience of common trading areas in East Africa and Latin America is that their survival in large part depends on the productive, technological and market equality of the trading area's member countries. Although European defence–industrialisation is a necessary first step, it will not be sufficient to realise the objective of unimpeded transnational collaboration across NATO boundaries. There also has to be an incentive for the US – the presently dominant NATO defence–industrial power, to make a substantive commitment to defence collaboration. Possibly, this now exists. For perhaps the first time, the economic rather than standardisation imperative of collaboration has become paramount. In the US, as in Europe, cost pressures are causing market restructuring through rationalisation and consolidation to emerge. This could precipitate technology and production sharing with other Alliance States.

Throughout the discussion it has been taken as given that NATO will survive the present crisis characterised by uncertainty. The form and role of the organisation may change, though its effectiveness will, as before, be measured by the yardstick of collaboration. Transatlantic collaboration between the two pillars will thus be essential.

Overall Conclusions

The purpose of this book has been to identify, explain and analyse the critical features of NATO arms collaboration. An objective approach has been adopted, evaluating the negative as well as positive aspects of the collaborative model. In providing a rounded picture of the subject, environmental factors were discussed in the introductory chapter. This scene-setting is an important task given the convulsive state of international affairs during the opening years of this present decade. But irrespective of the uncertainty, it is incontestable that a more benign security environment now prevails in Europe.

The balanced reduction of European military forces and equipment between NATO and the erstwhile WP countries signals in effect an entry into a new era: a preamble into the 21st century, based on optimism. NATO security and defence–industrial policy should be framed accordingly, both with prudence and enlightment. The contribution of this book in this regard has been to raise questions rather than to provide solutions, but searching enquiry is a stimulant to constructive debate. It is in this light that the following considerations are listed as change-agents shaping NATO policy through to the next century:

– the 1990s will be characterised by a downward spiral in military spending, with the structure of defence budgets changing to reflect increased emphasis on high technology defence systems;
– military forces will be dramatically reduced, but again there will be associated force structure changes, concentrating on mobility, flexibility and reconnaissance;

173

- the Central European front will become a relatively benign military environment, with NATO adapting to a new 'out-of-area' role, with perhaps Russian cooperation, and under UN auspices – *à la* operation 'Desert Shield';
- aerospace and, particularly, maritime forces will increase in importance, especially in relation to out-of-area operations;
- institutional arms reductions to specified levels will oblige advanced nations to coordinate their arms production and procurement planning;
- the obligatory raised level of cooperation that the above requires, especially in life-cycle syncronisation between NATO countries, should be viewed as a natural extension of the procurement liaison and joint planning already taking place in NATO committees;
- the CFE 'Cooperation imperative' when combined with reduced scale, higher production costs, and increased standardisation requirements from multinational force integration raises considerably the justification for arms collaboration;
- NATO European and North American defence–industrial bases will contract, and increasingly diversify into dual-use high tech production areas, progressively specialising as systems integrators;
- intra-European collaboration will become the norm, but will be supplemented where feasible by transatlantic cooperation. This will especially be the case in efforts to reduce R&D duplication;
- competing transnational defence–industrial consortia will become an important competitive mechanism; but for long-term viability 'losers' will need to be compensated;
- primarily civil oriented R&D will be emphasised in the future, with secondary bridge building objectives focusing on military application.

Taking these factors as a linked pattern of influences, the economic, political and military conditions have never before been as conducive as they are now for NATO arms collaboration. In the NATO European context incentives actually exist to go beyond this (viewing collaboration as an intermediate stage) towards a common defence market, with European-level agencies allocating, from a centralised fund, R&D and production contracts on the basis of revealed efficiencies. 'Two-way street' competitive consortia incorporating US and Euro elements then become a credible option, significantly, emphasising both the competition and scale aspects. These teaming possibilities become relevant not just on the Euro side of the pillar, but also at the US end. However, policy makers will need to meet the challenge, rising above what have become outdated parochial preferences for defence self-sufficiency. The cards are no longer stacked in favour of this game-plan. Time, as ever, will be the great arbiter, but now there has to be a realisation that NATO arms collaboration is finally about to come-of-age.

REFERENCES AND NOTES

Chapter 1

1 Almond, P., 'Clark Signals Fundamental Change Over Arms Research', *Daily Telegraph* (4 September 1991).
2 Parker-Jervis, G., 'Arms Firms Pay Price of Peace in USSR', *The Observer* (25 August 1991).
3 Morris, B., 'Why Soviet Chaos Will Not Deflect US Arms Cuts', *Independent on Sunday* (25 August 1991).
4 Taylor, T., 'What Sort of Security For Western Europe?' *The World Today* (Aug/Sept 1991) p. 139.
5 Anthony, I., et al, *West European Arms Production* SIPRI Research Report (October 1990) p. 20.
6 Morris, B., op. cit.
7 *World Armaments and Disarmament 1991*, SIPRI (1991) p. 296.
8 Cited by Col. Hempel and Lt. Ratter (East German MoD) in a paper, entitled: 'Central European Realities: the View from East Germany', presented at an Advanced Technology International Conference, London (June 7, 1990).
9 Callaghan Jnr., T. A., *US/European Economic Cooperation in Military and Civil Technology*, CSIS Georgetown University Monograph (1975) p. i.
10 *The Klepsch Report. Two-Way Street, USA–Europe Arms Procurement* (1979) p. 11.
11 See, Costello, R., 'Acquisition Office Shuffle Will Increase NATO Cooperation', *Armed Forces Journal International* (AFJI) (December 1988) p. 71.
12 Quoted by Covington, T. G., Brendley, K. W., Chenoweth, M. E., in *A Review of European Arms Collaboration and Prospects for its Expansion under the Independent European Program Group*, Rand N-2638-ACQ (July 1987) p. 1. Original source: *NATO Standardisation: Political, Economic and Military Issues for Congress*, Foreign Affairs and National Defense Division, Congressional Research Service, Library of Congress (March 1977) p. 28.
13 Walker, W., and Gummett, P., 'Britain and the European Armaments Market', *International Affairs*, Vol. 65, No. 3 (Summer 1989) p. 421.
14 Beardsworth, Major-General, S., 'Searching for an Aim: The Market Perspective', Advanced Technology Conference, op. cit.
15 See, *The Bulletin of Atomic Scientists* (January/February 1990) p. 19.
16 Ibid., p. 19.
17 Walker, W., et al, op. cit., p. 428.
18 Ibid., p. 423.
19 Roos, J. G., 'Eight Non-US Firms on DoD's "Top 100", But Allies Did Better a Decade Ago', *AFJI* (May 1990) p. 18.
20 Smith, D. R., 'Cooperate, Not Duplicate', *Defense* (July 1987) p. 397.
21 Ibid.

22 *The Financial Times* (3 April 1989).
23 Callaghan Jnr., T. A., *Pooling Allied and American Resources Within A North Atlantic Defense Market*, Speech given to 3rd NATO Marketplace Conference and Seminar, Brussels, Belgium (20 April 1989) p. 4.
24 *The Guardian* (23 March 1987).
25 *The Financial Times* (25 March 1987).
26 *The Financial Times* (23 March 1987).
27 Murphy, B., ' "Fair Return", Not "Buy European", Aim of Euro-Arms Program', *AFJI* (January 1989) p. 38.
28 *The Times*, London (18 January 1989). Note the comments made by Senor Francisco Fernandez-Ordenez when he recently addressed the European Parliament . . . 'The European Community may be forced to develop a common defence and security policy fully to exercise its potential influence in world affairs'. See, *The Times*, London (18 January 1989).
29 Vredeling, H., Report Chairman, *Towards a Stronger Europe* (IEPG) Vol. 1 (December 1986) p. 5. Italics added.
30 For example, NATO defence expenditure (1987) as a percentage of GDP (market prices) was 6.6 for the US; 4.7 for the UK; 4.0 for France; 3.0 for West Germany and Belgium; and around 2.0 for Spain, Italy and Canada. See, White, D., 'Squabbling over how to Share the Burden'. *The Financial Times* (25 November 1988).
31 *The Independent* (29 May 1989).
32 *The Financial Times* (7 July 1989).
33 See, Roos, J. G., 'US Revising Defense Trade Ratio Statistics', *AFJI* (July 1988) p. 23.
34 'Sunset at NATO', *The Washington Post* (2 March 1988) p. A2.
35 Roos, J. G., 'New Administration Should Chart a Two-Way Street', *AFJI* (December 1988) p. 57. *AFJI* (January 1989) p. 38.
36 *Towards A Stronger Europe* op. cit.
37 Fitzsimons, A., 'Current European Institutional Approaches to Security', *International Defence Review* (April 1989) p. 409.
38 Feldman, J., 'Collaborative Production of Defense Equipment Within NATO', *Journal of Strategic Studies*, Vol. 7, No. 3 (September 1984) p. 287. Note that MoUs, along with the Family of Weapons concept and Dual Production, form what is known as the 'Triad' of US cooperation measures.
39 In the nine years that the FWE has existed, tested items have led to US purchases amounting to more than $2 billion for 29 systems. The US has spent about $75 million evaluating all candidate programmes. In FY88 FWE was allocated $19.8 million against $43 million for NATO Comparative Testing. See, Roos. J. G., 'Allies' Success in US Programs Hinges on Equipment Requirements', *AFJI* (September 1988) p. 38.
40 Brandt, C. M., 'Armaments Cooperation and the Logistician: Boom or Burden', *Air Force Journal of Logistics*, Vol. 12 (Summer 1988) p. 10.
41 Data from, *World Armaments and Disarmament – SIPRI Yearbook 1988* OUP (1988). Data for 1987 – Tables on military expenditure, p. 177.
42 Ibid.
43 Carter, H., 'The Perils of Stealth is an Old-Time Melodrama', *The Wall Street Journal* (August 3, 1989) p. A15.
44 Roos, J. G., 'US Defense Contracting Changes Prompting International Teaming', *AFJI* (January 1989) p. 30.

Chapter 2

1 See, Cahen, A., 'Western European Union: Birth, Development and Reactivation', *Army Quarterly and Defence Journal* vol. 17, no. 4 (October 1987) p. 392. Note also, that on the creation of NATO, the BTO's military structure was absorped into that of the Alliance.
2 Cited from, 'Europe Seeks Identity for New Political Age'. The *Independent* newspaper (December 1, 1988).
3 Stanley, J. and Pearton, M., *The International Trade in Arms*, IISS (1972) p. 75.
4 Ibid., p. 75. Original source: *Arms Sales and Foreign Policy*, staff study prepared for the use of the Committee on Foreign Relations, US Senate (Washington Government Printing Office, 1967) p. 9.
5 Taylor, T., *European Defence Cooperation*, RIIA, Chatham House Papers, Routledge & Kegan Paul (1984) p. 16.
6 Cahen, A., ibid., p. 392.
7 Klepsch, E., *Two Way Street, US–European Arms Procurement*, Brassey's (1979) p. 27.
8 Klepsch, E., ibid., p. 28.
9 Donne, M., 'European Missile Group May Be Among World's Largest', The *Financial Times* (January 4, 1980).
10 Klepsch, E., op. cit., p. 18.
11 *Western Defence – The European Role in NATO* Eurogroup Publication (1989) p. 1.
12 Cahen, A., ibid., p. 394. fn.3 also details the relevant paragraphs of the Declaration adopted after the Rome meeting, thus:
para:(3) Conscious of the continuing necessity to strengthen Western security and of the specifically Western European geographical, political, psychological and military dimensions, the ministers underlined their determination to make better use of the WEU framework in order to increase cooperation between the member States in the field of security policy and to encourage consensus. In this context, they called for continued efforts to preserve peace, strengthen deterrence and defence and thus consolidate stability through dialogue and cooperation.
(4) The ministers recalled that the Atlantic Alliance, which remains the foundation of Western security, had preserved peace on the Continent for 35 years. This permitted the construction of Europe. The ministers are convinced that a better utilisation of WEU would not only contribute to the security of Western Europe but also to an improvement in the common defence of all the countries of the Atlantic Alliance and to a greater solidarity among its members.
(5) The ministers emphasised the indivisibility of security within the North Atlantic Treaty area. They recalled in particular the vital and substantial contribution of all the European allies, and underlined the crucial importance of the contribution to common security of their allies who are not members of WEU. They stressed the necessity, as a complement to their joint efforts, of the closest possible consultation with them.
(7) The ministers called attention to the need to make the best use of existing resources through increased cooperation, and through WEU to

provide a political impetus to institutions of cooperation in the field of armaments.

(8) The ministers therefore decided to hold comprehensive discussions and to seek to harmonise their views on the specific conditions of security in Europe, in particular:
- defence questions.
- arms control and disarmament.
- the effects of developments in East–West relations on the security of Europe.
- Europe's contribution to the strengthening of the Atlantic Alliance, bearing in mind the importance of transatlantic relations.
- the development of European cooperation in the field of armaments in respect of which WEU can provide a political impetus.

They may also consider the implications for Europe of crises in other regions of the world.

(9) The ministers recalled the importance of the WEU Assembly which, as the only European partliamentary body mandated by Treaty to discuss defence matters, is called upon to play a growing role.

They stressed the major contribution which the Assembly has already made to the revitalisation of the WEU and called upon it to pursue its efforts to strengthen the solidarity among the member States, and to strive to consolidate the consensus among public opinion on their security and defence needs'.

13 Cahen, A., 'Unity Through Common Defence – Western European Union', *NATO's Sixteen Nations* (June 1986) p. 43.
14 'UK Takes Over Presidency of Western European Union', The *Financial Times* (July 1, 1988).
15 Reed, C., 'IEPG-EDIG – For an "Open" European Defence Market', *Defence* (September 1989) p. 707.
16 Cited from, 'Fair Return, Not Buy European, Aim of Euro-Arms Program', *Armed Forces Journal International* (January 1989) p. 38.
17 See, Greenwood, D., *A Policy For Promoting Defence Technological Cooperation Among West European Countries*, EEC Document 1499/80.
18 Fitzsimons, A., 'Current European Institutional Approaches to Security', *International Defence Review* (4/1989) p. 409.
19 'Spain Presses for Common Defence and Security Role', *The Times* (January 18, 1989).
20 Fitzsimons, A., op. cit., p. 410.
21 Reed, C., '1992: A Minefield for the European Defence Industry', *Defence* (June 1989) p. 409.

Chapter 3

1 Hartley, K., and Hooper, N., 'Economics: The Ultimate Arms Controller?' *NATO's Sixteen Nations* (Dec. 1988–Jan. 1989) p. 35.
2 Heisbourg, F., provides a good review of the Issues Involved in his paper: 'A European Defence Industry: Dream or Reality?', *NATO's Sixteen Nations* (Dec. 1988–Jan. 1989) pp. 24–7.

3 See, for example, an article by Hartley, K., Hussain, F., and Smith, R., in *Political Quarterly* (January 1987).
4 Smith, A., *An Inquiry into the Nature and Causes of the Wealth of Nations* (1776) p. 423. Cited in Wells, S. J., *International Economics*, Allen and Unwin (1969) p. 25.
5 Notwithstanding his aversion to barriers of free trade, it should be noted that Smith did appear to accept that foreign trade restrictions might be necessary for reasons of defence. See, Wells, S. J., ibid., pp. 24n–5n.
6 Holloway, D., 'War, Militarism and the Soviet State', *Protest and Survive* (eds) Thompson, E., and Smith, D., Penguin (1980) p. 158.
7 Hartley, K., *NATO Arms Cooperation – A Study in Economics and Politics*, Allen and Unwin (1983) pp. 51–2.
8 Ibid., p. 51.
9 Hartley, K., 'The European Defence Market and Industry', *The European Armaments Market and Procurement Cooperation* (eds) Creasey, P., and May, S., MacMillan (1988) p. 54.
10 Creasey, P., and May, S., 'The Political and Economic Background', Ibid., p. 17.
11 Hartley, K., 'Value for Money in Defence: Strategic Choices and Efficiency Savings', *Public Money* (March 1986) pp. 35–36.
12 *Ministry of Defence: Collaborative Projects*, National Audit Office (NAO) London: HMSO (February 1991) p. 2.
13 Hartley, K., *The Economics of Defence Policy*, Brassey's (1991) p. 100.
14 See, Hartley, K., *Nato Arms Co-operation*, Allen and Unwin (1983).
15 Hartley, K., *The Economics of Defence Policy*, op. cit., p. 161.
16 Hartley, K., ibid., p. 101. Note that the author qualifies this conclusion by reference to several conditioning assumptions (pp. 102–3).
17 Feldman, J., 'Collaborative Production of Defence Equipment Within NATO', *Journal of Strategic Studies*, vol. 7, no. 3, (Sept. 1984) p. 284.
18 See letter from Lord Inglewood MEP in *The Financial Times* (26 June 1991).

Chapter 4

1 Taylor, T., and Hayward, K., *The UK Defence Industrial Base*, RUSI–Brassey's (1989) p. 1.
2 Ibid., p. 3.
3 'Half of Top 50 Firms Have Military Links', *The Independent* newspaper (January 29, 1990).
4 See, Matthews, R., 'Japanese Militarism: A British Perspective', *Rivista Internazionale Di Scienze Economiche E Commerciali*, Vol. 29, No. 7 (1982).
5 Matthews, R. and Bartlett, J., 'The Stirring of Japan's Military Slumber', *The World Today*, Royal Institute of International Affairs (May 1988) pp. 79–82.
6 Draper, A., *European Defence Equipment Cooperation*, RUSI–MacMillan (1990) p. 104.
7 See, Tucker, A. R., 'The Toyota Army', *Armed Forces*, Vol. 7, No. 12, (Dec. 1988) pp. 542–45.
8 Haglund, D., and Busch, M., ' "Techno-Nationalism" and the Contemporary

Debate Over the American Defence Industrial Base', in (ed) Haglund, D. G., *The Defence Industrial Base and the West* Routledge (1989) p. 237.

9 See, *Statement on the Defence Estimates: 1990* SDE, Vol. I, CM-1022-I, p. 33, and, Brzoska, M., 'The Federal Republic of Germany', in (eds) Ball, N., and Leitenberg, M., *The Structure of the Defense Industry*, Croom Helm (1983) p. 118.

10 Ibid., STE. p. 33.

11 Anthony, I., et al, *West European Arms Production*, SIPRI Research Report (October 1990).

12 Ibid., p. 6.

13 For example, the research being undertaken at the moment on 'Dual Use Industries in Europe' by the Directorate General for Internal Market and Industrial Affairs, European Commission (1990).

14 Taylor, T., et al, op. cit., p. 16.

15 *Aerospace Report*, Keynote 6th Edn. (1989) p. 16.

16 Ibid., p. 17.

17 *Aerospace Report*, keynote, op. cit., p. 17.

18 See, Freedman, L., 'The Case of Westland and the Bias to Europe', *International Affairs*, Vol. 63, No. 1, (Winter 1986-7) pp. 1-20.

19 'Fighting Allies', *The Economist* (March 4, 1989) p. 93.

20 Hobbs, D., 'Research and Development in NATO: The European View', *NATO's Sixteen Nations* (Dec 1989-Jan 1990) p. 29.

21 Ibid.

22 'Towards A Stronger Europe', IEPG Study Team Report, Vol. I (Dec 1986) p. 2.

23 Matthews, R., 'The Neutrals as Gunrunners', *ORBIS* (Winter 1991).

24 Ibid.

25 The table includes Ireland, which is not, of course, a NATO member state.

26 See, Matthews, R., (1991) op. cit.

27 In 1989 it was announced that Norway's arms controls were being liberalised to boost flagging defence exports. The restrictions were imposed some thirty years before, after the authorities discovered that Norwegian arms were being channelled to Cuba and Israel.

28 Sweden's defence exports amounted to US $1612 m between 1982-86, which is substantial for a neutral country supporting 'peaceful coexistence'. (See, Juusti, J., and Matthews, R., 'Finland's Defence Posture', *Defense Analysis* Vol. 6., No. 1, (1990) pp. 85-89); it should also be noted that in the electronics sector Finland has some of Europe's biggest multinational companies.

29 For instance, the *Penguin* Mark III air-to-surface missile (for F-16 fighters), and air-to-air missiles in collaboration with B.Ae.

30 IEPG Report, op. cit., p. 1.

31 Heisbourg, F., 'Public Policy and the Creation of a European Arms Market', in (eds) Creasey, P., and May, S., *The European Arms Market and Procurement Cooperation*, Macmillan (1988) p. 65.

32 Hobbs, D., op. cit., p. 27.

33 Ibid., p. 28.

34 Heisbourg, F., op. cit., p. 73.
35 Anthony, I., et al, op. cit., p. 11.

Chapter 5

1 Getler, W., 'Europe's New Aerospace Conglomerates are on the Rise', *International Herald Tribune* (August 22, 1988).
2 Moravcsik, A., 'Defence Cooperation – The European Armaments Industry at the Crossroads', *Survival*, Vol. 32, No. 1 (January/ February 1990) p. 72.
3 *AFJI* (January 1989) pp. 73–4.
4 *AFJI* ibid., p. 30.
5 'Electrical Brief-Fighting Allies', *The Economist* (4 March, 1989), p. 93.
6 Callaghan Jr., T. A., 'NATO Still in the Throes of Structural Disarmament', *AFJI* (December 1988) p. 61; original source: Senate Armed Forces Committee (May 1987).
7 Ibid., p. 64.
8 *Jane's Defence Weekly* (10 June, 1989).
9 See, 'The Race to Develop Technology', *The Christian Science Monitor* (18 July, 1989) p. 9.
10 Getler, W., op. cit.
11 *The Financial Times* (13 June, 1989).
12 'Defence Industry Braces for American Invasion', *The Sunday Times*, London (12 February, 1989).
13 Ibid.
14 *The Financial Times* (22 March, 1989).
15 *The Financial Times* (17 March, 1989).
16 Note current conjecture over Vickers (UK) and Krauss–Mafei (FRG) combining their tank manufacturing activity, given the likelihood of declining tank orders.
17 See, *Business Ratio Report*, ICC (1989) p. 1.
18 Ibid., p. 3.
19 See, *The Economist* (March 4, 1989) p. 93.
20 *The Financial Times* (August 30, 1989).
21 *The Financial Times* (March 20, 1990).
22 *The Financial Times* (August 9, 1989).
23 *The Financial Times* (March 20, 1990).
24 Ibid.
25 *AFJI* (January 1989).
26 Greenwood, D., 'The European Defence Industry Stakes', *International Defense Review* (November 1989) p. 1573.
27 Marsh, D., 'Cross-Shareholdings in Defence and Aircraft Urged by Daimler', *The Financial Times* (December 1, 1988), and *The Times*, London (July 20, 1989).
28 Albrecht, U., 'Spin-Off: A Fundamentalist Approach', fn. 25, p. 56, in *The Relations Between Defence and Civil Technologies*, (ed) Gummett, P. and Reppy, J., NATO ASI series (1988).
29 Ibid., p. 41.

30 Maddock, (Sir) I., *Civil Exploitation of Defence Technology*, Report to the Electronics EDC, London: Electronics Economic Development Council (1989).
31 Cited in Hartley, K., *The Economics of Defence Policy*, Brassey's (1991) p. 133. Original source, ACOST 1989, *Defence R&D: A National Resource* (HMSO, London).
32 *The Financial Times* (March 4, 1988).
33 'A Tokyo–Stuttgart Axis?', *The Economist* (March 10, 1990) p. 100.
34 Greenwood, D., 'Competition and Collaboration in West European Arms Procurement', *The International Defense Review* (April 1989) p. 512.
35 Moravcsik, A., op. cit., p. 77.
36 Jackson, J. H., 'Reshaping of the Defence Industry', *Jane's Defence Review* (November 25, 1989) p. 1154.
37 Ibid., p. 1154.
38 'Ministry of Defence: The Profit Formula – 1987–88', *52nd Report from the Committee of Public Accounts*, House of Commons (November 1988) p. 3.
39 Jappie, A., 'UK's "Ridiculous" Bidding Policy', *Jane's Defence Weekly* (October 21, 1989) p. 887.
40 Kennedy, G., 'Strains and Prospects in Defence Procurement', *RUSI* (Summer 1989) p. 48.
41 Jappie, A., op. cit., p. 887.
42 Goodman Jr., G., 'DoD's Acquisition System Has Industry on the Ropes', *AFJI* (June 1988) p. 46.
43 Ibid., pp. 46–8.
44 Roos, J. G. 'US Defense Contracting Changes Prompting International Teaming', *AFJI* (January 1989) pp. 30–32. The study in question was conducted by Vollmer, Staff Vice President, General Dynamics Defense Initiatives Organisation.
45 Goodman Jr., G., op. cit., p. 46.
46 Ibid., p. 46.
47 Ibid., p. 46, and, 'Spending Up in the Land of the Rising Gun', *Far Eastern Economic Review*, (October 13, 1988) p. 67, and 'Now Japan is Up in Arms', *US News and World Report* (August 8, 1988) pp. 41–5.
48 *Towards A Stronger Europe*, Vol. 1, IEPG Study Team headed by Vredeling, H. (December 1986) p. 12.
49 Kennedy, G., *The Military in the Third World*, Duckworth (1974).
50 *Towards a Stronger Europe*, IEPG, op. cit., p. 13.
51 It should be emphasised, however, that even for those developing economies that have been producing military equipment for decades, they still remain dependent on the advanced industrial countries for the design of sophisticated systems. On this, and related points, see, Matthews, R., 'India's Growth Industry: Militarism', *RUSI* (Spring 1988); 'The Development of South Africa's Military–Industrial Complex', *Defense Analysis* (Spring 1988); 'The Development of India's Defence–Industrial Base', *Journal of Strategic Studies* (December 1989).
52 Taylor, T., *Defence Technology and International Integration*, Francis Pinter (1982) p. 155, cited in Cooper, R., *Collaborative Defence Procurement by Smaller Industrial Nations* RMCS–CIT MDA Dissertation (1987) p. 32.
53 de Donnea, F., 'The Cost of Defence Equipment – A Dilemma Facing Smaller Nations', *Jane's Defence Weekly* (June 27, 1987) p. 1372.
54 Ibid., p. 1372.

183

Chapter 6

1 Anthony, I., et al, *West European Arms Production*, SIPRI Research Report (October 1990) p. 5.
2 Ibid., p. 5.
3 Taft, W. H., 'Armaments Cooperation Today and Tomorrow', *NATO's Sixteen Nations* (Dec 1989–Jan 1990) pp. 15–16.
4 Feldman, J., 'Collaborative Production of Defense Equipment Within NATO', *Journal of Strategic Studies* vol. 7, no. 3, (September 1984) p. 285. Original data source: Thomas Callaghan's US/European Economic Cooperation in Military and Civil Technology (Washington DC: Centre for Strategic and International Studies, Georgetown University, March 1976).
5 Cordesman, 'Defense Can't Be Hostage of Deficit Debate', *Los Angeles Times* (March 4, 1988) p. 11. Note also what the writer has to say on missiles . . . 'During 1984–86 alone, the Soviet Union produced 300 new ICMBs; NATO, including our British and French Allies, produced 10 . . . In the case of the short-range ballistic missiles not covered by the INF Treaty, the Soviet Union produced 1350; NATO exactly 1'.
6 Perry, W. J., *The Department of Defence Written Statement on NATO-Improved Armaments Cooperation*, submitted to the Research and Development Sub-Committee of the Committee on Armed Services of the United States 96th Congress, 1st Session (April 4, 1979) pp. 14–15.
7 Second Report from Expenditure Committee (Defence and External Affairs), *Defence* HC155, HMSO, London (1976) p. Iiv. Cited in Hartley, K., 'NATO Standardisation and Nationalism; An Economists' View', *RUSI* (September 1978) p. 58.
8 Kozicharow, K., 'US Spurring NATO Standardisation', *Aviation Week and Space Technology* (July 14, 1980) p. 97.
9 Expression borrowed from Hussein, F., 'Rationalising NATO', *New Scientist* (May 10, 1979) p. 9F.
10 Callaghan, T. A., Jr., *Pooling Allied and American Resources Within A North Atlantic Defense Market*, speech given at 3rd NATO Market Place Conference, Brussels (April 20, 1989) p. 3. See also *Report for the US Department of Defense* (1988).
11 Roos, R. G., 'New Administration Should Chart Two-Way Street', *Armed Forces Journal International* (AFJI) (December 1988) p. 56.
12 Heisbourg, F., 'Public Policy and the Creation of a European Arms Market', (Eds) Creasey, P. and May, S., *The European Armaments Market and Procurement Cooperation*, MacMillan (1989) p. 62.
13 *AFJI* (January 1989) pp. 73–74.
14 *AFJI* (December 1987) p. 71, and Evans, M., 'The Defence Entente Grows', *The Times*, London (November 22, 1988).
15 Roos, J. G., 'Allies Success in US Programs Hinges on Equipment Requirement', *AFJI* (September 1988) p. 38.
16 Taft, W., 'Cooperate, Not Duplicate', *Defence* (July 1987) p. 396.
17 *AFJI* (April 1986) p. 30.
18 Starr, B., 'USA Looks for Safer Nunn Projects', *Jane's Defence Weekly* (JDW) (November 25, 1989) p. 1147.

19 Famiglietti, L., 'Nunn Success Prompts US Review', *JDW* (March 4, 1989).
20 Feldman, J., op. cit., p. 288.
21 Callaghan, T. A., op. cit., p. 4.
22 Creasey, P. and May, S., 'The Political and Economic Background', op. cit., p. 2.
23 Moravcsik, A., op. cit., p. 78.
24 Ohlson, T.,
25 Feldman, J., op. cit., p. 292.
26 *Los Angeles Times* (August 7, 1988) p. VI, 10:1.
27 Rogers, M., 'One Europe, One Policy', *Jane's Defence Weekly* (17 August 1991) p. 290.
28 Taft, W. H., op. cit., (Dec 1989–Jan 1990) p. 17.
29 Murphy, B., 'Fair Return, Not Buy European, Aim of Euro Arms Program', *AFJI* (January 1989) p. 38.
30 Facer, R., 'The Alliance and Europe: Part III Weapons Procurement in Europe – Capabilities and Choices', *ADELPHI* series no. 108, IISS (1975) p. 32.
31 *AFJI* op. cit., (January 1989) p. 38.
32 'EEC Duties May Burden Defence Bill', *The Guardian* (January 4, 1980).
33 'US Warns EC Over Plans for Tariff on Arms Imports', *The Financial Times* (August 1, 1988). Note that the complaint against the RAF is that it paid no duty on the Lockheed Tristars it bought as tanker aircraft in the early 1980s, and that duty should have been paid because the Tristars were essentially civil and could be returned to a civil role.
34 Ibid.
35 *The Guardian*, op. cit. (January 4, 1988).
36 *JDW*, op. cit. (November 25, 1989) p. 1147.
37 *AFJI* (December 1988) p. 64, and Adams, J., 'Pentagon Cuts Hit British Contracts', *The Sunday Times*, London (February 21, 1988).
38 *AFJI* ibid.
39 *The Sunday Times* (February 21, 1988).
40 *AFJI* (December 1988) p. 56.
41 Roos, J. G., 'Lots of Talk, Little Action in US; Europe Forging New Order', *AFJI* (December 1989) p. 49.
42 Ibid.
43 Ibid., p. 50.
44 Famiglietti, L., op. cit.
45 Taft, W. H., op. cit. (Dec. 1989–Jan. 1990) p. 16.

Chapter 7

1 Note that a distinction should be made between 'licensing', where one country is dependent on another for defence technology, including design, and 'co-production', where two or more partners share more or less equally in the production of military equipment. 'Integrated design and production' is, of course, where all participants to the project share in the development and production of the weapon, e.g. Tornado.

2　See, 'Collaborative Weapons. Can They Work?' *Flight International* (1 June 1985) p. 128.

3　Hartley, K., 'Public Procurement and Competitiveness: A Community Market for Military Hardware and Technology?', *Journal of Common Market Studies* (JCMS), Vol. 25, No. 3 (March 1987) p. 244.

4　Quoted in Moravcsik, A., 'Defence Cooperation – The European Armaments Industry at the Crossroads', *Survival* (January/February 1980), Vol. 32, No. 1, p. 75 and fn. 33. Original source: Delpech, Jean-Laurens, 'La Standardization des Armements', *Revue de Defense Nationale* (May 1976).

5　Facer, R., 'The Alliance and Europe: Part III Weapons Procurement in Europe – Capabilities and Choices', *Adelphi Series No. 108* International Institute For Strategic Studies (1975) p. 37; also cited in the *Klepsch Report*, Brassey's (1979) p. 43.

6　Hartley, K., 'NATO Standardisation and Nationalism: An Economist's View', *RUSI* journal (September 1978) p. 59.

7　James, R. R., 'Standardisation and Common Production of Weapons in NATO', *Adelphi Series No. 3* (1967) p. 19.

8　Cohen, E., 'NATO Standardisation: The Perils of Common Sense', *Foreign Policy* (Summer 1978) p. 82.

9　Ibid., p. 82.

10　Hartley, K., *JCMS*, op. cit., p. 240.

11　See Cohen, p. 8. A major problem in the Roland collaborative programme was the conversion from French to US standards. For example, Hughes expected to receive 25,000 supporting documents during the transfer, it eventually received 145,000, 80 per cent of which dealt with changes to the original documentation. See Covington et al, *Rand*, p. 26. The system was supposed to require only $95 million for testing and coproduction planning, but its R&D was driven to over $400 million because of US modifications and the need to qualify 100 per cent of its parts for production in the US. See, Basil, R., 'Rules of the Road for the Two-Way Street', *AFJI* (December 1987) p. 79.

12　See, Boyes, R., 'The Tornado Rattles Bonn's Defence Planners', *The Financial Times* (21 August 1980), and 'Cheaper Weapons – Europe Does it the Second-Best Way', *The Economist* (21 June 1986) p. 23.

13　Ibid., p. 23.

14　Ibid., p. 23.

15　Hartley, K., *NATO Arms Cooperation*, Allen & Unwin (1983) pp. 153–4. The author also suggests that . . . 'One "rule of thumb" states that the collaboration premium on R&D is equal to the *square root* of the number of partners, with total development time approximated by the *cube root* of the number of participants' . . . (p. 153); author's italics.

16　Ibid., p. 154.

17　Cohen, op. cit., p. 81.

18　*AFJI* (June 1989) p. 24.

19　*The Financial Times* (26 March 1987).

20　*Jane's Defence Weekly* (27 May 1989) p. 991.

21　*Defense News* (16 March 1987) p. 13.

22　*The Times*, London (18 February 1988).

23　*The Financial Times* (6 September 1988).

24 Cohen, op. cit., p. 81.
25 See, *Flight International*, op. cit., pp. 129–30.
26 *The Economist*, op. cit., pp. 19–20.
27 Cohen, op. cit., pp. 77–78.
28 Covington, T. G., et al, *Rand*, op. cit., p. 22.
29 Ibid., p. 22.
30 Ibid., p. 32.
31 Cohen, op. cit., p. 80.
32 Covington, T. G., Brendley, K. W., and Chenoweth, M. E., *A Review of European Arms Collaboration and Prospects for its Expansion Under the Independent European Program Group*, RAND, N-2638-ACQ (July 1987) p. 47.
33 Fouquet, D., 'Cooperative Shipbuilding Project is Embarking on a Critical Phase', *Defense News* (16 March 1987) p. 13.
34 Boyes, R., 'Alliance Battles Against Duplication', *The Financial Times* (18 October 1979).
35 *Defense Attache* (January 1987) p. 9.
36 Covington, T. G., et al, *Rand*, op. cit., p. 22.
37 *Jane's Defence Weekly* (1 July 1989) p. 1345.
38 *AFJI* (September 1988) p. 81.
39 Covington, T. G., et al, *Rand*, op. cit., p. 22.
40 *The Economist*, op. cit., p. 20.
41 Ibid., p. 23.
42 Cohen, op. cit., p. 90.
43 Hall, Sir Donald, 'European Cooperation in Armaments Research and Development', *RUSI* journal (Summer 1988) p. 57.
44 *The Times*, London, (28 January 1989).
45 Taylor, T., *European Defence Cooperation*, Royal Institute of International Affairs, Chatham House Papers No. 24 (1984) p. 21.
46 Covington, T. G., et al, *Rand*, op. cit., p. 45.
47 *The Guardian* (30 January 1989).
48 *AFJI* (June 1989) p. 62.
49 This section draws heavily on, Steven J. Zaloga's 'Eastern Bloc Two-Way Street Has Its Share of Potholes', *AFJI* (December 1988) pp. 52–3.
50 Foss, C. F., 'Romanian Weapons Detailed', *Jane's Defence Weekly* (August 5, 1989) p. 224.
51 Ibid.
52 Zaloga, op. cit., p. 52.
53 Foss, op. cit., p. 224.
54 Zaloga, op. cit., p. 53.

Chapter 8

1 Weisser, U. (Capt.), 'Plans and Projections in the Germany of Tommorow', Paper presented at the Advanced Technology Defence Conference, London (June 8, 1990).
2 Lewis, P. (Dr), 'Verification Technology Opportunities', Paper presented at the Advanced Technology Defence Conference, London (June 8, 1990).
3 Ibid.

4 Interview with McNamara, R., *Analysis*, BBC Radio 4 (October 6, 1989). Quoted in *Security After the Cold War – Redirecting Global Resources*, Safer World Foundation (March 1990) p. 16.
5 Calculated from, UK *Statement of Defence Estimates* 1989.
6 Calculated from data contained in, Lovering, J., 'The Employment Crisis in the Defence Industry', *Diversification of the Defence Industry* Safer World, Proceedings of a Seminar held at the House of Commons (March 8, 1990) p. 11.
7 Ibid., p. 12.
8 See, IEPG's, *Towards A Stronger Europe* (1987); 'A NATO Weapons' Agency', *The International Herald Tribune* (6 May 1987); and Heisbourg, F., 'European Defense Cooperation and NATO's Future', *NATO in the 1990s*, (ed) Sloan, S. R., Pergamon–Brasseys (1989) p. 222 – Note the author makes mention of an embryo centralist R&D organisation, Institut Franco–Allemand de Saint Louis, already existing since 1958 between France and West Germany.
9 See, 'Europe's Companies After 1992 – Don't Collaborate, Compete', *The Economist* (June 9, 1990) pp. 23–6.

APPENDIX A.

The 100 largest arms-producing companies in Western Europe, 1988[a]

Figures in columns 5, 6 and 8 are in US $ million; figures in column 7 are percentages.

1 Rank	2 Company	3 Country	4 Industry[b]	5 Arms sales	6 Total sales	7 5 as % of 6	8 Profits	9 Employment
1	British Aerospace	UK	AC EL MI	5 470	10 045	54	277	131 300
2	Thomson S.A.	France	A EL	4 470	12 567	36	201	104 000
2	Thomson CSF (Thomson S.A.)	France	A EL	4 320	5 626	77	495	41 400
3	GEC	UK	ENG EL	3 850	11 005	35	803	157 000
4	Daimler Benz	FRG	AC ENG MV EL	3 420	41 852	8	969	339 000
5	Rolls Royce	UK	ENG	2 500	6 259	40	460	40 900
6	Aérospatiale	France	AC	2 300	4 700	49	16	34 250
7	Direction des Constructions Navales	France	SH	2 210	2 215	100	–	28 000
8	IRI	Italy	AC ENG EL SH	2 100	37 813	6	731	358 213
9	Dassault-Breguet	France	AC	2 080	2 965	70	66	13 818
10	MBB	FRG	AC EL MI	1 990	4 054	49	57	40 000
11	Lucas Industries	UK	AC EL	1 760	3 548	50	301	59 047
12	EFIM	Italy	AC MV EL	1 520	3 552	43	-20	37 405
13	FIAT	Italy	ENG A MV EL	1 500	34 041	4	2 492	277 353
13	AEG (Daimler Benz)	FRG	EL	1 370	7 619	18	15	89 600
14	INI	Spain	AC A MV EL SH SA/O	1 290	14 966	9	269	–
15	Thorn EMI	UK	EL	1 200	6 003	20	529	65 400
16	Ferranti-International Signal	UK	EL	1 170	1 464	80	65	26 980
17	GIAT	France	A MV	1 150	1 151	100	-84	14 740
18	Matra Groupe	France	MI	1 040	3 240	32	57	19 480

Appendix A *continued*

Figures in columns 5, 6 and 8 are in US $ million; figures in column 7 are percentages.

1 Rank	2 Company	3 Country	4 Industry^b	5 Arms sales	6 Total sales	7 5 as % of 6	8 Profits	9 Employment
19	Philips	Netherlands	EL	1 010	28 371	4	1 040	310 300
	MTU (Daimler Benz)	FRG	ENG	970	1 868	52	18	17 200
20	Oerlikon-Bührle	Switzerland	AC A EL	930	2 891	32	−24	27 750
21	Nobel Industrier	Sweden	A EL MI SA/O	910	3 481	26	152	22 101
22	Plessey	UK	EL	880	2 948	30	237	26 216
	Aeritalia (IRI)	Italy	AC	880	1 410	62	53	14 177
	Bofors (Nobel Industrier)	Sweden	A EL MIS A/O	870	873	100	44	5 994
	Matra (Matra Groupe)	France	MI	840	1 178	71	26	5 586
23	VSEL Consortium	UK	MV SH	830	830	100	28	10 782
24	Siemens	FRG	EL	800	33 823	2	791	353 000
25	SNECMA	France	AC	770	1 722	45	−42	13 482
26	Krupp	FRG	MV EL	680	8 391	8	−115	63 391
27	Hawker Siddeley	UK	AC ENG	680	3 327	20	198	42 000
	FIAT Aviazione (FIAT)	Italy	AC ENG	660	802	82	−53	4 749
28	Rheinmetall	FRG	A SA/O	650	1 851	35	47	15 460
29	Diehl GmbH	FRG	MV SA/O	610	1 361	45	–	14 200
30	Thyssen Industrie	FRG	MI SH	600	9 564	6	212	128 700
31	SAAB-SCANIA	Sweden	AC EL MI	570	6 934	8	26	48 500
	Dornier (Daimler Benz)	FRG	AC EL	570	1 093	52	24	9 800
32	Eidgenössischen Rüstungsbetriebe	Switzerland	AC	550	595	92	1	4 900
33	Smiths Industries	UK	EL	530	1 256	42	176	5 300
	Oto Melara (EFIM)	Italy	A MV MI	530	539	98	14	2 329
	Electronique Serge Dassault (Dassault-Breguet)	France	EL	510	678	75	19	4 100
	CASA (INI)	Spain	AC	500	697	72	−52	10 372

	Company	Country	Arms					
34	FFV	Sweden	EL SA/O OTH	490	984	50	5	10 037
	Agusta (EFIM)	Italy	AC	490	678	72	23	4 316
35	Racal Electronics	UK	EL	480	2 831	17	261	33 702
	Krupp Atlas Elektronik (Krupp)	FRG	EL	460	569	81	11	4 200
36	Westland	UK	AC	450	638	71	31	9 163
37	Devonport Dockyard	UK	SH	450	–	–	–	8 000
38	Hunting Associated Industries	UK	EL SA/O	440	714	62	33	5 596
39	Dowty Group	UK	EL OTH	410	1 068	38	141	13 710
	Hollandse Signaalapparaten (Philips)	Netherlands	EL	410	455	90	–	5 300
40	SD-Scicon	UK	OTH	390	–	–	–	–
41	Ericsson	Sweden	EL	390	5 108	8	214	65 000
42	Vickers	UK	ENG MV SA/O	390	1 383	28	1	16 731
43	Krauss–Maffei	FRG	MV	380	723	53	1	5 100
	EN Bazan (INI)	Spain	ENG SH	380	464	82	9	10 908
	Mercedes Benz (Daimler Benz)	FRG	MV	380	31 261	1	934	182 100
	SAAB Aircraft Division (SAAB-SCANIA)	Sweden	AC	380	666	57	9	6 490
	Selenia (IRI)	Italy	EL MI	380	564	67	3	6 716
44	SAGEM Groupe	France	EL	350	1 607	22	31	17 484
45	Renault Véhicules Industriels	France	MV	340	5 708	6	168	34 000
	Thyssen (Thyssen Industrie)	FRG	MV SH	340	2 790	12	–1	34 969
46	Ascom Holding	Switzerland	EL	330	1 640	20	–	14 000
47	Standard Elektronik Lorenz	FRG	EL	320	2 286	14	95	23 000
48	HDW	FRG	SH	310	638	49	8	4 600
	Fincantieri (IRI)	Italy	SH	310	1 392	22	–107	20 748
49	DAF	Netherlands	MV	290	2 631	11	74	16 561
50	Société Nationale des Poudres et Explosifs	France	A	280	566	49	9	6 900
	FIAT IVECO (FIAT)	Italy	MV	270	3 665	7	93	21 942
51	Dynamit Nobel	FRG	SA/O	260	626	42	–	7 000

191

Appendix A *continued*

Figures in columns 5, 6 and 8 are in US $ million; figures in column 7 are percentages.

1 Rank	2 Company	3 Country	4 Industry[b]	5 Arms sales	6 Total sales	7 5 as % of 6	8 Profits	9 Employment
52	Mainz Industries	FRG	MV	260	–	–	–	5 770
53	Wegmann	FRG	MV	260	–	–	–	5 930
	Blohm & Voss (Thyssen Industrie)	FRG	SH	260	683	38	–9	7 890
54	ENASA (INI)	Spain	MV	250	999	25	–56	4 168
55	FN Group	Belgium	SA/O	240	610	39	–2	3 000
	Turboméca	France	ENG	230	384	60	27	2 900
	FFV Aerotech Group (FFV)	Sweden	EL SA/O OTH	230	–	–	–	2 000
	MAK (Krupp)	FRG	MV	230	512	45	–	4 000
56	Landis & Gyr	Switzerland	OTH	210	–	–	–	–
57	United Scientific Holdings	UK	EL	200	215	93	42	4 165
58	SEP	France	ENG OTH	180	613	29	13	2 698
59	Aermacchi	Italy	AC	180	198	91	4	2 044
60	Norsk Forsvarsteknologi	Norway	A EL MI	180	210	86	10	–
61	Union Española de Explosivos SA	Spain	A OTH	170	182	93	17	800
63	Astra Holdings	UK	SA/O	170	171	99	17	1 238
62	Fr. Lürssen	FRG	SH	170	–	–	–	–
64	Pilkington Optronics	UK	OTH	170	–	–	–	2 735
	Santa Barbara (INI)	Spain	A SA/O	170	175	97	–76	4 586
65	GKN	UK	MV OTH	160	3 384	5	–	2 677
66	Südsteyerische Metallindustrie	Austria	MV SA/O OTH	160	–	–	–	–
67	Crouzet	France	EL	160	391	41	14	5 000
	BPD Difesa e Spazio (FIAT)	Italy	OTH	160	270	59	57	2 189
68	Volvo	Sweden	ENG	150	15 772	1	1 345	78 614

69	STC	UK	EL	150	4 198	4	410	34 904
70	Creusot Loire Industrie	France		150	269	56	–	2 600
	Matra Manurhin (Matra Groupe)	France	SA/O	150	153	98	1	1 698
	Thomson Brandt Armements (Thomson S.A.)	France	A	140	151	99	5	1 300
71	Vosper Thornycroft	UK	SH	140	166	84	12	2 000
72	AWD Bedford	UK	MV	140	–	–	–	1 250
73	Short Brothers	UK	AC MI	140	–	–	–	4 400
74	PRB	Belgium	SA/O	140	144	97	–49	1 533
75	SIG	Switzerland	SA/O	140	–	–	–	7 000
76	Rhode & Schwarz	FRG	EL	140	473	30	–	–
77	Electronica	Italy	EL	130	139	94	5	1 344
78	KHD	FRG	ENG	130	2 569	5	–56	18 800
79	Bremer Vulkan	FRG	SH	130	635	20	–63	7 680
80	Iveco Magirus AG	FRG	MV	130	1 287	10	59	6 755
81	Bosch	FRG	EL	130	15 758	1	–	165 700
82	NEI	UK	–	120	–	–	–	15 000
83	Luchaire	France	SA/O	120	333	36	8 716	4 065
84	Swan Hunter	UK	SH	120	145	83	6	–
	Breda Meccanica Bresciana (EFIM)	Italy	–	120	126	95	7	736
85	Messier Hispano Bugatti (SNECMA)	France	–	120	308	39	–	2 659
86	Heckler & Koch	FRG	SA/O	110	–	–	–	–
	IABG	FRG	OTH	110	–	–	–	–
87	Zahnradfabrik Friedrichshafen	FRG	MV	110	3 172	3	48	32 600
88	Panhard	France	MV	110	111	99	–	480
89	SFIM	France	–	110	193	57	7	1 447
90	Piaggio	Italy	AC ENG OTH	110	161	68	1	1 934
	Hispano Suiza (SNECMA)	France	–	110	268	41	–6	2 861
91	A.B. Hägglunds & Sons	Sweden	MV	100	391	26	33	4 137

Appendix A *continued*

Figures in columns 5, 6 and 8 are in US $ million; figures in column 7 are percentages.

1 Rank	2 Company	3 Country	4 Industry^b	5 Arms sales	6 Total sales	7 5 as % of 6	8 Profits	9 Employment
92	Fokker	Netherlands	AC	100	1 040	10	7	11 690
93	Raufoss	Norway	ENG SA/O	100	229	44	9	2 518
94	EXPALSA	Spain	A OTH	100	100	100	–	420
95	GAMESA	Spain	A OTH	100	125	80	–	450
96	Bodenseewerke Gerätetechnik GmbH	FRG	EL MI	100	211	47	9	1 600
	ELSAG (IRI)	Italy	EL	100	313	32	9	1 844
97	FR Group	UK	OTH	90	234	40	40	2 797
98	Carl Zeiss	FRG	OTH	90	2 323	4	–	32 000
99	Eurometaal	Netherlands	SA/O	90	90	100	4	976
100	IWKA	FRG	MV EL	90	695	13	11	6 800
	Officine Galileo (EFIM)	Italy	OTH	90	126	71	–	1 272
	SAT (SAGEM Groupe)	France	EL	90	458	20	–	5 376

^a Numbered entries are ranked according to total arms sales (column 5); entries whose sales figures in column 5 are identical are ranked according to unrounded values. Unnumbered entries are subsidiaries whose arms sales are included in the figure in column 5 for the holding company. Subsidiaries are listed in the position where they would appear if they were independent companies, but are not allocated a rank number.

^b Key to abbreviations in column 4: A = artillery, AC = aircraft, EL = electronics, ENG = engines, MV = military vehicles, MI = missiles, SH = ships, SA/O = small arms/ordinance, OTH = others

Sources of data: The data presented in this table are based on the following sources: company reports, a questionnaire sent to 300 companies, corporation news published in the business sections of newspapers and military journals. In addition, company archives, marketing reports, government publication of prime contracts and country surveys were consulted. In many cases exact figures were not available, mainly because companies often do not report on their arms sales or lump them together with other activities. Estimates were therefore made.

Arms sales: The criterion for the rank order of companies is their arms sales.

Coverage: The data are for 1988. The fiscal year for companies is not always the calendar year. No calculations have been made to adjust fiscal to calendar years.

APPENDIX A

Exchange rates: Most figures collected were given in local currencies. To convert figures into US dollars, the period-average of market exchange-rates of the International Monetary Fund, *International Financial Statistics*, were used.

Profit: Profit after taxes is shown for the entire company, not for the arms-producing sector alone. For figures taken from journals and periodicals, it was not always clear whether profit was given before or after taxes.

Employment: The figure shown is either a year-end or yearly average number, as published in the sources used.

Note: The authors would like to acknowledge the assistance of Bernard Harbor, (London), Sami Faltas (Eindhoven), Ernst Gülcher (Antwerp), Peter Hug (Bern), Evamaria Loose-Weintraub (Stockholm), Arcadi Olivares i Boadella (Barcelona), Mario Pianta and Giulio Perani (Rome), Paul Rusman (Haarlem) and Werner Voß (Bremen) in the data collection. Three interns assisted in the preparation of the appendix: Lisa Moore, Ivo Sarges and David Wiley.

Source: Anthony, I., et al., *West European Arms Production*, SIPRI Research Report (October 1990), Appendix A.

INDEX